THE LAST DISCO

THE LAST DISCO

The story of the Stardust tragedy

Sean Murray, Christine Bohan and Nicky Ryan

First published by Eriu
An imprint of Black & White Publishing Group
A Bonnier Books UK company

4th Floor, Victoria House,
Bloomsbury Square,
London, WC1B 4DA

Owned by Bonnier Books
Sveavägen 56, Stockholm, Sweden

🅧 – @eriu_books
📷 – @eriubooks

Trade paperback – 978-1-80418-481-3
Ebook – 9781-80418-506-3

All rights reserved. No part of the publication may be reproduced, stored in a retrieval system, transmitted or circulated in any form or by any means, electronic, mechanical, photocopying, recording or otherwise, without prior permission in writing of the publisher.

A CIP catalogue of this book is available from the British Library.

Typeset by IDSUK (Data Connection) Ltd
Printed and bound by Clays Ltd, Elcograf S.p.A.

1 3 5 7 9 10 8 6 4 2

Copyright © Sean Murray, Christine Bohan and Nicky Ryan 2024

Sean Murray, Christine Bohan and Nicky Ryan have asserted their moral right to be identified as the authors of this Work in accordance with the Copyright, Designs and Patents Act 1988.

Every reasonable effort has been made to trace copyright holders of material reproduced in this book, but if any have been inadvertently overlooked the publishers would be glad to hear from them.

Eriu is an imprint of Bonnier Books UK
www.bonnierbooks.co.uk

For The 48 who never came home,
and all those who fought for them

Stardust Floorplan

SCOTT'S FOODS

TOILET

TOILET

EXIT 6

EXIT 5

SHED

BAR

EXIT 4

CHANGING ROOM

CH. RM.

B GENTS

CHANGING ROOM

PRIMARY LIGHTING

MAIN SWITCH ROOM

NORTH ALCOVE

ROLLER BLINDS

UP

UP

BAR STORE

STAGE

DANCEFLOOR

EXIT 3

GENTS TOILET

LADIES TOILET

BAR

SPIRIT STORE

CLOAK ROOM

CASH OFFICE

EXIT 1

COLD ROOM (STORE ROOM AND LAMP ROOM ON UPPER LEVEL)

BAR

HOT PRESS

FIRE FIRST SIGHTED HERE

ROLLER BLINDS

WEST ALCOVE

CIGARETTE MACHINE

STAIRS TO 1ST FLOOR OFFICES

PASSAGE

EXIT 2 (MAIN ENTRANCE)

KITCHEN

PASSAGE (HIGH LEVEL)

SILVER SWAN

ROLLER BLINDS

LANTERN ROOMS

WASH UP AREA

EXIT FROM KITCHEN

EXIT 1 FIRE ESCAPE STAIRS

DOWN

Prologue

AT 2.04PM, THE CORONER walked in. 'If you have a seat, please take it,' she told the 200 or so people packed into the Pillar Room at Dublin's Rotunda Hospital on 18th April 2024.

The jury filed in and took their seats. The 12 gave nothing away in their expressions, keeping their faces deliberately neutral. At the other end of the huge room, family members of the victims held hands and took deep breaths. The only people with phones out were the reporters who had managed to find a space to stand in the room. A member of the coroner's staff discreetly placed small packets of tissues on some of the desks where the families were sitting.

After almost exactly one year, the jury at the inquests into the deaths of the 48 young people who died in the Stardust disco fire was about to deliver its verdict.

* * *

The story of the Stardust is not just a story about Artane in Dublin, although it is that too. It's also a story about Ireland.

The inquests which began in April 2023 were the first time that the full facts about what happened that night –

and before and afterwards – had been made public. Some of it was known already. Some 846 young people had gone to a disco on the Kilmore Road in Dublin 5 on 13th February 1981. The Stardust was one of the biggest venues in Dublin – and Ireland – and it was hugely popular. It had only been open for a couple of years and was known initially for its cabaret shows before pivoting to discos and gigs. It was a broad church: everyone from Joe Dolan to The Specials had played there.

That night at 1.41am, just after a disco dancing competition had ended, people spotted a small fire on some chairs in a part of the ballroom that was partitioned off. It wasn't big. Some people went back to the dance floor once they'd alerted staff. It looked like it was going to be put out very quickly.

At 1.43am, the first 999 call was made from the venue. The fire was growing, quickly and lethally. As people started to make for the emergency exits, they found some of them had locks and chains over them. At least one was completely locked. As people desperately tried to get out, the fire had become like a tornado, fuelled by the carpet tiles which decorated the walls. When the first fire engines arrived just eight minutes later, the fire was already past its peak. Inside, 40 people – many of them teenagers, the oldest just 27 – had died. Four more were pronounced dead on arrival when they reached the hospital, and another four would die in hospital over the coming days and weeks. Hundreds were injured.

Afterwards, it would be found that the Stardust had not been designed by an architect, that there were major problems with the emergency exits being locked when people were inside the venue, and that it had never been visited by fire safety inspectors – who would have spotted the problems with it – in the entire time it had been open.

As families grieved and searched for answers, then Taoiseach Charles Haughey almost immediately announced a tribunal which would investigate the fire. The Tribunal worked fast, but when it published its final report, it declared that the 'probable' cause of the fire was arson, meaning that someone in the venue or from the area had most likely deliberately set it ablaze. The verdict was to have repercussions for decades.

Families who questioned the lack of evidence found for arson were dismissed; the official narrative had been handed down and most politicians didn't see the need to fight it. Families were later asked to accept some financial compensation and move on. But they couldn't, and wouldn't, when there were still so many unanswered questions.

The inquests that took place in 2023 and 2024 also provided new information about what had happened. Many first responders spoke in detail about their work on the night and what they had seen in the worst blaze in this country's history. Witnesses who had not previously come forward told their stories. And for the first time in over 40 years, the Stardust's manager, Eamon Butterly, answered questions about what had happened that night, taking to the witness box for almost a week.

It somehow took 43 years for the State to officially acknowledge how the 48 died, even though the details were public knowledge within hours of the fire happening. It is not the only time that people have had to wait years for justice in this country, but it is possibly the most egregious. Over those four decades, a community had to deal with shattered lives, intergenerational trauma and a generation of children gone for good.

Years after the Stardust disaster, a lawyer at the inquiry into the Grenfell Tower fire in London spoke about how it showed how badly successive governments handled important issues. 'Grenfell is a lens through which to see how we are governed,' she said.

She could just as easily have been talking about the Stardust.

You can draw a straight line between the Stardust and all the other times when the Irish State fumbled and failed when it was meant to be helping people who had experienced injustice: the Kerry babies case, Tuam, the Mother and Baby Home survivors, the Magdalene women, the Whiddy Island disaster, the Dublin-Monaghan bombings. Each time, there was the original tragedy and then the one inflicted by the State afterwards. This is not a uniquely Irish situation – Grenfell and Hillsborough are two of the most high-profile examples in Ireland's nearest neighbour – but it is a common theme across successive governments.

The inquests were a chance to put this right and bring closure after all this time. Not assigning blame or finding anyone guilty, but simply to answer one question: why exactly did these 48 people die?

*   *   *

Back in the Pillar Room on that April day in 2024, the room was quiet chaos, less than five minutes before the jury was due to come back in.

More than 200 people were already inside the grandiose Pillar Room at the Rotunda Hospital, a space that usually accommodates around half that number, and more were trying to enter. Some spilled out into the lobby and court-yard outside. Some people doubled up, sharing seats with each other. Others lined the back wall of the room, pressed in tightly together. At one stage a member of the coroner's staff moved a group of people standing in front of an emergency exit, urging them to stand against a wall instead.

All of the legal teams had given up their seats at their tables so that the families would have somewhere to sit, and now a large group of lawyers clustered together, hovering nervously beside the coroner's desk in the centre of the room.

Unusually for an Irish court, the public was able to watch proceedings live online. It was a similar situation there too: the Zoom meeting's capacity had been set at a maximum of 500 attendees, and now no new viewers could enter until someone else left.

Families had been arriving since mid-morning to get a seat in the room, along with people who had been at the disco on the night and who had given evidence to the inquests over the past year. 'I'm nervous. We're nervous,' said Errol Buckley, whose brother Jimmy died in the blaze. 'Hopefully today is the day.' Bridget McDermott, the 87-year-old woman who lost three children in the fire, had spent the morning sticking to her usual routine, not wanting to get her hopes up.

Lawyers for the families had tried to lower expectations in the days before the verdict, saying that the inquests themselves had been a victory for allowing the full facts of what happened on that night to be laid out. But the families were hoping for one specific outcome.

The jury filed back into the room at 2.05pm.

Dr Myra Cullinane, the coroner, began by having the foreman of the jury read out the exact cause and place of death for each of the 48 victims. She then ran through more questions with them about the details of the fire before moving to her final questions.

'Members of the jury, your foreman has indicated that you've reached a verdict at these inquests and that you'll be returning the same verdict for each of the 48 deceased. Is that correct?' she asked.

'Correct,' replied the foreman.

'So, therefore, foreman of the jury, I will ask you now to announce the verdict of the jury, which refers to verdicts in each of the 48 persons who lost their lives,' said Dr Cullinane.

The foreman paused for the briefest of moments. Then he began to speak.

Chapter 1

THERE IS A TENDENCY WHEN things are over to remember how they were at the ending, but for a brief time, the Stardust shone brightly.

One of the only videos of the Stardust from before the fire is a fragment of a Dickie Rock concert broadcast on RTÉ in June 1980, just months before it all happened, and it captures the excitement and the energy of the club in its heyday.

The clip is 5 minutes and 36 seconds long, and in it the Stardust is *buzzing*. This is a cabaret gig: there are tables in front of the stage with groups of friends sitting around each one, as lounge girls weave in and out between them. The men wear suits and the women are in long dresses and it all looks very relaxed. It's the audience: they're chatting, drinking, laughing, taking their seats, watching the stage as the show kicks off. You can't see anyone actually smoking, but with the low ceilings, the dark walls and the late-night atmosphere, it just *looks* smoky. It looks fun.

The stage is large and T-shaped, somewhere between the size of the stages at the Olympia and Vicar Street, except much closer to ground level. There are at least 15 musicians on stage, including four saxophonists, a drummer, a horn section and someone playing the electric guitar. Many of the photographs of the Stardust taken after the fire are black-and-white, a constraint of newspaper print at the time. This is different. It is a jolt to see it in full colour, the silver tinsel curtains catching the light behind the musicians.

The music kicks off with a jaunty big band swing. It's confident. It's lively. After about 40 seconds it takes a pause and kicks up a gear as six disco dancers run out onto the stage wearing hot pants and bandeau tops made out of shiny material, each wearing a different colour. They're called the X-Appeal Dancers, a dance troupe from Belfast who performed at some of Dickie Rock's shows, and it's clear why they're there: they're a bridge, translating the music that has dominated Ireland's live music scene for the previous 20 years into something modern and danceable for a younger audience who want something different from their parents. They have pudding-bowl haircuts with differing levels of volume, they are lithe and gorgeous and fun, and you wonder whose idea it was to have everyone sitting down at tables rather than up dancing.

And then they run off and a voice announces, 'Ladies and gentlemen! Live from the Stardust! In concert! Mr Dickie Rock!'

You hear him off-stage before you see him. 'Music was my first love, and it will be my last,' he sings. He walks out on stage to loud cheers, wearing an all-white suit with a slim white belt, a wine-coloured shirt with the top few buttons open and a thick gold chain around his neck. The music starts out croon-y, but then the beat kicks in, the electric guitar joins in with the horns and suddenly it's like a disco track filled with energy and life.

Dickie Rock owns that stage. He has done this a million times before – he is only 43 but has already been doing this for 20 years, including representing Ireland at the Eurovision in 1966 – and he knows what he is doing. He swings the microphone wire around in his hands. He shimmies. At one stage there's a side kick of his leg in time with the beat. He looks like this is his favourite gig that he's ever played, which is probably how he looks at every performance he's ever done. The whole thing is a very different Ireland from today. It's Frank Sinatra at the Sands vibes, except with Tom Jones as the performer.

The video ends immediately after the final line ('I got the music / The good old rockin' music / I got the music in meeee') and you don't get to hear the applause but you know it's coming.

The Stardust only existed for two years and 11 months, but in that time, it established itself as *the* place to go for young Dubliners. When the owners applied for the licence, the judge told them it was the biggest premises he had ever granted a licence for. When people who went there talk about what it was like before the fire, they talk about how it was buzzy and it was cool. It filled a gap for them; it was their place to go to that wasn't home or work or school, where they could be with their friends and have a good time.

It managed to follow the zeitgeist of the time too, giving people what they wanted. When it opened, it rode the end of the wave of Ireland's showband and cabaret boom. Joe Dolan was the first act to play there in March 1978, playing a residency for six nights in a row. Eurovision star Dana, comedian Tommy Cooper and US crooner Gene Pitney all graced the stage in the months that followed.

They played to packed shows in most cases, giving the audience exactly what they wanted.

As the decade turned, though, the business proposition did too: the bottom fell out of cabaret at the end of the 1970s as teenagers and people in their twenties were less enamoured by seeing a live performance and just wanted to hear music they could dance to.

'When boys and girls went to a disco, as opposed to seeing a live band, *they* became the stars,' said Tony Johnson, a DJ who ran some of the earliest discos in Ireland, in a documentary about disco in Ireland. 'They got on the floor. They were showing their moves, they were showing their clothes. They didn't have to wait for a guy to finish one tune, tune up, have a chat with his mate, and then do another one, [while] you stand there with your hands in your pockets and maybe applaud if he was good or not. It was no longer looking up to anybody else. Disco . . . has always been that the punter is the star.'

The owners of the Stardust, the Butterly family from north county Dublin, had always intended for the venue to move with the times. The original plans for it filed in 1972 with Dublin Corporation (the precursor to Dublin City Council) had included a bowling alley – bowling was in its 'golden era' in the 1970s – as well as a pub and a restaurant. As the planning process stalled and restarted over several years, the application was rejigged, and at some stage, the bowling alley was dropped in favour of a venue for concerts and cabarets.

When it became clear that tastes were changing and there was an audience for a different style of show, the original seating that was fixed to the floor was removed in favour of non-fixed seating, and a larger dancing area was created in front of the stage.

And so, in February 1980, just weeks after the Dickie Rock show had been recorded and almost two years after it had first opened as a venue, the Stardust held its first disco.

* * *

The going-out scene for young people in Ireland in 1981 was radically different from today.

Nowadays there are options, whatever your interests might be. Going out-out might mean a restaurant, a pub or a club. Or maybe it's quieter: the cinema or a comedy show or one of the many, many gigs on any night of the week around the country. There are choices, in other words.

The competition doesn't just come from other venues either. A television ad for clothes from the early 1980s not-so-gently mocks a girl who wants to stay in and read on a Saturday night. 'Don't be a plain Jane!' the voiceover sternly tells us. Staying in wasn't seen as an option back then – or at least, not an aspirational one – but with streaming, food deliveries and dating apps, staying in has become a very real and often very appealing substitute to going out.

The obvious difference between then and now is that people – and venues – have more money, which means more choice. Back then, there was not a lot of either.

Ireland had undergone radical changes in the years leading up to the early 1980s. Not as dramatic as other countries, perhaps, but the country saw demographic and economic rollercoasters in the 1960s and 1970s: an increase in population plus the growth of the suburbs meant there were now a lot more teenagers and people in their twenties in new estates around the country, particularly in Dublin, looking for things to do.

Artane, where the Stardust was, was a prime example of this.

In the early 1950s, when it was mainly farmland, there were just over 2,000 people living there, and it felt far removed from Dublin city. By the time of the 1981 census, there were around 35,000 people – an increase of almost 30,000 people in just a couple of decades. 'It still would have been considered a very new suburb, even by the early 1980s,' said Cormac Moore, one of Dublin City Council's historians-in-residence. It was a broadly working-class suburb: local factories such as Tayto, Cadbury and Chivers were good employers, and most people worked in trades, shops or manual labour.

The whole of Dublin had grown massively in this post-war period, adding almost a quarter of a million people in less than three decades. This wasn't spread evenly: the city centre area saw its population flatline and then decrease, while the suburbs on the northside and southside boomed. A lot of this would have been the result of internal migration in Ireland: people moving from rural Ireland up to Dublin for jobs, but also people moving – or being moved – from unsafe and overcrowded tenements in Dublin city centre. According to Moore, this meant a mixture of age groups in these new areas: younger people moving to Dublin from rural Ireland, and families and older people moving out from the tenements.

Dublin Corporation had carried out a massive house-building project across Artane and Coolock and the surrounding areas, in part for the people moving out from the tenements. These suburbs are not far from Dublin city: Artane is just under 6km from O'Connell Street and you could walk it in under an hour and a half. For people moving there from Dublin city centre, however, it felt like they were going to the moon. 'I've heard stories myself that when people who lived in the city centre said they were moving to Coolock, families were saying, "Well, we'll never see you again",' archivist Karen de Lacey, who has been researching the area, told the *Dublin Inquirer* newspaper.

This shift in population completely upended the type of country Ireland was. The historian Erika Hanna has noted that Dublin is a city that mainly dates from the middle of the 20th century: before that, Ireland had been predominantly rural, with 60% of people living in the countryside or a small town or village in the late 1940s. As this migration to Dublin's suburbs took place, however, the numbers swelled, and by 1971, Ireland's population tipped over to become more urban than rural for the first time.

All of these people, all of these young families moving to a growing suburb meant there were a lot of people looking for things to do.

* * *

By the early 1980s, a one-stop shop for a night out was big business. The Stardust and venues like it held an outsized role in their areas; like many similar places, the

Stardust was a concert venue and a place for discos. But it also had a pub and a function room attached to it – the Silver Swan and the Lantern Rooms – meaning that there were three venues all under one roof, providing a smorgasbord of entertainment options catering to whatever its local audience wanted. On the night of the fire, as well as the disco in the Stardust, there was a crowd in the Silver Swan pub and a meal being held for the Marine, Port and General Workers' Union in the Lantern Rooms – teenagers and people in their twenties at the disco, a mixed crowd in the pub and work colleagues in the function room. These one-stop shops were a staple of towns and suburbs around the country – and, in some cases, they still are. It was partly about geography and partly about economics: casting a large net meant it could appeal to as many people as possible, both from the local area but also further afield.

There was another factor too. Ireland's going-out scene was somewhat unusual compared to other countries, probably in large part because of the influence of that particularly Irish phenomenon from the previous generation: showbands.

In the 1960s, while other countries were going through a social and cultural revolution, Ireland was doubling down on the short leash it held on people. The emergence of showbands marked a significant cultural and musical shift from the music of Josef Locke and Andy Williams that the older generation would have listened to. Combining elements of traditional Irish music with popular rock and pop influences, particularly country and rock 'n' roll, showbands found huge audiences across the country, providing entertainment and escapism. The bands followed a circuit through Ireland's towns, villages and cities, often playing in dance halls and church halls with strict no-alcohol policies. At their peak, almost 600 showbands were on the road around Ireland, including The Drifters, The Miami Showband and The Freshmen.

The showband circuit was sweet, chaste and alcohol-free, except it was populated by people in their late teens and twenties, so how much of these things could it really have been? The dance halls were more than just venues for music: they became places where people forged friendships, fell in love and danced. But despite their massive popularity, showbands couldn't last. As the 1970s progressed, newer musical genres like punk and disco gained traction, attracting the attention of younger audiences. The boom in television ownership provided stiff competition too, leading to declining attendances at dance halls.

As the economic downturn in the 1970s and 1980s hit Ireland hard, many dance halls closed down and many showbands disbanded or shifted to different musical styles. Venue owners began to look at their options. In the suburbs of Dublin, and large towns around the country, large venues that could hold many different types of events – functions, gigs, discos, pubs – began to spring up.

It was a world of flux for the entertainment industry, which led to a mash-up of genres at venues across the country. U2 are listed as having played at the Stardust just before Christmas in 1978, when they opened for The Greedies, a supergroup consisting of members of Thin Lizzy, The Boomtown Rats and The Sex Pistols. The month before the fire, soon after the Dickie Rock concert, The Specials played a gig at the Stardust that the *Irish Times* later described as being 'somewhere between a fracas and a fascist rally'.

In this search for ways to bring in a crowd, discos hit the sweet spot of appealing to both punters and venue owners.

Former 2FM DJ Will Leahy has described discos as 'the main communal pastime' for the generation of people born in the 1960s and 1970s. Far more people have gone to a disco than have played a hurling match or read *Harry Potter*, he says in his 2015 documentary about discos, but they don't have the same place in the cultural memory.

One of the first discos in Ireland had actually happened in 1965, when Danny Hughes – who 16 years later would be the main DJ at the Stardust on the night of the fire – rented a space on 16 Lower Mount Street in Dublin city for £10, telling the landlady that it would be a crowd from Trinity. Several months before, a disco night in a venue that held up to 1,500 people had opened in a basement on Burgh Quay in Dublin city centre. The club, called Sound City, ran on Sunday nights from 9pm until 1am and a flyer from the time describes it as 'Ireland's only rhythm and blues club for with-it people'.

What marked these out from every other night out at the time – particularly the showbands – was that, rather than having live music, only records were played. This was both a draw and a drawback – it was a novelty, sure, but people were used to live music. This might explain the slow progression of discos in Ireland.

In Dublin, there were a small number of discos throughout the late 1960s and early 1970s, but it was the mid-1970s when they really began to take off. Tourism had been decimated at the time because of the Troubles, so hotels were looking for business and desperate to fill their function rooms. Besides, there was not much else happening in these new large suburbs besides GAA or tennis clubs. 'From around 1973 to the end of the 1980s, every hotelier wanted to have his own nightclub,' said DJ Michael McNamara in the Will Leahy documentary.

There were between 200 and 300 nightclubs around the country between 1973 and the 1980s and almost every town had a hotel with a disco in it. Touring musicians and showbands tried to take action through their union to compel hotels to still employ them – and, more importantly, pay them – as their livelihoods had been so impacted by the growth of discos, but the hotel owners refused.

Discos were flourishing: they had become a fashion and a culture as well as a night out. People wanted to hear what was in the charts. The DJs would mix huge disco tracks, like the *Saturday Night Fever* soundtrack, with harder New Wave music like The Jam or Madness. Importantly too, they were affordable. Ireland was in a bad place: unemployment was running at 9.9% in 1981, stretching to almost 15% for people aged 15–24, and almost 1 in 8 people under 20 would emigrate by 1986, so for those who could afford it, going out had a feral appeal. It cost £3 to get into the Stardust on the night of the fire, at a time when the average industrial wage was around £112 per week.

The first *Late Late Show* of 1980 featured a segment about a young woman who had won the Irish Disco Dancing competition at the age of 19, winning a Toshiba colour television and a massive £1,000 in cash. Gay Byrne described her as 'presumably' the most outstanding exponent of disco dancing in Ireland at that time. She had represented Ireland at the World Championships in London, where she scooped third place and a further £1,500.

As her performance ended, Byrne noted dryly: 'Amanda Gibson, 19, from Palmerstown with the New Ireland Assurance Company. All I can say is that in my day in insurance, if you engaged in that sort of carry-on, you were asked to leave the next morning at nine o'clock, and your pension rights would go with you.

'But there you are. That's what they're up to, you see, folks. That's what they're up to.'

* * *

Patrick Butterly had a problem. The businessman owned a pub on George's Quay in Dublin city centre and he'd just opened up a disco in the building at the back called The Two Ages. This was at the time when discos were just starting out in Ireland. Butterly was not of the entertainment world but he could always spot an opportunity. It wasn't long before the disco was bringing in around a thousand pounds a week.

However, there had been no planning permission granted to turn the building into a disco. 'We just went ahead and did it,' Butterly said later. And now he wasn't able to get the planning permission because of fire safety issues with the building. It needed another fire escape, and there was no space available to put it in.

Butterly did what he often did in situations like this: he turned to people he knew in Fianna Fáil to help him. 'We were all Fianna Fáil-ers,' he said. 'What you had these people [politicians] for was to help get things. If you wanted to know something about your business or you wanted someone who could do something, you didn't get answers by writing into the papers. You asked these people.'

So he asked. He turned to Kevin Boland, the Minister for Local Government, who Butterly believed had the final say over planning permission decisions. The two men knew each other well. Boland's offices were close to the George's Quay pub, so they would meet for a coffee and a chat 'nearly every morning,' Butterly said. It was bad news, however. Boland told him he could do nothing about it: he couldn't go against decisions made by fire safety officers. If they had decided that the disco wasn't safe then that was that.

Butterly knew two things: the disco couldn't continue where it was and the business opportunity was too promising to stop for good.

He had recently bought a huge factory in Artane called R&W Scott's Ltd that was producing and packaging fruit, vegetables, jams and chocolates, but it wasn't working out. It was producing more stock than could be sold, and it was losing money, which Butterly hated. He could see an answer: if he closed the factory and converted it into a disco, it would solve both problems.

This is how the Stardust ended up in a converted warehouse in Dublin's Artane, and how Butterly – at one stage the biggest grower of tomatoes in County Dublin – would end up also owning a huge nightclub complex.

Patrick Butterly was born in 1919 in Rush, the coastal town that was – and still is – a major supplier of fresh vegetables to the rest of Dublin. Butterly loved Rush so much that he would holiday in the town, even while he was living there. 'This was all Butterly country around here,' he would later say. His family was poor but no poorer than the other people around them. He left school at 14 when he already had a few years of working under his belt: he would take the fruit and vegetables grown in his aunt and uncle's one-acre garden, along with produce from his neighbours, and travel by pony into Dublin Corporation's fruit and vegetable market in Smithfield in the city centre to sell it all.

He was, as he said himself, 'always a divil for money'. In his teens, he had managed to save up enough to buy a second-hand car to get him into the Smithfield market faster than the pony, meaning he'd get there earlier and secure the best place to sell his vegetables. From the car, he traded up first to one lorry, and then two; he soon had a couple of men working for him. He bought a farm and then another one, and soon he was growing and packaging huge amounts of vegetables.

He wasn't precious about what he traded in: at one stage he was also selling turf and imported coal from Poland. 'People say, "how did you make your money, Paddy?" Well, it wasn't making money. I did a lot of business. I grew a lot of stuff and sold it in the right markets,' he said. A lot of things he tried worked out but when they didn't – farming cows and sheep didn't prove successful, nor was a short-lived hotel on the Dublin–Belfast road – he would step away. He would never blame himself for any business failures, though. 'Not everything I did worked out, when other people were involved.' Buying the factory in Artane had been a huge expansionary step and one he was proud of, but he was smart enough to know that it needed to pivot if it was going to make money.

He and his wife Eileen had six children – Eamon, Colm, Donal, Padraig, Deirdre and Maeve – most of whom ended up being involved in the large web of family businesses.

The 1960s and 1970s were a busy time for them. There were at least four companies involving two or more family members set up in this time. One of his sons, Eamon, who would later hold a position at the Stardust, was a director at two of the companies.

Eamon had initially intended to be a farmer. Patrick had sent him to agricultural school in Meath when he left school at the age of 14 in 1959, but it hadn't worked out. Patrick wasn't impressed with the teachers – priests – who he thought were too slow. He pulled Eamon out after six months and sent him to learn how to weld in Dublin instead. For years afterwards, Eamon would work in the family businesses, going where his father wanted him. When Butterly decided to convert the factory into an amenity centre in 1972, and build an industrial estate around it – Butterly Business Park – he could see a role for Eamon in it.

The initial plan that was submitted to change the use of the factory was for it to be used as a bowling alley, pub, restaurant and warehouse. This changed along the way, and instead, the plan was to have a pub, a restaurant/function room and a venue for cabarets and concerts all under one roof, as well as one part of the building that would continue to be used as a food factory.

Patrick Butterly hired a man to prepare architectural drawings of the building to go along with the planning application. William White was not actually an architect; the Tribunal into the fire would later note that, 'while he described himself as an architect, he was not a graduate of any university or a member of any of the generally recognised professional institutions in this country or the United Kingdom'. He was a fellow of the Irish Architects

Society and had studied building construction at Bolton Street for six years. He had worked at Dublin Corporation for years before going into private practice as a draughtsman, preparing technical drawings of buildings.

As well as doing the drawings, White was instructed by Butterly to get permission from Dublin Corporation for a change of use for the building. White lodged his drawings and request with Dublin Corporation and the Butterlys waited for a response.

In January 1973, the Corporation refused the initial application for the conversion and the Butterlys immediately appealed. In June of that year, the Minister for Local Government, Labour TD James Tully, gave outline permission for the conversion to go ahead, subject to two conditions, one of which was to submit detailed plans of the building for approval.

William White stopped working for the Butterlys when he and the Butterlys had a disagreement over his fees, and a new draughtsman, Harold Gardner, was hired. Gardner was given one of White's drawings and made revised drawings of his own, which he lodged with Dublin Corporation. Like White, Gardner was also a draughtsman. 'As far as I was concerned about Mr Gardner, he was quite capable of doing the job,' Eamon Butterly would later say. When asked about the fact that Gardner was not an architect and was not employed 'in the way an architect would be employed to supervise a project', Butterly noted: 'He was not an architect and still he was dealing with the Dublin Corporation as an architect, they accepted him. I didn't know what his actual qualifications were, but he did his job.'

More than three years later, on 29th October 1976, Dublin Corporation finally granted full permission for the conversion. The approval was based on 10 conditions. Some of these are tick-box exercises (the first condition was that the development would be carried out in accordance with the plans lodged with the application). Others were not. One stated that the applicants would consult with the Chief Fire Officer and comply with requirements about preventing a fire hazard in the development.

In June 1977, work on the conversion started. The venue was large and was expected to be able to cater for upwards of 1,500 people, and potentially up to 2,000. Together, the three venues, including the kitchen, toilets, cloakroom and corridors, made up 2,944m² of the ground floor of the building, most of that (1,853m²) taken up by the Stardust. The Stardust was connected to the Lantern Rooms (the function room) by a corridor running between the kitchen and the West Alcove, and to the Silver Swan (the pub) by a door at the back of the main bar.

Eamon Butterly acted as the contractor, as well as the client, and hired eleven companies to work on it, ranging from plastering and electrical installation to plumbing and seating units. He had some limited experience of building warehouses and factories and he kept overall control of the work as it proceeded. There were no architects or engineers involved in supervising any of the work being done, apart from a company of engineers that was responsible for strengthening the roof.

Harold Gardner, the draughtsman, would drop by roughly once a week. He didn't think of himself as supervising the construction, he later said. He would have told Eamon Butterly if he saw anything wrong being done, but this never actually happened, he said.

On 6th March 1978, the Stardust, the Lantern Rooms and the Silver Swan opened. That month, the Butterlys got an ordinary pub licence for the three venues, followed by a restaurant certificate later that year. Two years later, in November 1980, they got a licence to allow dancing on the premises, seven months after the first disco had been held at the Stardust. Before that, they had had to operate under a temporary licence; Dublin Corporation had initially objected to the licence for dancing because the roller blinds that were used to separate the alcoves in the room weren't made of flame-proof material. The objection was withdrawn once the Butterlys produced a certificate to show that the blinds complied with British standards.

While Patrick was behind the project, his son Eamon was the most hands-on member of the family when it came to the day-to-day running, eventually coming on board as the manager. This was very much a family affair. Patrick was the principal shareholder and one of the directors of the company that owned the building; Eamon and his brother Colm were the other two directors. The company that owned the building, Scotts Food Ltd, initially (as of November 1970) had its shareholding divided between Patrick Butterly (29,999 shares), his son Colm Butterly (1 share) and a company called Patrick Butterly & Sons Ltd (30,000 shares). Over the following years there were various transfers of the shares, and by the end of 1978, the ownership of the company was divided evenly between Patrick Butterly and a company called Butterly Enterprises Limited, which listed as its shareholders the eight members of the Butterly family. Patrick and his wife Eileen had the most number of shares, with the rest divided among their six children. Each of the four sons (Eamon, Colm, Donal

24

and Padraig) had double the number of shares as the daughters (Maeve and Deirdre).

To add to the already somewhat complicated set-up, the three venues – the Stardust, the Silver Swan and the Lantern Rooms – were let to a company called Silver Swan Limited, which was owned by Colm and Patrick Butterly, sometime in 1978. There was no lease or tenancy agreement until after the fire, but Patrick and Eamon Butterly said the company paid £1,000 per week.

In practice, Patrick Butterly made clear that his son Eamon had responsibility for the management and control of the premises. When asked if Eamon had any particular qualifications or experience that made him suitable to run the Stardust, Patrick said: 'He did not need any special qualifications to run that business. . . all he needed was common sense and he had that.'

* * *

Financially, the Butterlys did well. Their focus was on the bottom line. In 1981, Eamon Butterly would tell a tribunal that he was brought in as the manager of the Stardust very soon after it opened. It was initially managed by someone else, but he noted that it 'wasn't going very well . . . financially'. (In perhaps a sign of things to come, when he was asked about this again in 2023, he would contradict his own evidence. 'I don't remember that,' he told Bernard Condon SC at the inquests into the deaths of the people who died at the Stardust. 'I don't remember any problems with finances.')

Accounts for Butterly Business Park Limited, the holding company behind the Butterly group, showed that in 2010 the company – whose primary business was described as the 'development and selling of real estate' – had total assets of €10.9 million. Colm Keena noted in the *Irish Times* that this figure 'may be a significant underestimate'.

If this were another type of story, the Butterlys could be written about as an example of an Irish family who, during some of the most difficult decades economically for this country, grew a small market garden business into a multi-million-euro entrepreneurial operation, spanning a food processing business, a property company, a business park and a huge entertainment venue, among other things. But that is not how the name will be remembered.

Years later, Eamon Butterly would be asked at the inquests into the deaths of all the people who died at the Stardust whether he had any regrets about what had happened.

'Is there anything you would do differently?' Michael O'Higgins SC asked Butterly on 28th September 2023 as he wrapped up his questioning of the witness.

'I would never [have] got involved in converting that factory into a nightclub,' Eamon Butterly responded.

Chapter 2

Sometimes people are surprised when they hear that the Stardust building is still standing. Most of the exterior was unaffected by the fire; it was the interior and the roof of the ballroom section that were devastated and had to be rebuilt. Now it's part of a large business park, with a Lidl and a Mr Price and an Asian supermarket all surrounding it and Artane Castle shopping centre right opposite.

It's an austere, grim-looking building these days. That's if you can spot it at all. There used to be a small green in front of it, leading you up to the Stardust. That's been replaced by a Texaco garage which has been plopped in front of the building, hiding it from the main road. If you're walking by and happen to look up above the petrol station canopy, you'll see the top of the building peeking over.

Looking at it now, more than 43 years on, it remains strikingly similar to how it looked for the young people queuing outside to be let in to dance and have fun with their friends at the weekend. It's two storeys high with an entrance in the middle of the front façade. It used to be a reddish-brown colour but now it's painted white. It's deceptively big – it would take a couple of minutes for you to walk all the way around it. Back when it was a disco, there was a large hand-painted sign at the top of the building saying 'STARDUST PRESENTS' above a cinema-style marquee board where the names of upcoming bands would go. Above the front door was an awning with 'STARDUST' on it. These touches were functional and did the job; they didn't need to be dramatic or beautiful. The disco nights it had and the bands it put on meant it shone like a beacon for the young people in the area. And from further afield too. People flocked from all around to go there. The Stardust was the place to be.

'It was almost like a community there because you knew everybody,' said Lorraine McDonnell, who used to go there with her sister Teresa. Part of this sense of community was because the people who went would go a lot. It was a regular part of their routine. 'All the build-up would be for the Friday night,' said Linda Bishop, who was also a frequent attendee. 'And then [you'd go] Saturday night and, if you still had the money, Sunday night.'

'It was a great bit of craic there,' said Errol Buckley, a fine dancer in his day who'd go to strut his stuff. 'It was a popular place, people came from everywhere. It was the new disco on the scene.'

The appeal of the Stardust wasn't confined to the local area. Maurice Frazer was from the other side of the Liffey in Sandymount, but he'd also frequent the Stardust, as would his sister Thelma and her boyfriend Michael Farrell. 'Everybody had friends in Coolock or wherever. Dublin was – still is – a small place, but even then, the Stardust was a magnet for young people, not only from Coolock but from all of Dublin. It was a great venue.'

These teenagers and young adults in their early twenties were living in an Ireland of high unemployment, high emigration and poor economic prospects. Many had left school early and gone out to work. 'Loads of people there at the Stardust that night would've all gone there from work,' said Linda. The unemployment rate was particularly high among young people and particularly in working-class areas such as those surrounding the Stardust on all sides. Taoiseach Charles Haughey had set a grim tone for the decade ahead when he made a televised address to the nation in January 1980, warning the Irish people that 'as a community, we are living away beyond our means'. This would have come as news to the young people in Artane, Coolock and Bonnybrook who frequented the Stardust, many of whom were already out working and handing money back to their families every week to help make ends meet.

This came up again and again at the inquests years later, when family members remembered the responsibility that these young people shouldered. Josephine Glen left school at 14, and her sisters described how she gave most of her wages to her mother, a single parent of four children. But even the money they had left over wouldn't be spent on themselves. When Michael Griffiths received his first pay cheque at the age of 16, he didn't spend it on himself; instead he brought his siblings to the cinema. Marcella McDermott got a job at Dunnes Stores and never came home without a little something for her mother. 'The last thing she actually bought her was a lovely cream cake,' her sister Selina told the inquests. Perhaps this accelerated growing up is why the Stardust meant so much to the people who went there. It was the place where people could have their first dance, go to their first gig, meet their first boyfriends or girlfriends, catch up with their friends, have a break from work. Coming into February 1981, it was all about the big disco-dancing competition on Valentine's weekend.

*   *   *

If you picked up a newspaper on the morning of Friday, 13th February 1981, you would have found some common themes of the 1970s and 1980s in the headlines: industrial action and political upheaval.

It was the period right before social partnership and national pay agreements were introduced, so strikes were common. The *Irish Press* carried details of a potential deal to get Electricity Supply Board drivers back to work after a five-week strike. Workers were being offered payments of up to £2,000 per person – almost €10,000 in today's money – if they returned to work immediately, the paper reported. Meanwhile, workers at CIÉ were also unhappy, seeking a meeting with the bosses at the state transport company over rumours that as many as 100 buses would be taken off the roads due to a cut in a government subsidy.

There was also talk of Fianna Fáil's annual conference – its Ard Fheis – opening that night and due to get fully underway the following morning. Gene McKenna wrote in the *Irish Press* that a massive portrait of Taoiseach Charles Haughey – who represented the constituency of Dublin Artane, home of the Stardust – had been erected in the main hall of the RDS, alongside the slogan 'Leading the Nation Safely Through' in almost equally giant letters. The paper highlighted that Ireland's policy of neutrality, up for debate as much then as it is in the 2020s, was set to be on the agenda. One issue delegates would be voting on at the party conference called for no nuclear missiles to be located anywhere on the island of Ireland.

These issues may not have been front and centre of the minds of many going to the Stardust that night. The disco-dancing competition final was taking place and the hype had been building for weeks. There had been rounds taking place every second Friday for several weeks now, with the winners all going through to the grand finale. Good numbers were expected for that Friday night, with people turning out to support their friends. Under its licence, the venue had a maximum capacity of 1,458. The cover at the door in 1981 was £3 (the equivalent of almost €15 today), so even if it was half or two-thirds full, there was still plenty of money to be made for the owners. In today's money, the takings between the entry fee and the takings at the bar on a good night would run well into five figures.

Across Dublin, people were getting ready to go out. Errol Buckley was practising in his house for the disco-dancing competition. The youngest in a family of 10, Errol shared his siblings' love of performing in front of a crowd. The 18-year-old had initially entered the competition for fun, but his moves were enough to land him a place in the final. He came from a family of performers; his sister was a go-go dancer, and his brothers were all singers, including his older brother Jimmy, who was something of a father figure to him. In their house that evening, Errol, Jimmy and the other Buckley brothers were hyping each other up ahead of the big night. They had some friends over to have a couple of beers and practise their moves, egging each other on to get up for a demonstration.

Dotted all over the city were these small moments of life, centred around the Stardust.

In Raheny, Marcella McDermott let her younger sister Selina in on her plan for the night: her parents thought she would be babysitting with a friend, but she was actually going to go to the Stardust. Selina was tasked with hiding Marcella's going-out clothes in a little bag in the alley beside the house. Her brothers George and William were going as well – George meeting a girl and wearing clothes bought specially for the night, Willie heading out with his mates – but they didn't know that Marcella would be there too.

Eugene 'Hughie' Hogan and his wife Marie were with Eugene's brother and sister-in-law. The couples had gathered to toast Hughie and Marie's future. Hughie, a carpenter who found himself out of work the previous year, had landed a new job in Kerry. The couple were due to move on Monday. After a couple of drinks, they planned to join Hughie's younger brother Bernard at the Stardust to finish off the evening.

Others who wanted to go had to navigate getting their parents' permission. 'I had to beg my parents to let me go, especially on the late nights,' Linda Bishop said. 'My dad was very strict. I had to plead with him. There were some people there and they were 15, 16 and I'd say, "why can't I go?" And he'd say, "that's only because I'm not their dad".'

Antoinette Keegan, who was planning to go with her sisters Mary and Martina, was hearing from friends who were having the same battle. 'I was ringing from my job to my sister Mary in her job,' she said. 'We were also ringing her friend Mary Kenny and other friends saying "what are you wearing?" It was the big build-up as usual. And other friends were telling us "I'm not allowed go, I'm told I'm grounded from the last time I got in late."'

That was the first battle. The next one was actually getting in the door. Even if you were allowed go to the Stardust, you still had to get past the bouncers. There could be a dozen or more on duty on the night. The Stardust was over 21s – on paper, at least. Many underage people were able to get in, though, and some as young as 15 even held membership cards, which usually guaranteed you would get in. This was a time when young people wouldn't have routinely brought their passports with them on nights out. Garda Age Cards didn't exist yet. In reality, it was more of a vibes-based approach from the doormen. If they didn't like the look of you, you wouldn't be getting in. If they recognised you from before, that would usually count in your favour.

Before heading into the Stardust when the doors opened at 10pm, some of its patrons would have a drink somewhere else, where they would meet their friends to kick off the weekend. The Silver Swan pub, which was attached to the Stardust, was an option. Pre-drinking didn't exist in the way it does now. 'We definitely wouldn't have been allowed drink in the house,' said Linda Bishop. 'We'd just go and have a couple of bottles of Carlsberg Special Brew. We all met up at about 8 or 9 o'clock in the Silver Swan. We'd normally meet in there because they were quite strict [at the Stardust].'

People had ways to get in. 'If there were a gang of fellas, the bouncers wouldn't let them in,' said Linda. 'We'd meet different fellas we knew from work or from the area. They'd say "will you walk in with me?" We'd only do it with fellas we knew. We'd walk in with different fellas just to pretend we were a couple and get in. You paid for yourself and then they'd go off with their friends and we'd go off with our friends. But otherwise, lads coming down on their own would always get refused.'

Errol Buckley had another trick: 'We used to have to wear a shirt and tie going in there. There was one night I went up and I had no tie with me. There was a bit of a ribbon hanging down off the canopy. I went around the corner and took the ribbon and put it on myself. The fella said "you were very quick", and I said "yeah, I got one off my mate". He said "come on in then".'

This need to look older was understood by many people who attended.

'We dressed up, high heels, makeup and the lot,' Catherine Darling, who used to attend with her sister Susan, said. 'Then we were allowed into the Stardust because we looked 18.'

Once you'd gotten to the point where they were letting you in, the doormen would pat down the guys and search the handbags of the girls in the small entrance hall of the Stardust looking for alcohol. Given the thoroughness of the searching, doorman John Furley remarked to a colleague that the place was like 'Alcatraz'. At a small booth inside the entrance on the right-hand side, you'd pay your entry fee and leave your coat at the next booth before entering the main ballroom. There was a staircase just inside the main entrance on the left as you walked in, but it only led to offices upstairs and not to the main event that lay inside. Eamon Butterly would sometimes head up to the landing and stand there with a cup of tea, watching as the doormen checked bags and coats on the way in.

When you walked into the main ballroom, the room would unfurl in front of you with all the noise and the lights and people milling around. The stage was on your right with the big dance floor in front of it. There was tiered seating on the left-hand side and at the back of the building – these sections were known as the West Alcove and the North Alcove. The latter area was far larger. Depending on the night and how many patrons were expected, management closed off these alcoves using a blind or shutter that could be brought down to near the ground. If an alcove was closed off, it wouldn't be uncommon for staff to have a plate of chips there on their break, or gather to have a quick smoke and a chat, as it was curtained off from the patrons. In the middle of the ballroom was a large number of tables and seats for people to sit and watch the show on stage or the moves on the dance floor – or just sit and chat with their friends, as many did. The dance floor was wide enough for dozens to dance comfortably.

There were three bars in the venue: a small one on the right-hand side as you walked in the main door, and another small one just beside the dance floor. The main bar was in the back left corner as you walked in, just beyond the West Alcove. Two drinks were very popular, with the men at least: Smithwick's and Harp. The crowds would begin to filter in from half 10 or 11pm. By midnight on a disco night, the place would be heaving.

But there would also have been sections of the Stardust that would've gone relatively unnoticed by the patrons who came for these disco dances. Your £3 entry fee also got you a ticket for a meal at the end of the night. The meal was an essential part of the club's operation: up until the year 2000, a venue had to serve a substantial meal to patrons if it wanted a late licence, and it had to be included in the cost of entry. This is the same 'substantial meal' that made a resurgence in Ireland as the country began to lift its Covid restrictions in 2020. Several witness accounts have suggested the food at the Stardust ranged from 'rank' to 'shite'. But it had to be served nonetheless, and to make the food the Stardust premises had a large kitchen immediately on the left-hand side as you came into the main ballroom.

Towards the end of the night, waitresses would begin serving the food en masse with sausage and chips or a curry dished out to patrons. You may not have noticed where the food was coming from, but it arrived nonetheless. There were other parts of the Stardust which would not have been visible to the average attendee, including the passageway beside the kitchen leading into the Lantern Rooms or the corridor behind the North Alcove linking into the Silver Swan bar. You would also likely never have seen the area behind the stage, consisting of dressing rooms and a passageway for DJs and bands to bring their gear in and out of the Stardust. Most importantly of all, dancing away and enjoying the night with friends, you may also not have noticed the emergency exits from the Stardust – all six of them – and not realised the significance they would have in the early hours of 14th February 1981.

* * *

On the stairway just inside the main entrance to the Stardust disco, Eamon Butterly had started to watch proceedings on a typical disco night when doormen were checking bags and patting down people at the door before they paid their entry fee and walked into the ballroom. He did this because there was a problem at the Stardust.

Butterly was concerned that the takings on the door weren't matching the number of people on the premises. Were some patrons getting in for free? And if they were, how was it happening? He believed that some people were paying the entrance fee on the way in but then opening emergency exits to let their friends in by the side without paying in themselves. But there were also suggestions that the doormen were letting people that they knew in for free, and even that the doormen were pocketing some of the entry fee money themselves.

Firing the doormen was one approach taken by the Stardust management. There had been such a high turnover that, of the nine on duty on the night of 13th February 1981, three had been working there for a month or less. One of these doormen, Leo Doyle, had been promoted to deputy head doorman just a few months into the job as 'no one else wanted it'. Other workers described how morale was 'on the floor' among staff. In any case, something had to be done if people were getting in for free. Doorman John Furley said he didn't know if Butterly was 'vexed' by the idea of people getting in for free, but he knew that Butterly 'didn't like to be bested'.

Eamon Butterly had considered his options and a decision was made between him and the senior staff: they would keep the emergency exits to the Stardust locked and chained when there were discos on, from the start of the night up until about midnight, when the doormen could unlock and unchain them. But even after they were opened, the locks and chains would be draped over the bars of the emergency exit doors in such a way as to give the impression that the doors were still locked. In later investigations, this practice became known as 'mock locking'. So if someone in the Stardust looked at one of those emergency exits at, say, 1am, they would see a chain on the door even if it was, in fact, unlocked.

According to Butterly, this practice was only in place for a few weeks prior to the fire. He said it was 'forced' on him by people getting in for free. Other evidence suggests that doors were being locked before this, and not just at the Stardust, but at the Silver Swan as well. A schoolteacher named William Bassett was in the Silver Swan and saw an emergency exit door chained and locked as early as August 1980. Staff members at the Stardust would later give detailed evidence of seeing doors with chains on them at times when the public were on the premises.

The doors weren't the only parts of the building Eamon Butterly had turned his attention to. In early 1981, massive steel plates were welded over the windows of the men's and women's toilets located next to the main entrance of the Stardust, blocking the frames and allowing the windows to open only a few tiny inches. This was ostensibly to stop people passing in drink or 'weapons', according to Butterly's statement to the gardaí. Head doorman Thomas Kennan would later say that he was aware that lads were passing out ties to their mates outside to help them get in.

Martin Donohoe wasn't too impressed with some of the things he saw when he visited the Stardust. Donohoe was an Inspector of Places of Public Resort for Dublin Corporation. Technically, his job was to inspect electrical systems in public buildings like restaurants, hotels and discos, but he kept his eyes open for other things too; he liked to look out for any fire safety regulations which were not being complied with.

Under the law, an inspector had the power to go into a premises and make sure it was up to standard. He went to the Stardust on 4th July 1979 and found that one leaf of an exit door in the adjacent Lantern Rooms wasn't opening fully. It was his job to draw the attention of the owners or managers to this fact, which he did. He went again in August and it hadn't been fixed yet. On that day, he also found loose tables obstructing one of the emergency exits in the Stardust. When Donohoe went again on 7th August 1980, he found that a portable platform – used to extend out the stage for cabaret shows, such as the Dickie Rock performance – was causing an obstruction close to another emergency exit, and there were also a number of loose seats obstructing the passageway on the east side of the building. When he went back again two weeks later, he found a plastic skip in front of one of the emergency exits full of empty bottles and placed in such a way that it could obstruct people trying to use that exit. The next time Donohoe went, just two weeks later, it was because a member of An Garda Síochána had made a complaint. This time, he found an exit door chained and locked in the Silver Swan pub. At the time, Eamon Butterly said he was not aware that the door should be kept open and that he would have it opened immediately.

Going north from the Dublin civic offices to the Stardust in Artane was becoming something of a regular occurrence for Martin Donohoe. In late November 1980 he inspected the nightclub again and found an emergency exit chained and locked, with the bolt on the panic bar mechanism broken and the upright piece of it hanging loose. Thomas Kennan said the bar had been broken during the evening and the door was 'locked and chained for security reasons'.

Donohoe told Kennan that if he was worried about security, he should put a man on the door rather than locking it.

Donohoe was back in again in January 1980. He timed it well. It was the night that The Specials were playing and the Stardust would soon be rammed. He found that the passage leading from the stage to another emergency exit was obstructed by a large box. He told Butterly and the concert promoter that it had to be moved. When Donohoe came back, the box was placed between two toilet doors in the ballroom. Again, he brought this up with Butterly and the box was taken away.

In all, Martin Donohoe visited the Stardust 30 times in just 18 months, raising issues and coming back to check if anything had been done about them. The Specials gig in January 1981 was something of a tipping point; the scenes that night prompted Dublin Corporation to write a rebuke to Patrick Butterly, warning him of the potential for legal trouble and the risk that the venue would be denied a licence in the future.

A planning officer wrote:

Dear Sir,

The Inspector for Places of Public Resort (Electrical) visited the above premises on 15th January, 1981, at 9.00 p.m. and noted the following:—

(1) Exit passageway at side of stage obstructed with cases, boxes, etc.

(2) Overcrowding—the number of persons present in the Cabaret Room was greatly in excess of the permitted number (of 1,400) for which exiting is

provided. This constitutes a very serious infringement of this bye-law.

Your attention is drawn to the requirements of Bye-law 38 of the Bye-laws relating to Places of Public Resort which require that special care shall be taken to ensure that the means of escape provided for all persons on the premises are at all times maintained unobstructed and immediately available.

Unless I receive your immediate assurances that the Exit ways will in future be maintained unobstructed at all times the public are on the premises and immediately available it will be necessary to institute proceedings against you for contravention of the above bye-law and also to raise the matter during the hearing of your application for renewal of your annual licence.

Eamon Butterly wrote back on 27th January, acknowledging what the Corporation had said. This letter was 18 days before the night of the St Valentine's Day disco:

The back exit in question was cleared immediately [sic] *it was brought to my attention and I assure you that it will not happen again. I personally take great care to make sure all exits are clear. Re overcrowding, I had discovered that tickets were forged for the show on that particular night and I have forged tickets if you wish to see them. This would account for the number of people who were on the premises. I have also decided not to stage concerts of this type again.*

Again, I assure you that all exits will be kept clear when the public are on the premises.

This letter did not impress Judge Ronan Keane, at least. In the Tribunal of Inquiry set up in the wake of the fire, he would find that this letter was a 'deliberate attempt' by Butterly to mislead Dublin Corporation into thinking all the exits would be kept in an unlocked and unobstructed condition while patrons were on the premises.

But even aside from Donohoe's inspections, a lack of oversight from the authorities was a key concern too. The fire prevention department at Dublin Corporation did not have nearly enough people working for it and was 'grossly understaffed' at the time that the planning permission was sought for the Stardust. At the time of the fire, there were three vacancies in the department. Fire officers said that, even if it had its full complement of seven people, this wouldn't have been enough and should have been closer to 12.

'The fact that there was no inspection whatever of this building by any member of the Fire Brigade, either in the Fire Prevention Department or fire-fighting service, from the day it opened until the fire, was one of the most disquieting facts to emerge at the inquiry,' Keane said.

Despite Donohoe's interventions, the inspection regime at the Stardust and warnings to the Butterlys didn't lead to compliance with bye-laws in place. Had it been inspected by the fire prevention department, the electrical and public lighting department or even during a disco night, issues may have come to light earlier and perhaps been addressed.

While, on paper, Ireland was superficially committed to ensuring standards for buildings, in practice the enforcement of this was lacking. And lacking substantially. In a letter to the *Irish Independent* in August 1980 after

10 people died in a fire at a hotel in Bundoran in County Donegal, the secretary of the Chief Fire Officers Association S.F. McDermott said he and colleagues had continually raised with government ministers the 'total inadequacy of qualified fire prevention staff, to seek, find and remedy the fire safety inadequacies of all types of premises in this country'.

The night of that Specials concert at the Stardust stands out. The numbers on the premises were well in excess of the 1,400 allowed capacity. Butterly had blamed people using forged tickets to get in. The crowd in the Stardust was rowdy and boisterous, and things got ugly. Bottles flying, stage invasions, punches getting thrown. The band, who were playing with The Beat, barricaded themselves in their dressing room. The Beat lead singer Dave Wakeling told Ed Power in the *Irish Times*: 'The band did a runner, and the fight carried over backstage. There was blood on the walls and broken glass on the floor. We noticed all the exits at the back were chained up and padlocked. There was no way out. So we went back into the dressing room and put up a sofa against the door until they had finished bottling each other. Later, we read about the fire.'

There were other events that caused disquiet in the run-up to 13th February 1981. Fr Dermot McCarthy was part of a group called the All Priests Show, which had performed in the Stardust the week before the fire, raising money for charity. When his part was over, he had tried to leave through an exit door at the back of the stage, but found the chains on the door were locked. He couldn't open the door, going out around the front of the stage instead to find an exit that was open.

There were power outages and electrical problems at the venue, too. Patrick O'Driscoll was performing at the nightclub with an Elvis tribute band when he saw a 'shower of sparks' coming from the ceiling at the backstage area. He said he believed it was a power surge and kept playing. Suzanne McCluskey noticed sparks 'flash down from the ceiling' during a gig that January. 'The flashes I saw were a purple colour, they were not a series of flashes, just an odd purple flash,' she said. And DJ Danny Hughes told the inquests that an electrical contractor setting up equipment informed him of a 'fluctuation in electrical supply' at the Stardust. Hughes said he never had problems with this equipment anywhere else.

* * *

People at the Stardust didn't know anything about the Corporation inspections or the rebukes made to Butterly over locking the doors. At the Valentine's disco, in the nondescript building with its locked and chained emergency exits, the steel plates welded over the toilet windows and with walls covered in carpet tiles, it was a busy night.

Staff were hard at work behind the scenes. It was no small operation. There was a cashier working at the entrance and a cloakroom attendant to take coats, jackets and bags from patrons. Twenty-three barmen were ready to pull pints, assisted by five washers who would make sure there was no shortage of glasses. Nine staff were working in the kitchen, with six waitresses and a catering manager. Fourteen lounge girls were on hand to dole out drinks, pick up plates and empty glasses, and keep ashtrays from overflowing. A supervisor kept the operation moving.

Danny Hughes arrived at around 8.30pm to get ready for his DJ set. He had five assistants who also got up on the decks at various points in the evening.

By 11pm, a queue of people stretched along the front of the building, waiting in the freezing cold to be allowed in. Susan Darling was wearing a red dress with short sleeves and a long, heavy grey coat. She had also convinced her mother to lend her one of her prized Aran cardigans to keep her warm. 'Now don't let anything happen to that,' she warned.

Inside, the atmosphere was electric. Hundreds of people had packed out the venue, dressed in their finery, out on the dance floor or sitting at tables and chairs, huddled together with friends, dishing out the latest gossip. Maybe some were seeing if they could find romance in time for Valentine's Day.

Catherine Darling remembers the question on everyone's lips: Who are you rooting for in the disco-dancing competition? She and her sister Susan knew a good few of the people taking part, but they had their favourites. One was Errol, another was Robbie Mulligan.

Like any nightclub, the Stardust wasn't immune to a bit of trouble now and again, but the night passed without much incident. Outside, four lads were trying to sneak in through the exit doors. Others who tried this method in the weeks before the fire were unsuccessful: one later told the inquests that he tried to get in at one door but it opened just a couple of inches because it was chained shut; another recalled trying and failing to prise a door open using steel bars.

The group of four checked Exit 6. Locked. They scaled a drainpipe to the roof of the building. This was a route sometimes used to sneak into the Stardust, so much so that independent security had been hired to keep watch, in addition to two car park attendants. They peered through a skylight to see if they could get in that way and tried in vain to force it open, giving up when they were spooked by a passing garda car.

They hopped down off the roof and made a final attempt to open a door using a beer keg they had knocked over during their descent.

It was shortly before midnight. A barman in the Silver Swan heard this commotion and rushed out, armed with the leg of a chair. The sight of this angry man was enough to make the youths scarper. They didn't return to the Stardust again that night. Later investigations heard repeatedly that this incident had had no bearing on events later in the night, but the story of the boys on the roof was to become one of many pored over in the search for the cause of the fire.

Inside, the night flowed on.

Phelim Kinahan, the floor manager, was working that night, as was Thomas Kennan, who was in charge of the nine bouncers on duty. These doormen were responsible for unlocking all the exits – and making sure they were locked in the first place. None of them were given specific responsibility for it, nor was there a specific time when it was usually done.

While the front door had a simple lock and key and could be covered by metal shutters, each of the remaining five emergency exits was secured with a padlock and chain. Each of these was strung through the panic bar, the horizontal mechanism seen on many emergency exits, which would open the door when force was applied. These bars allow people to get out quickly, and also means the doors will still open if the crowd pushes against them in a crush.

One attendee that night, Ann Horner, noticed the chains on the doors and joked with a boy she was chatting with that they'd been locked in. 'They haven't locked us in, they've locked them out,' the boy said, saying that people had been getting in for free.

On the night of Friday 13th, Exit 3, which was very close to the stage, was unlocked at around 8.30pm to allow the DJs to unload gear from a van, which was backed up to the doorway to allow for easy movement of the heavy equipment. The DJs weren't able to use their usual set-up, as they discovered on a few occasions that the electrics in the Stardust couldn't handle the power it drew.

Staff at a bar close to Exit 4 also had a key for it, as they needed to go to and from a shed outside to manage kegs. This usually happened within an hour of opening, and the door was kept unlocked.

But doors in the Stardust had a habit of becoming locked again.

Chapter 3

By 1.40am, in the early hours of Valentine's Day 1981, the big night at the Stardust had reached its crescendo. The winners of the disco-dancing competition had been crowned – their prize, a voucher from K-Tel Records.

The club was heaving. More than 800 people had turned out to see the competition, but some were now calling it a night. Finishing up their drinks, saying goodbye to friends. In the foyer, a small number of people were leaving, collecting their belongings from the cloakroom before heading on.

Peter O'Toole was there too. His girlfriend, Ann Roe, had lost her handbag, and Peter was using a payphone near the main entrance to report it to gardaí. He rang 999. The call was automatically recorded by the operator in Dublin Castle at 1.42am.

'I'm at the Stardust disco. Can you hear me?' Peter asked. The operator replied that they could, but Peter was rushing to get the words out: '. . . and my girlfriend's handbag was robbed'.

'Your girlfriend's handbag was robbed?' the operator repeated.

'She's the manageress in the shoe shop in Northside Shopping Centre.'

'Wait now, would you . . . Stardust?'

They struggled to communicate with each other, perhaps due to Peter's urgency or the din of the club. He repeatedly asked the operator if they could hear him; the operator tried to get his name and a location where he could meet the gardaí.

Then, a noise in the background halted the call. Peter hung up.

* * *

Forty minutes earlier, at 1am, the bars had stopped serving for the night. It was time for the dancing competition. This was the big moment. The 36 contestants took to the floor and everyone else vied for a spot to watch, crowding around the edge of the dance floor, standing on tables and chairs, craning their necks. A few of the staff members drifted over to watch as well.

For all of the hype leading up to it, the contest itself would be over quick: just one song, meaning the contestants had only a few minutes to give it all they had. Danny Hughes, the DJ for the night, chose 'Born to Be Alive', a hit by French disco artist Patrick Hernandez, as the deciding track. The song had been released in late 1978 and quickly became a hit in the United States and across Europe. In Ireland, it spent a week in August 1979 at 21 in the music charts.

It's everything you would imagine for a disco-dancing contest. Think 'Boogie Wonderland' by Earth, Wind & Fire and you're in the right ballpark. Pumping bass octaves drive it forward, with four-on-the-floor drums and an open hi-hat on the off beats. There's a frenetic riff from a clean electric guitar, and you get a burst of brass every so often.

'We were born to be alive,' Hernandez sings. 'Born, born to be alive.'

Two of Danny's assistants were the judges, and they studied the dance moves carefully. They passed their judgement to the DJ before the six-minute edit of the song came to an end: Errol Buckley and Paula McDonnell were crowned the winners.

Paula's two sisters were thrilled, cheering on their big sister's win. Errol couldn't believe it. He and Paula stepped up on stage in front of the crowd, hundreds of people looking on. Errol wasn't that interested in the prize he had won; it was the thrill of the moment he enjoyed. He went into the back dressing room behind the stage with his big brother Jimmy, who was telling Errol how proud he was of him. Photographs were taken of the winners before Errol and Paula collected their prizes and were brought back on stage for an encore. Colm O Briain took over as DJ and urged the crowd to get back out and join in with the winners, spinning 'Born to Be Alive' one more time.

The dance floor filled again, but this was also the cue for some to head on. If you weren't calling it a night, you were maybe bursting for the bathroom and headed in that direction or went back to your table to finish the last of your drinks, returning to the chats and the craic. Lounge girls were picking up what was left of the plates of sausages and chips.

It was time for 20-year-old John King to go home. He'd had a few and wanted to get back to his bed. John went to the main door at around 1.30am, but the outside shutters were down and the door was locked, so he couldn't get out. There were two bouncers in the foyer. One of them, John Fitzsimons, asked the other, Frankie Downes, for the keys, which Downes used to open the door, pull up the shutters and let John out. He heard the shutters being rolled back down behind him as he walked away.

Linda Bishop and Sandra Hatton weren't interested in having a dance. They were back with friends at their table near the main stage, sitting beside a blind running from floor to ceiling – one of five identical shutter blinds in a row that cordoned off the West Alcove, which wasn't in use that night. The pair hadn't shaken off the chill of the night outside and were trying to catch the attention of bouncers as they passed. 'Any chance you could turn the heating on? This place is freezing,' Sandra asked one of them.

Linda suddenly felt a warmth. She glanced at her watch – brand-new, with a light-up face – and saw it was 1.33am. Surely they didn't actually turn the heating on, she thought, sure the night is nearly over. One of their friends, not wanting to spend the final songs sitting down, encouraged them out onto the dance floor. They relented and left their table.

Over at the bar, the staff were tidying up after the busy night. Gerry Guilfoyle was counting the takings and putting bottles of spirits away. Nearby, Declan Burnett was washing glasses when he got a whiff of something, similar to burning rubber. This type of smell had been noticed before in the Stardust by another glass washer, just a few months previously. He had searched the venue to see if he could find the source, going upstairs to the lamp room, where he noticed it was stronger. He still couldn't find exactly where it was coming from, and it faded away after a while.

Another night, three weeks before the competition, staff saw what appeared to be smoke hanging in the air, lit by a lamp over the stage, shortly before the club opened. On that occasion, there was no smell, but it sparked concern among the workers who saw it. Again, the source of the smoke couldn't be found, and it was gone by the time they started letting people in. A waitress witnessed something similar at one of the bars a week prior. 'Someone said the smoke was from the heating,' she said.

Burnett mentioned the smell to Guilfoyle. Probably just cigarettes, he said. The pair continued with their work. The crowd in front of them danced to 'Lorraine', a track by English ska band Bad Manners.

At 1.40am, around seven minutes after Linda Bishop and Sandra Hatton had felt the increase in heat, their friends were back at the table beside the West Alcove. Among them was Frances Winston, in the Stardust for the first time. The gang wasn't long sitting down when Frances also smelt something like smoke. She asked if anyone else noticed it – no, Valerie Walsh replied.

Then Sharon O'Hanlon asked the same question: could anyone else smell something burning? Their attention quickly turned to the shutter blind beside their table. It was glowing, illuminated by something behind it in the empty seating area in the West Alcove. They peered in.

What they saw didn't look too serious: a small fire, a few inches high, a couple of feet at most, on two or three seats in the back right corner. On the other side of the wall was the main bar, where staff had noticed a strange smell. The flames were bright orange with a blue tinge, and there was little or no smoke coming off it. One eyewitness later agreed that the flame – multicoloured, dancing, lively – was similar to 'when whiskey on a Christmas pudding is set on fire'. The sort of thing that could be put out with any of the several fire extinguishers dotted around the building. Everyone who saw the fire in that first minute said the same thing: it didn't look like something to be too worried about and would be put out quickly. Jacqueline McCarthy spotted the flame after looking under the blind, and immediately went to tell a nearby doorman, pointing him in the direction of the fire. He shouted to other doormen to ring 999 and then ran back to look at the fire for himself. The flames were running the entire length of a seat now. To some, it looked like other rows might be catching fire too.

The smell started to get stronger, and the glow behind the blinds intensified. People at other tables noticed or stopped to look as they were walking by. Some didn't even see the glowing curtain; they just saw something was happening – a fight, maybe – and started to drift over to the West Alcove from the dance floor or other parts of the ballroom to see what it was. The blind was divided into five sections, and someone raised the one closest to the main bar, revealing the fire to more people. That's when it caught Linda's eye from the dance floor. She could see what looked like a sofa on fire, but still nothing serious. Maybe they'd just go for a smoke while they put it out, she thought.

The alarm was raised among other staff. Maria Brady, the lounge girl supervisor, was collecting empty bottles and glasses when she saw the glow behind the blind and rushed to tell barman Laurence Neville. 'Larry, come out, there's a fire,' she shouted. He ran out to see what was happening. The flames had now spread to adjacent seats. He watched for a matter of seconds before running to the Silver Swan. He stood in the doorway of the pub and shouted: 'There is a fire in the Stardust!' Eamon Butterly was among those in the Silver Swan at the time. Years later, a doorman told a court that he heard Butterly say 'the bastards started a fire'. He and others followed Neville back into the Stardust.

In the foyer, where Peter O'Toole was in the middle of ringing 999 about his girlfriend's stolen handbag, two people ran in to alert the doormen guarding the main entrance about what was happening inside. One of these doormen, Leo Doyle, went into the ballroom to look before coming back and grabbing a fire extinguisher from the wall. The other doorman there, Frankie Downes, who had let John King out to go home just minutes before, was still manning the main entrance, unlocking it as people left. Once the shout came in that there was a fire, he unlocked the doors, keeping one side open by slipping a doormat underneath to hold it in place.

Lorraine McDonnell was unaware of what was unfolding. She had sat back down after the competition and was engrossed in conversation with a man she had met. Her sister Teresa, who had been sitting by the main door, suddenly appeared beside her and interrupted the pair: 'Lorraine, get out. There's a fire!' 'Go, just go now,' Lorraine said, and Teresa darted away.

There were seven fire extinguishers in the Stardust and staff were now rushing over to the seating area with them. Among them was doorman Patrick J. Murphy, one of the only two staff members who had ever used one before. He trained his extinguisher at the flames, but it didn't seem to have any effect. The fire continued to grow. Barman Colm O'Toole also managed to grab a fire extinguisher, but the liquid seemed to drive the flames on rather than put them out. Instead of quelling the fire, it was like the liquid was splitting the flame into two. Even though the fire had now spread to other rows of seats, it still looked like something that could be brought under control. Despite its small size, the intense heat of the fire kept forcing the people with the extinguishers back, and they struggled to stay close to the fire. The heat seemed to be emanating from the air or ceiling above them and singed the hair on the back of Patrick's neck. Another doorman felt like he was being sunburnt by the heat.

Something like jelly started dripping from the ceiling above them. It left a strawberry-coloured stain on clothes. Some of it was falling down in little fireballs. The music continued, although a crowd had drifted off the dance floor to watch what was happening.

Little more than two minutes had passed since the fire was first seen when Neville returned to the ballroom from the Silver Swan. He watched as, suddenly, the fire started to take on a life of its own. It grew and gained speed, shooting like a fireball across the seats, forcing the bouncers and doormen fighting the fire back. The carpet tiles that covered the walls of the ballroom caught alight, propelling the fire higher and wider, and it spread left and right around the seating area. Black smoke poured from the fire. It was thick and acrid, tasted slightly sweet, and burned the throats of people standing around the West Alcove.

Neville ran to the Silver Swan pub to call 999. Vital seconds were lost as the phone was set to only call numbers within the Stardust complex itself, and he couldn't find the switch that would enable it to dial out. The call was recorded as having happened at 1.43am, less than three minutes after the fire was first seen. 'Would you come down to the Stardust Club in Artane as fast as you can,' he said, 'there is a large fire. There is over 800 people in the place. For God's sake come quick, it is getting out of control!'

The officer on duty at the control room in Dublin's Central Fire Station at Tara Street, around the corner from College Green, took his number and said Dublin Fire Brigade was on the way. The officer wrote the details of the call on a docket, in accordance with the normal procedure, and passed the docket to the senior fire officer on duty.

Unease in the club had been slowly spreading as the fire grew, revealing itself to more people. It now looked like it was getting out of control as smoke swirled through the ballroom 'like a tornado'. Linda Bishop noticed that in the space of just a few seconds – not even minutes – people had started to move faster towards the doors and then run. A friend of hers, Valerie Walsh, appeared in front of her. 'I have your coat and your bag – we're gone,' she told Linda.

Some people were getting out of the emergency exits dotted around the building. Others made it to Exits 3, 4 and 5, only to find that they couldn't get out. The first to arrive at Exit 4 found a lock and chain draped over the panic bars. Kicking or shouldering the door, it started to ease open by a few inches, but there was no more give. It was a similar scene at Exit 5, where the crowd swelled to more than 40 people in front of the closed doors. Exit 3 was shut with a padlock and chain. Three women who spotted the fire after leaving the ladies' bathroom headed straight for this exit. 'The bloody door is locked,' one shouted. Three men arrived at the exit as well and started kicking the door – kicking and kicking, but it barely opened. More and more people started to arrive at these exits. 'Get that chain off the door, for fuck's sake!'

The situation in the ballroom was getting out of control. More staff arrived with extinguishers and sprayed foam on the flames. It still wasn't having any effect. 'Please open the door!' someone yelled at Exit 3.

Staff were escaping through other exits, some through the Silver Swan. Others who left through the kitchen found the corridor filled with smoke and were pushed back, heading instead to the Lantern Rooms.

All efforts to fight the fire had been abandoned in the West Alcove. The heat was, somehow, growing even more intense, the smoke more dense, and the flames looked as though they would spread out to the ballroom at any second. The ceiling started to melt beyond the alcove. Droplets fell on people, burning their clothing, sticking to their skin. 'The door is shut!' someone shouted at Exit 4.

All through this, the music played, with many on the dance floor facing the stage with their backs to the West Alcove, still unaware of what was unfolding in the densely packed club – either how serious it was or the fact that there was a fire at all. If you couldn't smell the smoke or had a view of the fire through the open blind, the smoke drifting across the ceiling looked like special effects, like dry ice.

The next series of events happened in rapid succession.

Colm O Briain was still up on the decks, playing a mix of different songs. He had been watching the growing intensity of the fire through the open section of the blind but could see now that people were starting to panic. He turned down the music and made an announcement, telling the crowd not to panic, that everything was under control and to head towards the exits. It was 1.44am.

Jimmy Fitzpatrick was on the opposite side of the crowd from the fire, still dancing. He remembers that 'Shaddap

You Face', a number one in Ireland that month, was playing, thinking to himself, 'What's the point of this song?' Then, the announcement. He looked around: 'Where's this fire? What fire is he talking about?' He followed the crowd's attention. From his angle, all he could see was a flicker behind the blinds.

The dance floor began to empty after the DJ's announcement, with people running to exits that still weren't open. They kicked and pushed the doors, taking turns to save their strength. The smoke was thick enough at some exits that some started to succumb to smoke inhalation, collapsing to the ground.

Onlookers saw someone reaching down to the bottom of the shutter blind separating the alcove from the rest of the room. He released the bolts that were holding the remaining four blinds around the West Alcove in place, pushing them up with his hand. Now, the fire was visible to everyone in the room, leaving them in no doubt as to how serious the situation was becoming. It looked like every row of seats was ablaze. The flames were at ceiling height, and the carpet tiles on the walls were burning ferociously.

At almost exactly the same time, right as the entire ballroom was exposed to the unfolding emergency, the blaze accelerated. Pillowy, lethal, fast-moving black smoke gushed out – then, a ball of fire, shooting across the ceiling of the entire ballroom, rolling above the hundreds of people still on the dancefloor. This is a phenomenon known as a flashover: the air at the top of the club grew so hot that it was able to ignite other materials. It is feared by firefighters because of how quickly and intensely it causes flames to spread. One person looking at it thought it was like looking into hell. 'Jesus Christ, we are all going to die,' somebody shouted.

The temperature in the rest of the club rose sharply, burning skin and clothes, and the building started to fall apart. A portion of the ceiling in the West Alcove collapsed – one person described it as being like 'balls of fire falling' – and even more dense smoke billowed into the ballroom. People were jumping over tables and chairs to get out as the burning material from the melting ceiling fell on top of them, some of it twice the size of a fist. To Antoinette Keegan, it looked and felt like when a candle is held at an angle and drops of wax fall; as it hit people's faces and bodies, it felt like it was raining acid. Some described it as being like liquid plastic. As they tried to brush it off, it would stick to their bodies, pulling their skin off as they tried to get rid of it.

Jimmy Fitzpatrick ran towards the main entrance, passing two girls near the cigarette machine who were panicking. He kept going and got into the hallway – but stopped. He knew he had to help them. He turned back into the Stardust and towards the fire, through flaming droplets coming from the ceiling. Jimmy was strong, an amateur boxer. He grabbed them – 'Let's go, are you ready?' – and threw them with all his might towards the exit. As he got his bearings, he tripped and fell. Then, a bright flash of light and a loud bang. The lights went out, and the club was plunged into pitch darkness.

It's the moment everyone who was in the Stardust that night remembers probably more clearly than anything else. The lights failed so soon after the DJ's announcement that some people believed it happened at the same time. 'As he was saying that, everything just went black,' Errol recalls. Yvonne Graham was screaming at Christine and Anne, still on the dancefloor, to get out when 'everything just went black'. The last thing Antoinette remembers is 'the music stopping and the lights going out', leaving them 'in the pitch dark with thick black smoke and fire coming down on top of us'.

The ripple of panic that had been sweeping through the ballroom turned into a torrent. People were lost in the darkness, the roaring flames barely illuminating the club through the heavy smoke. Some – many – began to scream over the roaring noise of the fire, rushing, pushing and clawing their way through the darkness to an exit, any exit, as the fire advanced through more and more of the ballroom behind them. A small group started to pray the Our Father.

Catherine Darling knew the place like the back of her hand because of how often she went. She knew where every exit, toilet and bar was, but that was when the lights were on. 'How the fuck are we going to get out of here?' she thought to herself.

Deborah Osbourne was holding hands with her friends to get out. The surging heat hit the back of her neck, the fire like 'a monster, a living thing' coming after her. Their hands lost grip of each other, and Deborah screamed into the darkness, calling their names, before being knocked to the floor. She put a hand on a seat to try to get up, but melting material pulled the skin off her palm.

On the ground, she found her friend Sandra Lawless. They lay together and hugged and Deborah, giving up on the fight to get out, tried to comfort her: 'You're going somewhere nice. You're just reaching out to get to that place.' Another friend found them and shook Deborah, telling her to get up. 'To this day, I don't know why I didn't take Sandra with me,' she said later.

Christine Carr held her breath for as long as she could before she had to take a breath. The smoke was so thick it felt like breathing ash, immediately filling her lungs. She could feel the lack of oxygen suffocating her. 'Mammy, daddy, I'm going to die,' the 16-year-old thought. Her next memory was being outside, somehow, on the ground.

Antoinette, Mary and Martina Keegan had also formed a chain with their friends Helen Henby and Mary Kenny. They were almost at an exit when the heaving crowd pushed them to the ground. Antoinette fell to the floor, struggling to breathe as heavy smoke burnt her throat. The sisters continued to hold hands tightly, Antoinette repeating, 'Oh God, please help us, help us.' She looked up through the mass of people and could see some were struggling to get out of the exit nearest them. She fell unconscious.

Helen couldn't find them. She was caught in the burning droplets falling from the ceiling, which were setting clothes alight and starting small fires all around the ballroom. She crawled underneath a table where other people were also hiding. Some of them were on fire. Helen was burning too and had to get away. She went to a passageway near Exit 5 and just lay down, thinking she was dead, before someone came across her and carried her out.

The chains on the exit doors were just one part of the struggle to escape. Tables and chairs, which had been stacked near Exit 4 – beside the dance floor – had fallen over and were now strewn across the floor. People tripped and fell in the darkness. The pushing crowd caused a crush as bodies heaved desperately towards doors that wouldn't open. Exit 4 was forced open, pitching the pushing crowd out of the darkness and into the night air, and so was Exit 6. Exit 5 took another minute – a lifetime – to open. As people began to spill out, some found themselves forcing against a crowd of people who had already left and were trying to get back in to find their friends.

This was the exit through which Yvonne Graham escaped. 'It's a stampede,' she thought. 'It's like wild animals trying to get out.' She was carried by the weight of the crowd through the open doors. Outside, a skip used to collect empty bottles had been in front of the door and had been overturned. Yvonne tripped and fell over it, and others slipped on the bottles, cutting themselves on the broken glass. Yvonne stood at the door, screaming through the flood of people for her friends – soon, the figures of two, Christine and Anne, emerged through the crowd, 'as black as your boot'.

Exit 3 was the last of the emergency exits to open, the locked chains taking even more force to open than on other doors. People who got out found the DJ's van was parked right in front of the door. There were a small number of steps leading down from the door, with the back doors of the van pressed up against the bottom steps. A handrail to the left-hand side of the steps and a raised grass verge to the right made it even more difficult to get around. Instead of being able to swarm out, people were squashed into narrow lines, trying to get out to the left and right of the van. Henry Byrne had just managed to get out past the van and could see the problem it was causing. He dove into the van through the driver's door window, released the handbrake and then jumped out. Another man jumped into the van and steered it, as people rushed to push it up onto a nearby embankment, moving it out of the way.

Catherine Darling was close to the main bar and managed to make her way to Exit 1, which was beside the main bar, down a long corridor crammed with people, all using the wall to feel their way out. People behind them shouted 'keep walking, just keep walking' as they moved towards the chink of light from the open door at the end. When she got outside, everyone was screaming. The panic was everywhere.

It's human nature in this type of situation to try to leave the same way you came in, and that's what many people did; a lot of people in the room headed straight for the main entrance, known as Exit 2. This door had been opened as soon as word had spread that there was a fire and people had been able to leave through this exit without any difficulty. Sandra Hyland fled this way, but turned and went back inside – she was out, but her friends weren't. Suddenly she was caught by a funnel of people pouring out of the ballroom and carried backwards towards the exit again as more and more people filed into the foyer. Then Sandra heard the shout: 'They're locked!'

The main door, which had been wedged open with a mat underneath when the fire started, had closed over. People were now trapped in the foyer, hemmed in as others continued to squeeze in, the crowd heaving and pushing. Some people were knocked to the ground. Others were forced by the mass of people in the wrong direction, either up a set of stairs in the foyer or into the cloakroom. All the while, the intensity of the fire grew behind them. The West Alcove was now completely ablaze, and a section of the roof of the building was close to collapse. Smoke filled the lobby. Some people collapsed on the ground as they inhaled the fumes.

Doorman Frankie Downes didn't see this happening. He had been wedged in the corner of the foyer by the force of the crowd and eventually got out before the doors shut. Outside, he was attempting to stop people from trying to get back into the club, wrestling one man on the grass outside, when he glanced behind him and saw the doors had closed. The doors had to be kicked and pushed from inside to get them out again. 'I can't remember my feet touching the ground till the time I got back out the door again,' Sandra said. As people poured out, some turned back to see what they had escaped from. Five bodies lay on the floor.

Linda Bishop got caught in this bottleneck at Exit 2, the crowd of people much larger than the small opening in the doorway. She was pushed against the wall, where she could see, hear and feel the fire. As she stood there, she thought to herself that she would not be getting out of this exit, but she didn't know of any other way out. 'This is probably it,' she thought to herself.

At that moment, her friend Valerie found her, grabbed her arm, and started towards another exit, but they soon lost each other again in the dark. Making her way to that other exit, Linda fell over something – 'I hope it was just coats, I just always say to myself, I hope it was coats' – but picked herself up and kept moving. Each breath she took hurt. It was only because she bumped into a stair post that she knew she was near the door of Exit 1. She kept walking through the dark, desperate to get out of the smoke, desperate for a breath of fresh air as she reached the doorway. She fell on her hands and knees again, vomiting, but slowly found her way out the door.

Errol Buckley, the disco-dancing competition winner, didn't know how he got out, but he did. He and his girlfriend had been swept up in a crowd, and before they knew it, they were outside. He turned back to the exit and saw girls running out of the nightclub on fire. It looked like there was burning material stuck to their skin. Close to the exit Errol left through was a sand pit. He didn't know if it was the right thing or not, but he tried it: he threw one of the burning girls into the sand, and then another and then another, rolling them, trying to put the flames out.

Outside was mayhem. People had collapsed. Some were suffering from horrific burns. Some screaming for their friends. Others were carried motionless to a grassy hill outside the club. Some who looked back inside saw a furnace. The doors were open and it was just completely red.

Jimmy Fitzpatrick was still crawling on the ground inside, completely disoriented, being trampled by the crowd. The smoke, 'so thick you could chew it', meant he had no idea which way he was crawling, guided only by the material underneath. He felt carpet, then the wood of the dance floor. He was going the wrong way, deeper into the room.

He got up and ran blindly, falling again against the stage. He felt as though someone moved past him, so ran in that direction, and reached an exit that was still locked, surrounded by people screaming and trying to open the doors. Jimmy joined them – kicking, and kicking, and kicking. He wasn't even sure if it was the exit, or a wall, or the door to a toilet, but it burst open and they rushed out into the night.

Then, people heard the screams: people were still trapped inside, with no way out.

Chapter 4

NOT FAR FROM THE STARDUST, a Dublin Fire Brigade ambulance crew was preparing to make their way back to their station in the city centre.

Dave Fitzgerald and Paddy Cunningham had been dispatched to an emergency in nearby Darndale but received word over the radio that it was a false alarm. As they headed back, another call came in. The operator said the switchboard was receiving calls about a fire in the Stardust. A fire engine was on its way but Fitzgerald and Cunningham were to head across and check it out as well.

They were among the first of the emergency services to arrive at the fire, roughly 20 minutes after Linda Bishop first felt a rise in temperature in the club and 10 minutes after the first 999 call. The scene that greeted them as they pulled in off the Kilmore Road was unlike anything either of them had experienced.

It was hundreds of people but it looked more like thousands, swarming around the building – screaming, crying, in shock. Some rushing through the crowd frantically, trying to find their friends. Their faces had been blackened by soot, making it hard to recognise each other. Clothes were in tatters, covered in scorch marks. People were badly burned. The most severe cases were comforted while a vehicle that could take them to hospital was found.

People who were unconscious were being laid on a grassy area next to the club. Even at this stage, it was too late for some of them. Behind the crowd loomed the burning nightclub, smoke and people pouring out of the doors and windows. Anyone who tried to get back in to rescue friends faced a roaring, crimson furnace. The sky above was lit up red and orange. This is chaos, Fitzgerald thought.

The dense crowd started to swell as locals arrived to see what was happening and to try to help. Among the masses was Antoinette Keegan, who was starting to come to after being pulled out of the club unconscious. She was in immense pain, with burns on her face and hands. There was a pile of material – sand or soil – next to her, and she started rubbing it over her face in a desperate attempt to cool herself down. It stung her burnt skin. She was screaming for her two sisters. 'Where's Mary? Where's Martina?' she shouted.

In the scramble to escape, Lorraine McDonnell spotted an area inside the club where the smoke seemed less dense. She held her breath, ran, and managed to get out of the building. She went around the front, desperately gasping for breath in the cold night air. She soon found her sister Teresa's friends amid the pandemonium. They had the same question she did: 'Where is she?' It was like a sixth sense for Lorraine. She knew Teresa was gone.

Errol Buckley, who had won the disco-dancing competition less than an hour before, couldn't find Jimmy. He hurried through the screaming crowd, asking anyone he could if they had seen his brother. Someone told him that the rest of his family were out, but no one was sure where Jimmy was. Another said that Jimmy had gotten out of the fire but had gone back in to try to find Errol.

This is crazy, thought Errol, I don't know what is happening here.

Catherine Darling lost her sister Susan in the pandemonium. In the midst of it all, she came across a man screaming for help, trying to get his shirt off.

'As I was taking his shirt off, the skin on his back was coming off with the shirt,' Catherine said. 'He was screaming, he just wanted the cold air on his back.'

What was happening hadn't sunk in for Susan yet. She was talking to doorman Frankie Downes, explaining that she had to go back in to get a cardigan her mother lent her. 'I can't go home without it,' she insisted.

'My ma had said, "Don't let anything happen to it." Frank said we wouldn't be getting back in, and he wouldn't be surprised if one or two people are dead. I said, "Are you joking?"'

She broke off the conversation to find Catherine wading through the dense crowd. She managed to get back to the door she'd gotten out of moments before.

'It only seemed like minutes from the time I'd come out that door to go back in that way,' she said. 'And you couldn't get into it. You just couldn't get into it because of the flames. There's no way you could have walked back in.'

*　*　*

For many of Dublin's firefighters, the first they heard of what was happening was 'fire, Stardust, go'. As more information filtered in, it became clear it would be one of the biggest challenges that Dublin Fire Brigade had ever faced.

Moments after receiving the first 999 call from Larry Neville at 1.43am, the dispatch centre in Tara Street received a call from John Fitzsimons, a full-time fireman who was picking up some extra work as a doorman at the Stardust. He was working there that night. 'Look, we could lose up to 200 people here tonight,' Fitzsimons told the fireman who answered the call. He also gave them a crucial piece of information: this was going to be a district call. This was a way for Dublin Fire Brigade to triage how serious the incident was going to be. A district call meant that there was a threat to life, so two additional fire engines, an ambulance and an emergency tender carrying extra equipment would be needed. A brigade call was the next step up – it meant that not only was there a risk to life but even more fire appliances would be needed at the scene. A brigade call was unheard of for anyone working in Dublin Fire Brigade at the time.

The dispatcher immediately told Kilbarrack Station, the closest station to the Stardust, and North Strand Station, near Fairview, to send an engine each. After John Fitzsimons's call, they ordered engines to the scene from two more stations.

When the call was received at Kilbarrack, a fireman switched on the bells and a red light to alert the team on duty. They were on the road in 30 to 40 seconds, led by Station Officer Noel Mooney. As they approached, the crew could see the smoke rising in the sky above the building. They were still four minutes away.

Around the time of the first 999 call, Michael Kelly had heard a loud crackling noise coming from outside his home – the asbestos roof tiles on the Stardust were cracking from the heat. He went into his back garden and saw the smoke over the nightclub. Kelly took action: he grabbed a torch, jumped into his car and drove the two-minute journey to the club, running into the building through the Lantern Rooms. His route was blocked by a burning door, so he tried another. Suddenly, he found himself in the burning ballroom. He searched through the thick smoke with his torch, and the light soon found people on the ground in front of one of the bathrooms. Kelly picked one person up and managed to carry them out of the building. He ran back into the flames again and again, bringing people out each time.

At the same time, patrons, barmen, bouncers, anyone who could help were trying to rescue people they could see trapped just inside the exit doors. Once inside, they got low, underneath the smoke, crawling on the ground, searching with their hands in the dark.

Thomas Larkin was one of those pulled out after collapsing inside. He came to, took stock of the situation, and immediately went back in. A woman's white blouse caught his eye. He grabbed her, trying to pull her out, but she was clutching to something. Thomas kicked her hand free and dragged her out. It wasn't until decades later he discovered it was Antoinette Keegan, wearing the white blouse her sister Martina had lent her, and Antoinette had been clutching her hand.

Another group had just escaped through Exit 5 and looked back inside. There were people moving in the shadows. Harry Mahood was among those who rushed in and grabbed as many as they could, but a girl caught Harry's eye. She looked like she was lost, wandering aimlessly among the flames. It was only after she collapsed, within metres of the door, that he saw she was on fire.

The fire was still spreading outwards through the club. As it reached the exits, the flames grew too intense for rescue efforts. People had to be restrained from putting their own lives at risk to save their friends. Some could see people they thought they knew, just out of reach.

Michael Kelly was going back in again through the Lantern Rooms when he bumped into someone: a fireman. After what felt like an eternity, the fire engine had come roaring into the car park at 1.51am. Before they even arrived, the crew had seen dozens of people walking down the roads around the Stardust, giving a sense of the emergency's scale. They donned their breathing apparatus so they would be ready to get inside the building immediately.

The fire engine struggled to get through the crowd. People thumped on the windscreen and pointed at the Stardust to say their friends were inside. The next obstacle was a metal barrier, installed without planning permission to prevent cars from parking at the back of the building, blocking their way. The crowd saw the trouble the fire engine was having and physically forced the barrier open, allowing it to drive up to the building.

The fire was tearing the nightclub apart. Parts of the roof had fallen in, and flames soared into the night sky. Station Officer Mooney knew that the priority was to get anyone trapped inside out immediately. They also needed water. A blaze of this scale was going to require an immense amount to quench. The Kilbarrack appliance had a tank onboard, and the crew trained their hoses on the building immediately. It was empty after seven minutes – not unusual, as that time would be used to find a hydrant, but the firemen searched and couldn't see any. They had no idea there were three close to the Stardust, as two were missing the distinctive plate labelled 'H' above them, and one was mislabelled. The clock was ticking. They knew by rule of thumb that they would find hydrants close to a road junction and left to continue their search on the road outside the Stardust. Crucial minutes were lost trying to find water; at one point, as many as 10 firefighters were focusing on this rather than efforts to get into the building. As they made their way through the crowd – and away from the fire – they were accosted. People couldn't understand why they appeared to be leaving the scene instead of rescuing their friends.

One crew were lucky. Beneath the club was a massive water tank, dating back to when the complex was first built and used as a factory. Eamon Butterly maintains that he informed the first crew to arrive about this.

This all played out while more appliances arrived. The second, from Tara Street Fire Station, arrived almost immediately after the first. The firefighters' primary focus was on the people trapped in bathrooms at the front of the building, who could be heard screaming for their lives behind the steel-plated windows.

Deirdre Dames was trapped there in the ladies' toilet; when the lights failed, she fell and became disorientated, and crawled on her hands and knees towards what she thought was an exit. She could see flames licking underneath the door frame to the bathroom. People inside were splashing water on their faces in an attempt to cool down. Jean Hogan was pulled by another girl towards what they thought was Exit 2, but it was the gents' bathrooms. Ten other people were trapped inside the smoke-filled room, coughing violently, some of them vomiting. People were frantic, beating their hands on the windows, screaming to the people outside for help.

One firefighter, Acting Station Officer Patrick Hobbs, went over and shouted to some of the people trapped in the bathrooms at the front of the building if there was any way for them to get out the windows. He could see it was going to be impossible. The crowd outside grew desperate and tried in vain to remove the plates or pry them open with whatever they could find – iron bars, a sledgehammer taken from a fire engine, their hands – as people on the inside shouted that they were burning. Firefighters stepped in, and attached a steel rope to the windows with the other end tied to their appliance, but even the powerful vehicle couldn't make a difference. It was no use. The firemen had to go in and get them out.

Fireman Noel Hosback was already trying to do this. He saw his chance: a small window into a narrow storeroom that led to a bar, where the entrances to the bathrooms would be on either side. Hosback climbed in and fought through the smoke to the men's bathroom, kicking down the door. People were still alive inside. He ran back to the storeroom and shouted that he needed a breathing apparatus. This crucial piece of equipment was in short supply, as the first engine carried fewer than it normally should have.

He found one and dived back in. Time was ticking. People were starting to succumb to smoke inhalation, too weak to get out on their own. Hosback risked his own safety and shared his breathing apparatus with them. One by one, they were passed to Fireman Brian Parkes in the storeroom, who brought them to the window.

Hobbs was among another group of firefighters who managed to reach the other bathroom; the fire in the main entrance had mostly been put out, allowing them to get in this way. They were in luck as well: the people were in shock and panicking, while another lay unconscious on the ground, but alive.

The firefighters still had to get into the depths of the ballroom itself. The intense heat made it impossible to get in through some exits, but it was comparatively cool at Exit 3. A crew made their way into the club this way, fighting fires as they went, but the building was unfamiliar to them. Some knew it from going to the Stardust themselves as patrons, but other than that, they had nothing to go on. Fire stations in the area were not required to familiarise themselves with the layout of buildings like the Stardust, a venue that posed a high risk of disaster if something went wrong. They soon found themselves in a room behind the stage. There were a number of people lying there, unconscious. They were maybe too late for some of them.

The firefighters noticed something unexpected. Inside, the building was still ablaze, but the fire was well past its peak. A building of this size would normally be expected to burn for hours, but it had been gutted within minutes by the speed and intensity of the inferno. The collapsing roof had also vented the fire, releasing hot air. More and more firefighters were now getting inside. As Brian Parkes passed Exit 4, he noticed a chain draped over the panic bars.

It was a hellish scene. Tables and chairs throughout the ballroom were engulfed in flames. Unrelenting smoke made it difficult to see. They felt their way inside with the lights of their torches. Almost immediately, as soon as firefighters stepped in the exit, they began to uncover the toll of the fire, tripping over bodies unseen beneath their feet. The further they went, the remains of people whose lives had already been claimed by the fire lay on the ground. Some were still on fire, others were burnt beyond recognition, but each one was carefully brought outside as they were found. They moved deeper into the ballroom, trying to put out any of the fire that was still burning intensely. The dance floor was now just a glowing pile of debris. It was clear they wouldn't find anyone alive there. The temperature was so intense that their ears – the only parts of their bodies left exposed by their old-style breathing apparatuses – began to burn. In the centre of the dancefloor, amidst a tangled mess of wire and rubble from the collapsed ceiling, a group of people lay fused together in a huddle.

* * *

Outside, Lorraine McDonnell had been watching the firemen take body after body out of the building. A line was now forming along the east side of the Stardust. She went over to try to see if one of them was Teresa, just so she would get an answer, but a fireman pulled her away.

Laurence Duffy was trying to make sense of the scene. He was a garda motorcyclist based a few kilometres away at Santry Garda Station. When he stepped out of the station after receiving the call about the fire, he could already hear the commotion in the air. He sped across within minutes and was one of the first gardaí on the scene, with a patrol car pulling in behind him.

Duffy was limited in what he could do. He spoke to the other gardaí and scanned the crowd. He spotted the growing number of taxis that had arrived at the scene, who were taking the walking wounded to hospitals around

THE LAST DISCO

Dublin. His training kicked in: in an emergency like this, you need to get the wounded off-site as soon as possible. He rushed over and urged the drivers to gather as many people as they could, explaining that he would lead them in a convoy to the hospital – they would have to stick close to him, as he would be the only outrider.

Ambulances, gardaí, taxis – anyone with a car was trying to help with this mammoth task. Nick Nolan found four people suffering from smoke inhalation and sped into town but was pulled over for speeding.

The garda approached the car and shone his flashlight into Nick's face, asking where he was going. Nick answered: 'Shine your fucking torch in the back seat and you'll see where I'm going.' The garda saw the people, faces blackened by smoke, still struggling to breathe, and said, 'Follow me', and gave them an escort into town.

Dave Fitzgerald and Paddy Cunningham's ambulance was still trapped in the middle of the panic. As soon as they parked, the crowd opened the back doors and desperately piled inside. The drivers got out and realised the grave injuries they were dealing with. They needed to leave immediately with whoever they could.

Cunningham stayed in the back while Fitzgerald got in the driver's seat and started the engine. The ambulance wouldn't move. It was overloaded, sitting flat on its suspension. Fitzgerald hopped out and tried to convince anyone not seriously injured to get out of the ambulance. The clamouring crowd grew tighter and tighter around him, jostling him. It looked to Fitzgerald like crowds coming out of Croke Park, hundreds and hundreds of people around him, pulling at him, asking to go in the ambulance. Someone started repeatedly poking him in the back.

He spun around to snap at the person to stop distracting him. The boy in front of him was standing with a girl in his arms. 'Can you look after my girlfriend?' he asked. Fitzgerald looked down. She was 18 or 19, unconscious, with extensive burns. She's in serious trouble, Fitzgerald thought. He took her from the boy and put her on the floor of the ambulance.

Garda Laurence Duffy was speeding his escort of taxis through Dublin's quiet streets to the Mater Hospital. As soon as they arrived and the injured were unloaded, Duffy went inside. He rushed through the hospital to find his sister-in-law, a nurse, to tell her what he had seen. This was a major emergency, the likes of which is rarely seen in Ireland. She had started to realise this too, as she watched the hospital fill up with patients, but lines of communication in 1981, before social media and mobile phones, were different. Neither the garda nor the nurse had any idea if authorities were fully aware of what they were facing, but they knew there was a procedure in place at times like this, something known as the Major Accident Plan. For Dublin, this meant as many resources as possible would be mobilised for an incident involving 25 or more seriously injured casualties. All of Dublin Fire Brigade's available ambulances would be dispatched to the scene. Each of Dublin's six major hospitals would make beds available. Duffy and his sister-in-law found phones and started making calls to their superiors, who had the authority to activate this plan.

These wheels were already turning; the decision for the first stage of the plan to be implemented was made by Joseph Kiernan, a third officer with Dublin Fire Brigade, less than 15 minutes after the first fire engine arrived.

THE LAST DISCO

Kiernan had surveyed the scene himself and went into the building to do a final check of the bathroom at the front of the club. The loss of life was becoming apparent. The line of lifeless bodies outside was still growing. At 2.12am, just six minutes after the first stage was launched, Kiernan told a garda to radio headquarters to launch stage two of the Major Incident Plan, and that the City Morgue needed to be opened. Dublin Airport, the Defence Forces, the Irish Red Cross, St John's Ambulance Brigade, the Order of Malta and the Blood Transfusion Service Board were all to be alerted.

But back in the command centre, there was confusion over what this plan involved.

The Department of Health and Dublin Fire Brigade both had different versions of the plan. The copy in the garda communications centre was different again.

Here is the call logged at 2.06am, edited for clarity:

[An Garda Síochána] Guards here again. One of our units came in to say that one of your chiefs said that this is a major something? Phase 1. Major Accident Plan.
[Dublin Fire Brigade] . . . Major Accident?
[AGS] . . . Plan.
[DFB] Phase 1.
[AGS] Yes. Hang on just a second will you . . . We have word back through our car from one of your chiefs that this is a Major Accident, Phase 1.
[DFB] What?
[AGS] That's correct, you . . . What does that mean in our language?
[DFB] It means that you will have a list there. You are in [the control centre], aren't you?

78

[AGS] Yes.

[DFB] You have a list there. Who to notify; all the hospitals; dangerous buildings. We'll do most of it anyway.

[AGS] All hospitals?

[DFB] Yes, now the only way you can help us out is if you get CIÉ with the single-deck buses for the non-urgent cases up there or any of your cars that are available to shunt them into some of the hospitals.

[AGS] Yes, we have all our mobiles on the way out there to get them in.

The time is now 2.12am. Kiernan is calling in Stage 2.

[DFB] Yes, we've had 10 ambulances. That's the best we can do.

[AGS] We have our cars taking them in also . . . but all we have to do is . . . you have notified the hospitals, is it?

[DFB] We are looking after that end of it [. . .] Have you got a direct line to any of the army barracks there . . .

[AGS] To where?

[DFB] . . . to see if they can help with any ambulances? Any of the army barracks.

[AGS] What's stage 2? Now he says Major Accident Phase 2.

[DFB] That's it. The shit has hit the fan so.

[AGS] What?

[DFB] The shit has hit the fan.

[AGS] Is that right? What does that mean?

[DFB] It means everything is notified, army, the whole lot.

[AGS] You want everyone notified?

[DFB] Yes.
[AGS] Right you are. Thanks.

This plan was going to make little difference for the emergency crews at the scene. The fire was essentially out, with only small pockets of flames remaining. The rescue operation would also soon come to an end, but it had dragged on. As late as 2.15am, firemen entered through Exit 5 and came across another previously unknown bathroom. A shout went out: 'There are people in here.'

They found a pile of bodies, eight or ten people, blackened by the fire but not burnt, lying on the floor. It wasn't clear if they were dead or alive; all firefighters were wearing breathing apparatus, which meant their vision was limited, and they were working 'literally by hand'. The people were immediately passed outside. Fireman Paul Porter was helping bring these bodies out when he spotted a man fully clothed, unburnt, lying on the ground. He and another fireman dragged him to safety and immediately started resuscitation attempts. An ambulance crew soon took over.

There was no hope of finding anyone else alive. The rescue mission became a recovery operation.

Back at the Mater Hospital, Dave Fitzgerald and Paddy Cunningham had just arrived. Despite being one of the first ambulances at the scene, it took so long to leave that the hospital was already full. They were told to try another hospital. Fitzgerald wasn't taking no for an answer and was desperate for someone to treat the young woman he had been handed outside the Stardust. He stepped inside and found a nun, and told her it couldn't wait. She tried to refuse, but a doctor overheard and ran out to the ambulance with Fitzgerald.

There was no time for a stretcher. Fitzgerald took her up into his arms again and brought her inside. The doctor directed him to lay her down on a mattress and told the paramedics to bring the others inside, too.

The young woman passed away before Fitzgerald even made it back to the ambulance.

* * *

Slowly, the crowd was starting to thin out. The injured were on their way to hospital, and the people who stayed, transfixed by the disaster, began to make their way home. Gardaí, still trying to stop people from getting back inside the club to find their lost friends, attempted to clear the area. Linda Bishop, the first to notice the rising temperature in the ballroom, had found some of her friends, and the group stood watching the scenes unfold. She didn't need immediate hospital treatment – that would come later in life. She doesn't know how long they stood there for. Eventually, a young garda came over and told them, 'Come on, you need to move.'

Journalists were now arriving at the scene of the fire. One RTÉ reporter, who had been working in the newsroom for just a year, had been woken by his editor at 2am. 'There's been a major fire on the northside of Dublin, at a disco called the Stardust,' he said. 'Get yourself there as fast as possible.'

It would be a night that would stick in Charlie Bird's mind for decades. He drove across from north Wicklow, crossing the Liffey at Liberty Hall, still unsure of exactly where he was going. But turning onto Amiens Street brings you past the city morgue. Ambulances were busy coming and going. He followed emergency vehicles returning to the scene.

Bird pulled into the complex and saw the ground frozen – it was so cold that night that the water used to fight the blaze had already turned to ice. There was still a crowd gathered outside the Stardust, but now the panic and shock had passed. The screaming, the sirens and the incessant wail of water pumps were gone. A horrible silence hung in the air.

Another RTÉ journalist, cameraman Sean Burke, had been to the scene earlier while the fire was still raging and captured the scenes of chaos and rescue efforts – the firefighters rushing into the building and leaving carrying limp bodies. People with burns and blackened clothing, and others escaping through windows. The crowd is immensely dense in the footage, the camera being knocked as people run by.

Bird spoke to him and others at the scene, before finding a shop nearby with a phone he could use to file his first of many reports on the disaster.

*   *   *

Joseph Kiernan gave the order for the most difficult task: firemen, gardaí and ambulance crews were to carry out a systematic search of the building to find any remaining bodies.

Some remains had been left in place due to the severity of the injuries, trapped under wires and rubble from the collapsed ceiling. Firefighters had to carefully untangle this mess before passing the bodies to a stretcher.

The more they searched, the more they found.

Some of the dead were somehow untouched by the fire, having succumbed to smoke inhalation. In other cases, they were burnt beyond recognition, whether it was a man or a woman only clear from earrings or the type of watch they were wearing. Partial remains were found on the stage.

In the North Alcove, Fireman James Tormey found the remains of two people locked in an embrace, having spent their final moments holding each other.

After completing several more trips, speeding along icy roads, garda Laurence Duffy ran out of ambulances to escort to hospital, and was back at the Stardust. He was among those tasked with removing the remains of those who died. Portable lights arrived at the scene from Dublin Airport and shone into the dark building, offering an unnatural light to help direct the work. Four people were assigned to each body. Some bodies were still too hot to pick up without being doused with water first. Outside, ambulance attendants draped blankets over the remains.

Duffy remembers being given instructions as they walked through the smouldering rubble, but there was no forensic recording of where the bodies had been found. It was long before technical examinations of scenes became commonplace. Firemen were later simply asked where a body was found, and that body was assigned a number.

Vehicles arrived at the scene as part of the Major Accident Plan as late as 2.35am and were not needed. They were instead used to ferry these young people, who were trapped and couldn't get out in time, to Amiens Street.

Before the search was called off, there was one final sweep of the building. Fireman Parkes was scouring the club and noticed that one door of Exit 5 was now pushed inwards, likely by the emergency services as they went in and out of the building. He checked behind it and found a torso.

*   *   *

The silence that had fallen over the scene deepened once this work was complete, the fire crews packed up and the scene cleared of people, save for some gardaí manning a cordon. One tasked with this watch duty saw that Eamon Butterly, bar manager Brian Peel and three others were still on the premises, chatting in the foyer of the undamaged Silver Swan.

It was almost 6am. Laurence Duffy went home. He stepped inside and went to the bedroom where his wife was sleeping, trying not to wake her, but she stirred. The smell of smoke from his clothes filled the room. He told her what happened. She got up and brought him to the kitchen. She made her husband a cup of tea, and he shared what he had seen. They talked about it for an hour or more, listening to the radio as the first names of the dead were read out.

The next day, Duffy was back at the Stardust. And the next. And the next. 'Our counselling was being sent back to the Stardust to mind the place. We were there for a week or more. We were all sent up, we were all back out there, and it didn't matter that we had been there that night. "It's only bodies", we were told. Of all the things I've been through in the job, this has never left me. Never.'

Chapter 5

THE MCDERMOTT FAMILY KNEW that their sons Willie and George had been in the Stardust. They didn't know their daughter Marcella had gone too. Her parents wouldn't have let her go. She'd told them she would be babysitting.

It was the trio's younger sister Selina who told them.

'I suppose it was early in the morning,' she said. 'My da was a fireman on Tara Street D-watch. He was off duty that night. I was actually up in my eldest sister June's house. She lived a door away from the family house in Edenmore.

'There was a big commotion and my da woke my mother up. "There's a fire in the Stardust." He ran up to June's house. I was there and then it was "right, we know that Willie is there, George is there, we have to get over to the Stardust". And then they said "well Marcella is babysitting, she's with her friends".

'And then I said to my da, "no, she's not, she's at the Stardust". And he just sort of picked me up and shook me and then just said, "what do you mean she's at the fucking Stardust?" He just dropped me and they all just ran out the door. It was mayhem. Absolute mayhem.'

As the cold, dark night passed, the nation was waking up to the shocking news, with radio bulletins giving details of a nightmare in north Dublin.

But the parents of children in Coolmore, Artane, Bonnybrook, Coolock and beyond were woken up far earlier. Some to the news that their children were missing after a fire in the Stardust. Or they were woken up by their own children who had made it out of that place.

Linda Bishop, one of the first to feel the heat at her table which backed onto the West Alcove, had managed to escape the chaos. She remembers getting a taxi but had no money on her, after losing her coat and bag in the melee out the door.

'Next thing I remember, I was knocking at the hall door,' she said. 'I knocked once or twice and then the realisation was hitting me, so I started banging down the hall door.

'My youngest brother ran down the stairs and flung open the hall door as much to say "have you forgotten your keys? You're waking up the whole house." But I just fell into the hall and I started screaming. He brought me up to my parents. They're sitting in the bed. I said "there's been a fire in the Stardust, I've lost my leather coat."

'My father had been made redundant earlier in the year, so the leather coat is all I said. And he was saying "don't worry, I'll go down tomorrow and get it for you."

'I remember my mam went downstairs to make a cup of tea, and she said when she turned on the light, my face was black. I remember trying to wash the stuff out of my hair. It took forever.'

Errol Buckley still didn't know where his brother Jimmy was. In the chaos outside, he decided to bring his girlfriend home at around 4am in case her mother would be worried. His skin also bore the marks of the fire in the Stardust.

'I was trying to wash,' he said. 'I was black. I couldn't get the stuff off me. I came back to the house. My brother

Pat was there. I said I couldn't find Jimmy. My ma was living down the country, so she had to come up the next morning.'

Errol told his family that he'd heard Jimmy had actually gotten out of the Stardust a few times and that he may have been taken off in an ambulance. 'No one knew,' he said. 'There were no phone calls. We had a search party. We must've went to 10 hospitals.'

Catherine Darling recalled being out on the road that morning with the word filtering through and hearing 'such-and-such was missing'. It was to be a common refrain on the streets of north Dublin for days to come.

Lorraine McDonnell went home in the early hours. Without her sister Teresa.

'I went upstairs and called my dad,' she said. 'He eventually woke up and he was saying "what? what?" I said there's a fire in the Stardust and I can't find Teresa. My mother woke up as well and she came down and my friends then called to the house.

'I didn't realise. I can't remember if I told them I was going home. My dad said, "right, we'll go look for her". My mother thought she could go to the hospital and pick her up and bring her home.'

Lorraine's family went between Dublin's hospitals all day Saturday. They couldn't find Teresa. The hospitals were not pleasant places to visit. They were full of the injured, some of them unrecognisable due to injuries. Families with loved ones in hospital didn't know where they'd been brought.

'The whole day, we were giving the names to whoever was in charge and we were told she wasn't there. No one had given her name there. I don't know what time it was in the afternoon, but my dad came home. I remember him going upstairs and next thing I heard him crying.

'I went up to him and said "dad, dad, we'll find her", and he apologised. He was apologising for crying, I think because he was a man of his generation who had to be the big man, the strong man to look after his family.'

The panic and confusion spreading out of Artane wouldn't confine itself to that small part of north Dublin. Eugene Kelly was working on a freight ship that was making a round trip across the Irish Sea.

'I was on the Kilkenny ship from Dublin to Fleetwood,' he said, adding that he and some of the crew had been getting Valentine's cards for their wives to bring back. Eugene recalled one of the men saying he'd never heard of a captain pulling out of dock on Friday 13th.

'Coming into Dublin the next morning, people were saying there was a big fire in the Stardust,' he said. 'One of the crew members came and told me I was wanted down in the office.

'I went down thinking, "is something wrong?" He said "I got a call from your family. You've to go home straight away. Your mother and father have been out looking for Robert. He hasn't been found. All his friends were down in the house, they'd got out."

'I just broke down roaring and crying. Just something told me he was one of them ones that died in the fire.'

When Eugene arrived home, he walked through the door to find his mother in tears and convinced Robert had died. But they didn't know yet. They still hadn't found him, and their search would last for three more days.

Caroline McHugh had been invited along with her parents Maurice and Phyllis to a family wedding in Manchester, but she had chosen to stay behind as she was keen to go to the Stardust. Over in England, Caroline's parents woke up unaware of what had happened the night before.

Maurice said they were in a local shopping area that morning, when Phyllis's uncle came up and broke the news: 'There's been a phone call from Dublin. There's after been a serious fire in Dublin in the Stardust, and Caroline is missing.'

They tried to get a flight home immediately. The only flight available back that day was from Liverpool. Having driven over on the ferry, Maurice would drive them to Liverpool to get the flight home. Before they went, it was all phone calls, trying to get updates.

* * *

Anyone in Ireland old enough to remember 1981 remembers the Stardust fire. Hearing of so many dead in such circumstances stopped everyone in their tracks.

They remember hearing about it in their mother's kitchen that morning. They remember picking up the newspapers and seeing the horror the photographers had captured of people at the club. They remember being terrified for their own kids and worrying they too could go out and never come home. They remember being told they couldn't go out that night because of what happened. They remember the panic they felt the next time they went out for a pint or for a dance, thinking, 'Is this place safe?' They remember the niggling concern on nights out in the months or years that followed, always checking emergency exits or wondering what would happen if there was a fire.

The *Evening Herald* captured the mood with a headline that read simply: 'Why? Oh Jesus Why?'

Its lead story said: 'Dublin mourned its dead children today. A tangled mass of charred wreckage stood as their funeral pyre. A black pall of smoke hanging over a burnt-out nightclub was their shroud.'

The *Irish Press* led with 'Disco Fire Disaster' and had details of iron bars blocking windows, the 'crazy panic' inside and how parents were searching for their missing children. It described the 'heartbreaking scenes' all over Dublin as families went from hospital to hospital.

The paper reported: 'Those who could not find their children eventually ended up in the darkness beside the City Morgue in Store Street trying to identify charred bodies. Said a garda in Store Street, one of those trying to help the families: "It was a pathetic sight. People were out of their minds, all praying that they would not find their sons or daughters in the morgue."'

It was headline news across the world. Sunday's *New York Times* had it on the front page, along with a large image of a man carrying a woman in his arms out of the Stardust. He's shouting and the woman appears badly injured.

Pope John Paul II was among the hundreds who sent messages of sympathy to the office of the Taoiseach and the Archbishop of Dublin. 'I am deeply saddened by the news of the deaths and suffering of so many young people in the fire disaster in Dublin and I am at one with their parents and families in their grief,' the pontiff said. Condolences also came from Britain's Queen Elizabeth II and Prime Minister Margaret Thatcher. Up North, Ian Paisley sent condolences too.

The media coverage would be wall to wall for the coming days. It would prominently feature survivors' testimonies and stories of heroism, from both the first responders and the patrons who risked their lives to save others. It would detail the pressure on the government to take action, claims made over how the fire started, and how families had been plunged into grief by the tragedy.

One of the main tasks for the gardaí in the wake of the fire was identifying the victims. The fire was so intense and conditions so severe in the nightclub that the remains would not be easy to identify.

'I had 15 years in [to my career] and I'd seen a bit,' garda Laurence Duffy said. 'But there were young guards there and they were fantastic, and young firemen there weren't too long around. I don't know how they survived after it.'

To help them in their inquiries, gardaí began interviewing witnesses. They were also able to recover any of their belongings that gardaí had recovered from the debris.

After all her concerns about her mother's cardigan, Susan Darling eventually got it back. 'It was just a piece of wool,' she said.

'That was one of the saddest things in the day after the fire,' her sister Catherine said. 'Detectives came to the house and questioned you over and over. We had to go to identify our belongings. When I went down, my handbag was still intact. It was soaking wet but my photographs, my money, everything was still in it. Half of my coat was burnt. You're sitting there looking going, "all of our friends have died, and you're looking at these bits of coats". You're identifying a coat, and a mother was identifying a child. That was one of the hardest parts of that.'

The old Dublin City Morgue on Store Street was demolished in 1999. In those few days in February 1981, it became a grim, hideous site of pilgrimage for families of the victims of the Stardust fire. There were so many bodies the morgue could not accommodate them all. Dublin had never experienced anything like this. It took 19 ambulances to convey the remains of all the young people to the morgue. Members of the Defence Forces erected a tent in the yard outside the morgue.

Families would turn up frantic. Shocked. Numb. They'd have been searching everywhere for their loved ones.

Having exhausted all the hospitals and not found their loved ones, this was the last place many of them would have to go. That trip. The worst of trips.

The girls from Derry, including Yvonne Graham, had escaped the Stardust, and most of them found their way back to their digs at Nazareth House. Susan Morgan was not among them.

'It was the next day,' Yvonne said. 'After we'd gone around the hospitals, we decided to go to the morgue.' She walked around the building, trying to get some news about her friend. But then she took a wrong turn, into the marquee erected to accommodate the number of bodies. The scene would leave her with nightmares of burnt bodies trying to climb into her bed.

'I called back to Nazareth House and Susie still hadn't turned up. Then they got a phone call. It was like a dream, it must've been just shock. I had to go with the nuns. I had to identify her by Susie's clothes and her ring. I knew her shirt, it was Fionnuala's. Her ring, what was left of the trousers, her shirt. That's how we found out that Susie was dead.'

Maurice Frazer vividly remembers the scene on Store Street, with loads of people milling around, cigarette smoke dominating the scene.

'And people here and there, and you had nuns running around consoling people,' he said. 'The sounds you hear of mothers wailing and fathers cursing.'

They were calling out 'why, why?' he said.

'We were brought in and sat down at a table. A garda sergeant said, "Look, we think we know that Thelma was in the fire from the items of jewellery that you think she had."

'And he literally opened it up, and you know, you just can't describe it. These were taken from her body, and they were melted. Her watch. Her digital watch had no face on it and was all burnt. I was in denial. I was saying it couldn't be Thelma's. My brother says "yeah, that's what she was wearing".'

It would be dental records that would positively identify Thelma.

The morgue was where Lorraine McDonnell's family would identify Teresa.

'On the Sunday, my father went with one of my uncles down to a place you didn't go to,' she said. 'The city morgue. He went and identified her by a ring my mother had given to her for her 16th birthday which originally belonged to her. My father had given it to her when they were 16 years married. An eternity ring.

'It was just . . . a numbing shock. I'm sure this applies to all the families, but it was just like an earthquake going through your home.'

It wasn't until the Tuesday that the Buckleys found out that Jimmy had died. He was identified by his wedding ring.

'He was found at one of the doors,' Errol said. 'He was looking for me. He knew the Stardust like the back of his hand. He worked in Scott's Foods behind it, so he'd have known every door and every exit. People were saying, "he was out looking for you".

'I was sick.'

Maurice and Phyllis McHugh were still across the Irish Sea when they were told this was the trip they would have to make when they got home.

At around 1pm that day, they got through to Phyllis's sister and her brother-in-law.

'And he said, "look, she's in the morgue",' Maurice said. 'Just like that. That was it. The whole drive, there wasn't a word spoken in the car.'

When the McHughs arrived back home from Britain, they went straight to Store Street.

Having just left their 17-year-old daughter Caroline mere hours prior, they were going to identify her remains.

'They explained to us that Caroline was so badly burned that they advised us not to see the remains,' Maurice McHugh said. 'We were sort of in shock. We were going on with what everyone said to do, guide us along.'

The McHughs were given a piece of Caroline's jeans. The back pocket was soaking wet and contained a melted comb. They were also given a watch that was 'burnt to bits' and a chain.

Eugene Kelly had also arrived back in Dublin off the ship.

'The days went on, I was going in and out of the morgue,' he said. 'I always remember it was on the Tuesday. One of the gardaí came out to me, and he was holding out this material, like velvet. I always remembered Robert's velvet jacket and he said "can you identify it?" I said yeah, and I just remember collapsing.'

Eugene was brought home in a garda car to tell his mother.

'As soon as she heard me roaring and screaming through the door, she knew Robert was dead,' he said. 'It's a day I'll never forget.'

The scenes in the morgue shocked photojournalist Eamonn Farrell. His photos today capture the numbness and horror hanging over Dublin at that time.

'I went and sat down, I could see a lot of activity going on. I didn't take pictures of the people, as such. I took pictures of silhouettes. I took pictures of the bags of belongings. I took pictures of the guards kind of in doorways.

'It was absolutely horrific.'

The experience of the morgue would scar the families, adding to their pain at this time of unspeakable grief. Years later, families would speak of the heartbreaking moment they found out 'which number' their child or loved one was. With such a volume of victims, the many logistics to figure out, and the unrecognisable condition of some remains, investigators had simply reduced each identity to a number. They were assigned a number. Their humanity and lives stripped away while their families mourned.

*   *   *

And then there were those recovering in hospital. More than 200 people had been injured in the Stardust, some of them severely.

The Keegans knew that Antoinette was in a bad state in hospital. Her sisters Mary and Martina were missing.

Inevitably, the path for parents John and Christine led to the morgue too. Mary and Martina had died, but they weren't allowed to see them.

'[My mother] was told to remember them the way they were,' Antoinette said.

They were identified on the Sunday and buried on the Wednesday. All the while, Antoinette was recovering in hospital. Given her condition, her parents didn't want to tell her the news.

'I was in there for two and a half weeks,' she said. I wasn't allowed a newspaper, television, radio, nothing. I'd ask anyone who was coming up how Mary and Martina were, and my dad would say "oh fine, grand, grand". My mother and father were coming up and taking off their black mourning clothes and changing into ordinary clothes.

'I don't know how they did it, I really don't. It was one of those things that they were told they had to do because otherwise, I'd have gone into shock. The doctors had warned it was 50/50 for me to survive.'

The news was eventually revealed by an unknowing, well-meaning priest while Antoinette was still in hospital. Her father then confirmed the horrible truth to her.

Antoinette was just one of 124 people admitted to hospital, although later stats would put the number injured at roughly 200. Some who had inhaled smoke didn't go to hospital. In the kind of shock they'd been feeling, some even went into work the next day. In a daze. Dublin's hospitals were overrun and overwhelmed by the scale of the tragedy as victims poured in from ambulances and taxis and cars overnight.

Eighteen hospital consultants were responsible for caring for the patients admitted following the fire. Three patients were discharged the next day, but some stayed as long as 90 days. The average length of stay in hospital following the Stardust fire was a week.

As well as caring for the injured, they had to contend with the families who were frantically going to and fro from hospitals searching for news of their loved ones. This put further pressure on the health service. In Dublin Castle, a special phone line was set up to deal with queries arising from the fire, such as the names of the injured and where they were being treated. RTÉ was asked to include the number in its bulletins from that morning.

'A list of the injured was compiled in each hospital but this took time to be generally available and in some instances was incomplete,' a later report noted. Those injured had sustained a wide range of 'fire-related disabilities' affecting the eye, skin and respiratory systems.

The report looked at a sample of cases: '7% of the hospitalised sustained injuries to their eyes. A description of the burns, the sites affected and their degree indicates that this type of injury was extremely common.

'However, only 11% of the hospitalised required skin grafting. Other surgical procedures were carried out on 4% of the hospitalised. Respiratory problems of varying severity arising as a result of the Stardust fire affected a very significant number of those hospitalised following the fire.'

The scars for those who'd been in but survived the Stardust would go beyond merely the physical. And it would be some time before these scars faded, if they would ever fade at all.

* * *

The community had been left shattered by the disaster. So many families and friends were grieving for the loved ones they had lost. People who had survived were trying to come to terms with what they had experienced. The horrific human cost of all of this was driven home by the personal stories that were emerging. Eugene Hogan was at the Stardust with his wife. They had planned to move to Kerry the following Monday with their children, after Eugene – nicknamed Hughie – had gotten a new job. He never came home. Francis and Maureen Lawlor were a married couple who'd gone for a night out. Their little daughter Lisa was just a year old, and she would grow up an orphan because of the Stardust. Helena Mangan was a single mother who'd gone to the Stardust with her new boyfriend John Stout. They both died in the fire, leaving young Samantha, just four years old, without her mother. So many young people dead in one tragedy. Ireland had never seen the likes of it before.

Compounding this grief in the days and weeks that followed were the funerals. You could have several in one day, most taking place within a week of the disaster.

In many cases, families weren't permitted to see their loved ones. It was a closed casket. The constant refrain was 'Remember them as they were'. Families would later describe being told what funeral home their son or daughter was brought to and when the funeral would take place. At this time of tragedy, some had little agency in how they'd mourn their dead.

There were so many funerals. One after the other. It was an unfathomable loss of life. And these deaths were marked by how Ireland buried its dead. A big church service followed by a burial. All of these very visible. Very visceral. Very real.

Speaking to the Stardust podcast, RTÉ journalist Charlie Bird said there were five to six funerals a day. 'It's so hard to get your head around it,' he said.

Photojournalist Eamonn Farrell said: 'I think one of the pictures I took shows 13 hearses lined up outside the church in Kilmore. And then I remember when I was in the graveyard there were about five funerals taking place at the same time.'

The McDermotts were burying three of their children after they'd received the news, one by one, that William, George and Marcella had died.

Their younger sister Selina would recall their mother Bridget seeing the three coffins laid out, banging on them and pleading to be let see her children.

'She kept saying "why did He take three?"'

Linda Bishop said that it was difficult to make it to all the funerals of people you knew because there were just so many taking place so quickly. 'It was just horrendous,' she said. The Darlings went to the funerals, 'as many as we could cope with', they said.

Before Thelma Frazer was laid to rest, first came the funeral of her boyfriend Michael Farrell.

'One thing I have to say is the community across Dublin was fantastic,' Maurice Frazer said. 'You had locals and taxi drivers coming up and offering lifts. So we went across to Michael's funeral. Michael was a lovely, lovely chap – an amazing person. It was an honour to know him.

'That was the first funeral we came across for. That was soul-destroying. I knew his parents. We'd all go out for a drink together, they were lovely people. As I say, the community was so strong.'

Thelma's funeral would take place a day later after family from England travelled over.

'I think when you see the hearse come out of Store Street, that's when it hits you,' Maurice said. 'You know your sister is in that and that's basically it. That's probably the first time I broke down.' Thelma was one of only two victims who lived on the southside. Maurice remembers the moment Thelma's hearse crossed the Liffey. Traffic was stopped across the city centre, with gardaí everywhere manning the route, showing the respect Dublin was affording to their loss. 'My dad was very strong, but that's when it really hit me, personally.'

The funerals were covered extensively in the media.

The *Irish Press* reported on the Tuesday how 20 graves had been dug at St Fintan's Cemetery in Sutton to bury some of the victims.

'A robin swooped under the jaws of the two mechanical diggers as the earth was lifted and a seagull winged low across the sound from the strand where so many of the youngsters would have enjoyed summer days,' the article read.

On the front page that day, the paper carried details of the funeral of John Colgan (21).

'As a pall of sorrow hung over the whole country, and especially Dublin, the churches of parishes around the Stardust club last evening saw the start of the funeral services of many of the victims, the cards and red roses of St Valentine's Day replaced by funeral wreaths and messages of sympathy, the bright lights and music of the disco all changed to hesitant words of consolation and religious hope.'

'Fr John Delany, curate, stated that he had been told that John Colgan had gone continually back into the Stardust blaze to help others. "If that is not being a hero, nothing is, and it is something for his family to hold on to," he said.'

A few days later, on Friday, the newspaper also reported on the funerals of the McDermotts.

'It was the sheer magnitude of the McDermott loss that moved so many to tears.

'Flakes of snow fell as the coffins bearing the three McDermott children were carried to the graveside. The guard of honour of more than 200 firemen marched behind the three hearses as they arrived for burial and there were also guards of honour of Boy Scouts and the Civil Defence.'

Errol Buckley would later say that when they went to bury his brother Jimmy, he was still numb with the shock of it all at the time.

'I didn't know what I'd done the day of my brother's funeral,' he said. 'But when you're asked about it, when you talk about it, things click back into place. I know what I did after my brother's funeral. I went to another funeral.'

*   *   *

The response from the State to such an appalling event had to be swift.

This tragedy occurred in Taoiseach Charles Haughey's constituency. His Fianna Fáil party's annual conference, due to be held on Valentine's Day, was cancelled.

The government quickly decided to hold a Tribunal of Inquiry to investigate the disaster, announcing it just a day and a half after the fire.

This is Ireland's most significant form of public inquiry, reserved for matters of the utmost importance. The Whiddy Island disaster of 1979, where 50 died in an oil tanker explosion off the south coast, had its own Tribunal of Inquiry, with its report being completed in 1980. An example from recent years is the Disclosures Tribunal, which delved into allegations of a smear campaign against garda whistleblower Maurice McCabe.

Headed by a senior judge, the tribunal can investigate these matters thoroughly, and they typically cost the taxpayer millions of euros.

There was a parallel garda investigation, but a tribunal meant the State was sending a clear message: 'This is a horrible situation or event. The public deserves answers. So we'll call a tribunal to get to the bottom of it.'

The *Irish Times* reported on Monday 16th February that Minister for the Environment Ray Burke had provided assurances that the inquiry would 'cover any potential questions raised' and would 'satisfy any concern of the general public'.

Tuesday was a national day of mourning, and the Dáil was adjourned for a day as a mark of respect. That was not before a few brief remarks from the main party leaders, and it was full of the kind of words you'd expect from politicians after such a tragedy.

As hard as it may be to imagine such an event happening today, it is perhaps not too difficult to imagine the kinds of things that today's political leaders would say in such a situation. And it was no different in 1981.

Haughey said: 'Our hearts go out in sympathy to the parents, families and friends of all the victims who have been so tragically and so suddenly bereaved.

'We pray God will give them every consolation in their grief and loss, and we hope for a speedy recovery for all those who have suffered injury.'

Fine Gael leader and main opposition leader Garret FitzGerald said he could add little to Haughey's words:

'Yet, inevitably, and through no fault of his, his words cannot in substance convey the depth of the feelings that have overwhelmed all of us in the face of this tragedy.

'We have not faced anything quite on this scale before and no tragedy has been so concentrated in the area affected: none has affected such a particular age group in our society as this one has done. The feelings of everybody in the country seek expression and cannot readily find it in these circumstances.'

The last to speak was Noël Browne, the famed liberal politician and Minister for Health in the 1950s; at the time of the Stardust, he was a TD for the Artane area. He said: 'As politicians, word spinning is our trade and fine phrases are a part of that profession. Yet, skilled and experienced though we might be at the job, there is little or nothing we can do to comfort the unhappy parents in Artane for the sudden, terrible and tragic loss of their children.'

But the tragedy also focused some minds in a very practical way. Foremost for the public, along with the deep sense of mourning, was to ensure this couldn't happen again.

Minister for the Environment Ray Burke told the Dáil on Wednesday: 'I will be bringing forward, as a matter of urgency, proposals for improving the law on the fire service, in particular in relation to fire prevention matters. Draft proposals for a Bill are at an advanced stage.'

Burke said he'd asked all city and county managers in Ireland to inspect all potentially dangerous buildings immediately. This included dance halls, discos and other places of public entertainment in which people could be at risk of fire. Furthermore, he said that any premises not up to scratch should be closed pending the taking of 'remedial measures'.

Burke held talks with the Fire Prevention Council and set up a task force to liaise with local authorities to make sure this was done.

Haughey himself visited the site and the hospitals. The *Irish Times* on Monday described him as 'visibly shaken'.

Gary Murphy's biography of the former taoiseach said that when he heard of what had happened, he went to the Mater Hospital just before 6am with Bertie Ahern, a TD for Dublin Central and future taoiseach himself. They didn't stay long.

He gave his first response to the nation in RTÉ's 7.30am radio bulletin, before walking through the ruin with reporters.

'The appalling loss of life at the Stardust had a devastating impact on Haughey,' Murphy wrote. 'He knew many of the victims personally.'

Haughey would visit many of the victims and their families in the coming days. In some quarters, he was welcomed, but not all.

Phyllis McHugh recalled seeing Haughey after the fire, after Caroline had been brought to the church.

'My aunt was here and my sisters. They were all here, sitting down was Charlie Haughey and [Noël] Browne. My aunt asked them to leave. She said "you're not sincere, you're just here today". They just got up and left.'

There's a photo of Haughey leaving the Mater Hospital on the 14th. On the left of the shot is a man staring into space. It's Maurice Frazer's father.

'My father had gone to all the hospitals,' he said. 'You just know from the photograph. Being a soldier, he'd seen one or two things he shouldn't have. He's got that thousand-yard stare.

'It's an image I'm grateful to see. You know what sort of thoughts are going through his head. He's not going to see his daughter again. It's a tough one.'

*   *   *

Many of the staff of the Stardust met again in the Silver Swan the morning after the fire. The pub and Lantern Rooms function area were intact, but the Stardust attached to it was a smouldering ruin.

They were told two things: don't speak to the press, and speak to Eamon Butterly's solicitors before giving a statement to the gardaí.

That afternoon, Butterly's solicitor came down and took statements from the staff, and many of them subsequently made statements to gardaí.

It would've become immediately clear to the gardaí investigating what happened at the Stardust that some of the emergency exit doors were – at the very least – not easily opened when the fire had become widespread and people were trying to escape the building.

Testimonies emerged of men having to kick doors in to try to force them open. Big crowds gathering at exits trying to get out. Obstructions such as skips at the exits.

Were the doors locked in the Stardust? That narrative emerged almost immediately, and the focus then turned squarely to the staff and management about what state these exits were in.

Michael Kavanagh, a young man who'd been a doorman at the Stardust for less than a year, initially told journalists at the Stardust in the early hours that he had opened all the emergency exits on the night. He repeated this claim on RTÉ's *Today Tonight* programme on the Monday after the fire.

But before the week was out, he had gone to gardaí to give a new statement. This time, he said he hadn't opened the exits.

In this statement, made on Thursday 19th February, he said two of the doormen had visited his home the day prior.

Kavanagh said: 'Yesterday, the 18th February, 1981, Leo Doyle and P.J., another doorman, came to my house and asked my mother to tell me to go on television or to tell the papers that I got the keys and that I was responsible for opening the fire exit doors of the Stardust Club on the night of the fire.'

In his later evidence, he said that both men called and told his mother he should tell the gardaí that he had nothing to do with opening the exits. This whole tangled affair is complicated. And would remain complicated for many years. It begged several questions: why did Michael Kavanagh initially say he opened the exits, and then say he didn't just a few days later? For what reason did two other doormen go to his home to tell his family he must say he hadn't opened them?

The Keane Tribunal would later say: 'Mr Kavanagh said in evidence that he had told lies to the gardaí and on television because he was in a state of grief and shock following the death of his girlfriend in the fire, and because he was angered by the criticism in his neighbourhood of the conduct of the doormen during the fire, and what he considered to be the bogus claims of some of the patrons to have behaved heroically on the evening.'

The newer version of events was that Thomas Kennan, the head doorman and relative of Eamon Butterly, opened the emergency exits at 1:30am on the night, just before the fire was spotted. These accounts, only given to gardaí many days after the fire, would be treated with what the Tribunal would refer to as 'great reserve'.

These accounts would also anger families for decades. The conflicting accounts over the state of the doors would be compounded by another narrative that was being put forward in the immediate aftermath of the fire.

Butterly himself was alleged to have said 'the bastards started a fire' when he first heard about the fire on the night. It was a stance he would maintain in the days, weeks and months that followed.

The newspapers all ran quotes from him in the paper that Tuesday where he said the premises conformed to the required standards and that he believed arson was the most probable cause.

'My conscience is clear,' he said. 'I am a very upset man, but I did everything possible to make the place safe from the first day it opened.'

In any case, the Butterlys didn't hang around. Within a week of the fire, malicious damage claims worth over £4 million from companies owned by the Butterly family had been made against Dublin Corporation, according to media reports, although this figure was later reported as £3 million. These notices had to be served within seven days of the fire.

For that claim to come to fruition and payouts granted, it would need to be determined that the fire had been started maliciously, and not as a result of wrongdoing on the part of the Butterlys. The Tribunal of Inquiry, set up to get to the bottom of what had happened at the Stardust, felt like a good place to start looking for these answers.

* * *

The Stardust fire utterly devastated an entire community. The loss of each life touched so many, and their loss was so deeply felt.

The family of Julie McDonnell had been planning her 21st birthday for the next weekend. She was buried two days before her birthday.

Liam Dunne succumbed to his injuries a month after the fire. His family members would take turns to sit with him while others attended the funerals.

Jacqueline Croker's sister Alison told the inquests: 'It's not as simple as just one person being lost to our family. Everyone knew everyone in our community and each loss was felt by the community as well as the families. Living at home after the Stardust fire, you wouldn't be able to get onto a bus without seeing someone either with visible scarring from a burn or someone who had lost someone in the fire.'

Some families were not even granted the dignity of burying their own loved ones.

Five of the bodies of the deceased were unidentifiable. The solution arrived at was to bury them all together. Five coffins laid out. Their families not even sure which one was their son. Richard Bennett, Michael Ffrench, Murty Kavanagh, Eamon Loughman and Paul Wade.

Susan Darling broke down remembering the scene. 'Nobody knew who owned what child, which I thought was horrific to have your child and not even be able to bury your own child,' she said. 'It was absolutely heart-breaking, terrible, for their parents.'

In a powerful pen portrait delivered at the inquests, Terry Jones – sister of Murtagh (Murty) Kavanagh – outlined the effect it had. 'The Stardust fire ravaged our family,' she said. 'My father was a broken man. My sister sold her home and she and her family moved in with my father to care for him. This was an arduous task as everyone was suffering traumatic grief.

'We were all left devastated by the traumatic loss of Murty, the absence of a private funeral, and him being unidentified. But it was my father that was truly broken. Every day he would say "I would love to know where my son is buried." He would say this every day until his own passing, in 1985.'

An editorial column in the *Sunday Independent* on 22nd February made some prescient points. 'The tragedy of the Stardust will remain with us for a long, long time,' it read. 'A whole generation has been lost. Many families will carry their grief to the end of their days.'

The editors said lessons needed to be learned so that the chance of a 'similar holocaust will be greatly diminished'. It said legislation was needed to ensure that owners of public places carried out the required specifications in their premises, and there were some 'disquieting reports' from fire officers of their warnings being ignored.

'The Tribunal will be a traumatic experience for everyone,' it added.

THE LAST DISCO

The final death toll from the Stardust stood at 48 young people. The average age was just 19.5 years old.

A later analysis would reveal that, among the dead, there were at least six machinists or factory workers; six who worked as carpenters, painters or apprentices; three deliverymen; seven receptionists or typists; nine shop workers; two service workers; and three students or house-wives. That makes them sound older than they were; these were people at the very beginning of their lives, with many of them only having taken their first steps into the big, bad world.

In this, the newspapers hadn't given over to hyperbole. Dublin was indeed mourning its dead children. As the families laid their children to rest, their pain would remain and linger. Forever.

But the rest of the world would soon move on. Ireland had experienced a horrific tragedy, and the government had pledged to both get to the bottom of it and make sure something like this wouldn't happen again.

The Keane Tribunal was set up to do that. But it would take almost half a century before the families would finally get the chance at some true closure.

Chapter 6

ON A COLD, CLOUDY DAY just over seven weeks after the fire, Mr Justice Ronan Keane walked into a large room in the Law Society building in Dublin's Stoneybatter just after 11 o'clock in the morning and officially began the public work of the Tribunal tasked with investigating the Stardust fire.

It had all been set up incredibly quickly, especially by today's Irish standards, where tribunals have become a by-word for long-term and often plodding investigations. When Taoiseach Charles Haughey announced the Tribunal to reporters less than 36 hours after the fire, he was already clear about how it should look: it would be presided over by a High Court judge, it would be able to subpoena witnesses, and as well as looking at what caused the fire, it would 'have the power to make recommendations'.

On that first morning on Monday 6th April 1981, Mr Justice Keane sat at a table on a raised platform at the top of the large, high-ceilinged room. Sitting in a row alongside him were three expert assessors who were working with him to run the Tribunal: Professor David Rasbash of the Department of Fire Safety Engineering at the University of Edinburgh; Gunnar Haurum, the Chief Inspector of the Fire Service in Denmark; and Pierce Pigott, the Head of the Construction Division at An Foras

Forbartha, a now-abolished state agency tasked with planning and construction research.

In front of the judge and the assessors was another smaller table, where Tribunal workers sat, with a single desk to their right where witnesses would give their evidence. Several rows of desks faced the judge, split by an aisle down the middle, with people – lawyers – sitting on both sides of the tables. Members of the public could sit on chairs at the back of the room. Workmen had spent the weekend before the Tribunal began installing seating and a sound system in the room so everyone could hear what was said.

The room was beautiful. The 18th-century building, which had been a school for boys from poor families for almost 200 years – technically called the King's Hospital but generally known as the Blue Coat School because of the military-style blue uniform worn by the boys – had been bought by the Law Society 10 years before the Tribunal started and had undergone a massive renovation. It opened in 1978 as the headquarters of the solicitors' profession. The Tribunal was taking place in the Presidents' Hall, which had previously been the chapel of the school. The stained-glass window behind the judge and the assessors depicted Jesus Christ.

It was the ideal setting for the legal professionals, creating a triangle between the High Court and King's Inns at the centre of Ireland's law profession. It was less ideal for the families of the victims and for the survivors. Awkward to get to from Artane because of its location slightly away from the city centre, the building itself, with its imposing pillars above the entrance and large dome, can be intimidating for people not used to going into it – which is most people – rather than welcoming. The survivors were not cowed by it. One newspaper described how the young witnesses handled the 'ritual legal seriousness' and 'the bouts of questions in a decisive, determined way'.

On that first day, around 40 members of the public turned up to take their seats in the room, along with some 30 people who were working on the Tribunal. It was happening so quickly that many survivors and families were still recovering from the disaster.

Mr Justice Keane took diligent notes as the opening speeches were made. The 48-year-old had been selected by the Attorney General and the President of the High Court to oversee the Tribunal, and had widely been seen as a smart appointment; he was a star in the firmament of the Irish judiciary, widely considered to be one of the leading judges in the country. He is described in Ruadhán Mac Cormaic's *The Supreme Court* as being a 'tall man with [a] black Crombie hat who would get on [the DART] at Monkstown with the *London Times* under his arm and then stride purposefully up the quays to the Four Courts every morning'.

In his twenties, he had been part of a group of wonky recent graduates, including Michael D. Higgins, Garret FitzGerald and Donal Barrington, who had big ideas about how Ireland should change. The intellectual movement they formed, known as Tuairim ('opinion' in Irish), published papers and pamphlets suggesting new approaches for Irish social policy in areas like Northern Ireland, education and censorship.

Mr Justice Keane had become the youngest member of the High Court when he was appointed to it by former Taoiseach Jack Lynch just two years earlier and would go on to serve almost two decades there. He was seen as an intellectual but with a humane and practical side too; when he had been appointed a judge, he visited every prison in the country to see what the conditions were like for himself.

Now, on that first day, he listened as counsel made their opening arguments. Mr John Lovatt Dolan SC for the Tribunal began that morning by warning that 'it might appear at times that the Tribunal was taking a cold and rather unsympathetic approach'. However, this objective and calm approach would best serve the inquiry, he told the room. 'This is not the place for dramatisation or exaggeration,' he said.

The Tribunal was tasked with looking at the causes and circumstances leading to the fire, as well as the causes and circumstances leading to the injuries and deaths. This was a massive brief. It covered almost everything, including how the building had been furnished and how it was staffed; the bye-laws and regulations that were in place and whether they were adhered to; the fire safety inspections that had (or hadn't) happened; and a detailed look at everything that happened on the night.

This level of detail would require a large number of witnesses. A total of 363 people were to give evidence over the coming weeks, including 161 who were in the Stardust on the night. Each witness would be called by the Tribunal's counsel and questioned by him; they could then be examined by lawyers for any of the parties who were represented at the Tribunal. There were a number of these: the Tribunal had been given the power to compel anyone relevant to be represented at the Tribunal. In the end, this list was made up of the Attorney General, Dublin Corporation, relatives of the dead and injured, and the two companies owned by members of the Butterly family which had owned and leased the building containing the Stardust.

There was tension in the air on that first day. Even before the opening speeches began, a senior barrister told the room that he was withdrawing from representing 21 families of people who had died in the fire and 61 people who had been injured. The barrister, Garrett Cooney SC and his junior, Tom Morgan BL, instructed by Brian O'Reilly and Co. solicitors, had applied to represent these people within days of the Tribunal being announced and had sought to confirm that they would all be granted legal costs, as others were receiving. This did not happen; the government had appointed two legal firms to represent the families of victims, and that was it. Mr Justice Keane had indicated to Cooney at an earlier housekeeping hearing of the Tribunal that the people Cooney and Morgan represented would not have their legal costs paid.

On that opening day, Cooney told the Tribunal that he had no other option but to withdraw from representing these families and victims. 'In the interests of justice and equity, because [my] clients were of meagre financial income, they should not be denied the right to their own legal representation,' he told the Tribunal. Instead, his instructing solicitor had written to the 21 families and 61 people to give them the names of the solicitors appointed by the government, and had advised them to contact these specific firms instead. Page 1 of the *Evening Press* that day noted that 'families were angered and puzzled that the government wouldn't let them appoint their own legal representatives'.

There were broader issues too. The weeks between the fire and the Tribunal starting had been marked by turbulence. An editorial in the *Irish Independent* on that opening day said that the period should have been one of 'calm restraint' to help people prepare for the 'ordeal' of the Tribunal, as well as a period of preparation and 'confident expectation that the best possible actions were being taken'. 'It has been the opposite,' the editorial said.

It continued: 'Controversy has surrounded almost every aspect of the Stardust tragedy, including many details concerning the Tribunal itself. And much of the controversy has been attended also by bitterness, argument, recrimination, shortage of information, conflict over information and continuing public unease.' It noted that the main problem had been identified early on: was this Tribunal to be about the tragedy alone? Or was it to look more broadly at the implications of the fire and the shortcomings in the system itself, rather than just what happened on the night? The Dáil had opted for the latter, looking at what happened to the people who were there on the night but also the 'broader interest of the population'. The editorial was clear about what a good outcome would be: the 'best expectation' would be that the Tribunal would ensure that this could never happen again by recommending 'irreversible legislation and regulation'.

This broad scope – to hold a mirror up to Irish society and find out how this had been allowed to happen – is perhaps why the Tribunal ended up lasting for longer than expected. It had been due to sit for six weeks. Instead, it went on for 33. And even with this comprehensive investigation, one decision made by the Tribunal in its final report was to end up overshadowing all of the other work done by the inquiry, casting a shadow which was to last for decades to come.

* * *

The Tribunal jumped straight into the most contentious issues from the very first day, beginning with the matter of which, if any, of the six emergency exits had been locked or obstructed on the night.

Over several days, it heard from people who had been at the Stardust on the night and their experiences of trying to get out. With some minor variances, the same stories were heard again and again about the difficulties people had in getting out of four of the six emergency exit doors. It also heard evidence from the doormen who had responsibility for locking and unlocking the doors. Crucially, the Tribunal heard that no one had the specific responsibility of unlocking the exits after midnight. On the night of the fire, doorman Thomas Kennan said he had checked the emergency exits around 11pm and Exits 1, 3, 4, 5 and 6 were all locked with a chain and padlock. Another doorman, Michael Kavanagh, said he checked them soon after midnight and found the same thing. Kennan opened Exit 1 before midnight and draped the chain over it, and gave the keys to another doorman, Leo Doyle.

Were the doors actually locked or not? In trying to reach a conclusion on whether they were, the most compelling evidence came from a detective in the Garda Technical Bureau, Seamus Quinn, and from Michael Norton, an expert from the Forensic Science Laboratory of the Department of Justice. At Exit 2 – the main door to the Stardust – 22 of the 30 panes of glass in the door had been broken. Footprints were found on the door, suggesting that people had to kick it with their feet. One of the joints at the bottom of the door had opened and split the timber for almost 8 inches, suggesting a strong use of force.

At Exit 3, the door's locking mechanism had been subjected to such force that it had yielded and bent. Traces of blood were found both inside and outside the right-hand door. There would have been panic bars on both sides of the door: the panic bar was gone from the left side of the door, and on the right side, a chain with a Chubb lock was draped on top of the panic bar. At Exits 4 and 5, one leaf of each door was badly fire damaged, suggesting it had remained closed and impacted by the fire, while the other leaf was open. And at each of three of the exits – 1, 4 and 6 – a heavy chain with a lock draped over the panic bar was found by investigators after the fire.

If some of these doors weren't locked, and just had a chain draped over the panic bars, it might be thought that they would be easy to open. However, the expert from the Department of Justice, Michael Norton, conducted a test to see what would happen to a door if a lock and chain were draped over the panic bar. He tried 10 separate times and found that every single time when he tried to open the door, the chain would tighten, the door would jam, and the door would fail to open, giving the impression that it was locked. A garda repeated the test and found the same result. It took several attempts with several people to get the door open. For everyone in the Tribunal room that day, it was a visceral image of what the people trying to get out would have experienced.

As well as the locked and obstructed emergency exits, the Tribunal heard about three other factors which could have influenced the scale of the disaster: the problems with the main door, the rapid spread of the fire and the complete lack of preparedness at the venue for a disaster of any kind.

Five out of the six doors met the requirements for being used as an emergency exit. Whatever about their condition on the night, they were technically fine to be classed and used as emergency exits. Exit 2 – the main door into the Stardust – was not. Again and again, the Tribunal heard about the problems with this door, the one which hundreds of people walked through every night as they arrived for a disco or a concert or a cabaret. Its inner doors weren't sufficiently fire-resistant. It had a stairway up to the first floor right beside it, which was a breach of regulations and became a particular hazard when the fire broke out; in the confusion and darkness of the smoke, some people ended up going up the stairs instead of out the exit doors, and in some cases ended up being pushed up the stairs by the swell of people. Two of the people who died were found on the landing of the staircase. The cloakroom was also just beside Exit 2, which meant that if anything bad ever happened in the Stardust, there was likely to be congestion if patrons tried to get their belongings before leaving – which is exactly what happened on the night.

This could all have been spotted by William White and Harold Gardner, the men who were not architects but who had done the architectural drawings for the building when it was being converted from a factory and storage unit into a venue. Gardner told the Tribunal that he personally believed that the building was 'perfectly safe'.

THE LAST DISCO

They also could have spotted the problem with using carpet tiles on the walls. Again and again, these carpet tiles came up as a reason why the fire had spread so quickly and so devastatingly.

The fire had first been seen on three seating units in the West Alcove. Expert witnesses brought in from the UK's Department of the Environment to carry out research on the spread of the fire told the Tribunal that the burning of the seats would not alone have been enough to make the fire spread so rapidly – it was the involvement of the carpet tiles on the wall above them that contributed to it. The ignition of these tiles, the experts said, 'would have led to a considerable increase in the rate of heat output'.

Eamon Butterly had been the one to make the decision to buy the soon-to-be-discontinued tiles, which were manufactured by a company called Illingworth & Co. Ltd, a carpet manufacturer in Bradford, England. The carpet tiles were a shade of wine-red which the company called Buckingham Red, perhaps trying to invoke a sense of luxury. Less luxuriously, one company employee described the tiles as being 'hairy and tufted'. The tiles ended up being used everywhere in the Stardust: they covered almost all the walls of the ballroom and entrance foyer, from the skirting board up to the ceiling.

Butterly had gotten a bargain when he put in the order in early 1978 after meeting a salesperson who worked for the company's agent in Ireland who pitched to provide flooring for the Stardust. 'This particular tile had reached the end of its life and we were selling those particular tiles off,' the company secretary Graham Whitehead told the Tribunal. A company with the same name as the tile – 'State Room' – had asked the carpet company to withdraw the tile. Rather than just changing the name, Illingworth & Co. discontinued it. 'We were jobbing it off and we had another tile on the market to take its place,' Whitehead said. This was reflected in the price; they had been £1.28 per tile but this was reduced to 75p. Butterly ordered 3,749 of them for a total of £2,811.75. It was one of the biggest orders – if not *the* biggest – that Illingworth & Co. had ever had from an Irish company.

The problem was that the carpet tiles were never intended to be used in the way that they ended up being used in the Stardust. The company's technical team had said 'under no circumstances would we recommend these tiles for wall covering,' Whitehead told the Tribunal. The carpet tiles were for floors, not for walls, so they didn't have the flammability that wall coverings are supposed to have; they should have been class 1 (the highest level of fire resistance) but instead they were somewhere between class 3 and 4.

It was not clear who knew about putting the carpet tiles on the walls. The salesperson, Declan Conway, told the Tribunal that he had discussed using the carpet tiles on the walls of the Stardust with Eamon Butterly after Conway saw photographs of carpet tile being used on walls at a trade show in England. Conway said a sales representative for the company had told him that people in England used carpet tiles on walls in buildings like the Stardust because of the acoustic effect. After he told Butterly about this, he got some samples from Illingworth & Co. – and said that the company was 'well aware' that it was going to be used on walls.

Illingworth & Co. was adamant that it was unaware that they were going to be used on the walls of the Stardust.

'That is perfectly untrue,' Whitehead, the company secretary, told the Tribunal. 'We could not stop it being done but we have not recommended it.'

Whitehead said the company's tiles had always been advertised to be used on floors, never on walls. In one testy line of questioning, Whitehead described how the only time the company put carpet tiles on walls was at showrooms so that customers could see them being displayed.

There was also a lack of clarity over who knew about the flammability of the tiles. Declan Conway, the salesperson, told the Tribunal that Eamon Butterly had asked him to get a fire certificate from the company, which Conway said he did, and which he said showed the tiles met the British standard specification (there was no equivalent Irish standard at the time). A brief letter from the company enclosed the results of flammability tests on tiles. Whitehead told the Tribunal that this did not count as a fire certificate. 'We would never issue a fire certificate. We are not an appropriate body to issue a fire certificate.'

At the end of Whitehead's testimony, there was a question from Mr Justice Keane. 'Apart from your own products, which you say, Mr Whitehead, are only seen vertically on walls in your showroom for display purposes, have you ever seen any carpet tiling on walls in hotels or restaurants?' 'Not that I can recall,' Whitehead said. 'No.'

The first batch of the tiles were dispatched on 31st January 1978 and work on fixing them to the walls began almost immediately after they arrived in Artane in February; workers had to do 10- and 12-hour shifts to make sure that the tiles were fully installed by the time the venue officially opened on 6th March 1978.

And perhaps the final reason the Tribunal heard about why people hadn't been able to get out: none of the staff working there had a clue what to do in case of a fire. The Stardust employed a lot of people: 10 full-time barmen, all of whom were there on the night, plus at least 11 other full-time staff – cleaners, porters, clerical staff – as well as 62 part-time staff who were also working on the night: lounge girls, kitchen staff, waitresses and more bar staff, among others. Out of all of these people, only two had any training in anything even remotely to do with fire safety, and neither of them had learned these things at the Stardust: one of the doormen was also a fireman, while another had once done a course in hotel management which had included some details on what to do in case of a fire.

No fire drills were ever conducted in the whole time the Stardust was open. No evacuation plans were ever laid down or even discussed. There were seven fire extinguishers in the Stardust but most of the staff did not even know where they were located. The closest any of the staff came to any kind of plan in case of a fire was in the kitchen: the kitchen supervisor, Mrs Marley, had always told her staff that if there was ever an emergency, they should all go straight to the kitchen. Some of them did exactly that on the night, and got out from there.

Fire experts found that the entirety of the Stardust could have been evacuated in 2.5 minutes if it had been at capacity. Given that it was just over half full, it should have been more than possible to do it in this time and most likely even faster. Instead, the vast majority of people tried to get out of just two of the six emergency exits, one of which had 'serious defects' and should not have been used in that way.

THE LAST DISCO

Perhaps nothing showed the lack of training among the staff better than evidence given to the Tribunal by fireman and Station Officer John McMahon from the North Strand Fire Station. McMahon told the Tribunal how he had arrived at the scene and been brought into the building through the Silver Swan pub – which was not on fire – by the assistant manager of the Stardust. McMahon looked through the door between the pub and the Stardust and could see the scale of the fire in the main ballroom; he ran back to his appliance and brought in a hose through the main door with two of his colleagues, valiantly and desperately trying to hose down the ceiling in the main bar. Seeing that they needed more power to try to put out the flames, McMahon ran outside to get another line of hose. As he ran back towards the main bar, where the fire was burning fiercely, a colleague shouted to him that the assistant manager wanted to talk to him again. Assuming that it was urgent, McMahon went outside to speak to the man.

The assistant manager told McMahon that he had left a large sum of money in the building and needed help to either lock it up or get it out. He brought McMahon into the office of the Silver Swan and found that the money was safe. The assistant manager locked the door of the office – and then told McMahon that there were still people in the ballroom, which was completely ablaze. McMahon did not hesitate: he sprinted back to his colleagues at the main bar and told them they would have to make an attempt to go into the ballroom. The three immediately did so – and began to find bodies in front of the North Alcove.

The assistant manager of the Stardust on that night gave evidence to the Tribunal but was never asked about

McMahon's evidence, and whether he had really asked a fireman to help him retrieve money before mentioning that there were still people in the burning ballroom. If it did happen as the fireman said in his sworn evidence, it is a telling indication of the lack of knowledge or understanding among some employees working there on the night.

As well as the problems on the night, the Tribunal heard about larger, more systemic issues. In order to get planning permission, a building needs to comply with legislation, regulations and bye-laws. Under planning laws at the time, for example – the Local Government (Planning and Development) Acts, 1963 and 1976 – there was a specific requirement that wall linings should have a surface spread flame rating of Class 1, which the carpet tiles were far from meeting. There were also a large number of bye-laws that the building had to adhere to under Dublin Corporation requirements, everything from keeping emergency exits unobstructed to having designated roles for staff members in case of a fire. A building was supposed to comply with all of these rules in order to get planning permission from Dublin Corporation.

The local authority would have known when it granted planning permission that there would be a lot of people in the building and that fire safety would be important, particularly as there had been two big fires in the 1970s at similar venues in the Isle of Man and the US state of Kentucky which would have kept the issue at front of mind. And yet the Tribunal heard that some of its most vital departments were left understaffed and fighting to cope with the workload.

There were just five people working at the Fire Prevention Department who had to deal with between

1,100 and 1,800 planning applications each year for buildings looking to follow the relevant bye-laws. In practice, this meant that by the time they actually put together observations on what a building would have to do to receive planning permission, it was too late. This led to the practice since the mid-1970s of adding a condition to all planning applications requiring the applicant to find out the requirements of the Chief Fire Officer and comply with them. But the problem was this was 'a bit vague', as one witness put it. If an applicant didn't bother to check with the Chief Fire Officer about the requirements, nothing actually happened. And this is exactly what happened with the Stardust: the Chief Fire Officer had sent a letter to William White in 1976 with some observations, but neither the Butterlys nor Harold Gardner made themselves aware of what was in the letter – and at the same time, Dublin Corporation didn't do anything to enforce this.

All of this physical evidence painted a picture of why, perhaps, people died on the night. The medical evidence explained how they did. Dr John Harbison, the State Pathologist, had examined some of the victims himself and had read the post-mortems on the others. Most people had died quickly at the scene, he told the Tribunal: 40 of the bodies had been brought straight to the morgue at Store Street in Dublin city centre on the night. Four other people were brought to hospital but were dead on arrival. Four more died in hospital over the coming days and weeks.

He ruled out some narratives immediately: no, there was no indication that anyone had died from being trampled as people had tried to get out the exits, which had been suggested at one stage; there were no major crush injuries. No, alcohol did not contribute to the deaths. Just over half of the dead had consumed alcohol, just under half had not. Either way, it had not contributed directly to any deaths. Of the dead, 32 were charred to varying degrees, with many having lost portions of limbs. Three people were found only to have superficial burns on their hands, face or neck. Overall, he said that more than 80% of the people were not recognisable by their faces after the fire and had been identified by dental records, jewellery or clothing.

Almost one-third of the victims had a potentially lethal level of carbon monoxide in their bodies at the time of death. Of the 44 people who died that night, he attributed their death to shock due to extensive burns or from inhalation of smoke and fumes in the fire. For the remaining four who died in hospital, three died of bronchopneumonia and one died from irreversible brain and heart muscle damage as a result of shock from the fire.

A surgeon from Dr Steevens' Hospital, Mr Brendan Prendiville, who spoke on behalf of himself and five other surgeons who had treated the injured, gave evidence that some of the injured had a series of burns across the backs of their shoulders, just below their necks. This was not a usual finding in a fire, he told the Tribunal, and suggested that it could have been as a result of some kind of liquid or molten substance falling onto people from above.

While a lot of the evidence, particularly that from the medical experts, sounds like it could have been given today – indeed, at the inquests more than 40 years later, one expert witness noted that the policing investigation would be almost exactly the same nowadays as it was back then – some parts are jarring, particularly the evidence given by a psychology professor who interviewed 24 survivors.

The professor, named as J. McKenna, found the survivors had a wide range of symptoms in the months after the fire: nightmares, anxiety, sleep disturbances, increased alcohol intake, nervous tension, depressive reactions ranging from mild to severe and 'conversion neuroses [mental health issues causing physical symptoms] and hysterical symptomatology'. None of this was surprising given what they had been through. Most of them would be able to get over it, apparently, the Tribunal heard; some already had. '[Professor McKenna] was satisfied . . . that in the majority of cases the fire would become an unhappy memory and would not lead to any radical changes in their lifestyle,' the Tribunal report said. They would simply 'adjust to the new state of affairs'. 'Where such grief reactions continued, they would, in his view, be generally attributable to already existing personality weaknesses rather than the circumstances of the fire.'

What now comes across as pathologically cold and unhelpful typifies the response that many of the survivors and the families of the victims met with: paternalistic, victim-blaming and without any real substantive offer of help. McKenna's comments were later described as a 'failure of psychological understanding' in a government-commissioned report by the Eastern Health Board in 1991.

Over the course of its 122 days, the Tribunal heard from survivors, from firefighters and from gardaí; it heard from fire experts, Stardust staff, and the people responsible for making planning decisions across Dublin.

On the final day of the Tribunal in November 1981, lawyers for the Butterly companies asked for their legal costs to be paid for by the State. They were not alone: Dublin Corporation also made the same request. The barrister representing the Butterlys argued that public inquiries on matters of public importance were for the public benefit, and should therefore be paid for by the State, rather than having the cost incurred by individuals. Dublin Corporation's legal representative argued that the local authority only had a certain amount of money to operate each year and having to pay the legal costs would mean other areas of operation would be seriously diminished, including the fire services. Counsel for the Attorney General argued against awarding costs to either party.

The application for costs was the final thing that happened in the Tribunal. Once it was done, Mr Justice Ronan Keane reminded all present that contempt rules would still apply between then and the report being published. He praised the reporting of the Tribunal to that point as being 'both careful and responsible', perhaps encouraging this to continue.

And then at 1.20pm, he closed the Tribunal, saying that the report would be given to the Department of the Environment in due course.

* * *

The finished report was submitted on 30th June 1982, 16 months after the fire. This might be considered speedy by today's standards of Tribunal reports – Ireland's last two Tribunals (Smithwick and Disclosures) took eight and six years respectively between starting and producing their final reports. The Flood/Mahon Tribunal took 15 years. However, things moved at a different pace in the early 1980s. The tribunal immediately before Stardust, into the Whiddy Island disaster, took 15 months to produce its report. The one immediately after it, into the Kerry babies case, took 10 months.

And even with this speed, the Keane Report was a tome: 673 pages and over 210,000 words – shorter than *Ulysses*, longer than the New Testament of the Bible, closing in on *Crime and Punishment*. It was typed up by a team of typists from the Department of the Environment, who, the report noted, had had to go through 'many preliminary drafts' as well as the final one. When Minister for the Environment Ray Burke was given one of the first copies of the report, one newspaper report estimated that printing out all the remaining copies needed for distribution would take between six and eight weeks because of its size.

The language in the report is occasionally formal (at one point it puts 'disco' in inverted commas) but it is crystal clear throughout. This report was written to be read. It is precise and sharp; at one stage, when it describes how patrons reacted to the fire breaking out, the report notes that it uses the word 'panic' to describe the situation but putting it in quotation marks so that it isn't seen in a pejorative way or to suggest that people's behaviour was foolish or irrational. Instead, it says, much of what people did on the night was actually extremely rational: they tried to get to the nearest door, or to go back to the one they had come in through.

It frequently puts the experience of patrons and witnesses front and centre, dedicating one chapter to a timeline of the fire based on their appearances at the

Tribunal, and another to the evacuation of the building on the night. It uses their own words to piece together the picture of what happened to them and their friends.

So what does the report actually say?

It excoriates Eamon and Patrick Butterly. It takes them to task repeatedly and thoroughly for multiple failings. Some of the doormen working on the night also come in for harsh criticism. But the report also rakes Dublin Corporation over the coals and strongly criticises the Department of Environment too. It repeatedly points to systemic problems in Irish planning and fire safety at the time that could have prevented or alleviated the scale of the disaster in the years leading up to it, as well as the failings up to and on the night itself.

A significant amount of the report is focused on why the fire spread in such a catastrophic way. Again and again, it comes back to the unsuitable carpet tiles on the walls. They are mentioned 174 times in the report. They 'contributed substantially to the rapid spread of the fire,' the Tribunal report says. The use of the tiles was in breach of the requirements laid out by Dublin Fire Brigade, and contrary to the draft building regulations and fire protection standards, it found.

Using the evidence from patrons and staff and physical evidence from the doors themselves, the report concluded that two of the six emergency exits (Exits 2 and 3) had been locked when the fire broke out. One of them, Exit 3, showed signs of huge physical force. It had most likely been kicked open by people in the disco who had done what they were supposed to do when the fire broke out and ran for the emergency exits, where they then had to fight for their lives to get out. The other, Exit 2, had been

THE LAST DISCO

opened by one of the doormen shortly after the fire broke out, but had swung closed as people were trying to get out. The others all had a lock and chain draped over the bars to give the impression that they were locked. Additionally, three of the doors were obstructed, one by a skip outside, one by the DJ's van, and another by additional seating placed near it.

Notably, the Tribunal refused to use the evidence of some of the doormen about whether and when the doors were unlocked. The report says that the Tribunal had to treat the testimony of several of the doormen 'with great reserve', noting that several did not cooperate fully with gardaí, which was 'deplorable and indefensible'.

The report was blistering about the role Eamon Butterly played. In paragraph after paragraph, it details the failings of the Stardust manager. Butterly's policy of locking the doors was done 'with a reckless disregard for the safety of the people on the premises'. The report notes that he could simply have employed more doormen if there was actually an issue with people trying to let their friends in for free. The policy, such as it was, was sloppy. No one person had the specific responsibility of unlocking the doors after midnight, meaning it was possible, the report says, that on a number of occasions all of the exits could have remained locked during the entire time that the public were on the premises.

At times it even casts doubt on his evidence. It describes how, shortly after Christmas 1980, Eamon Butterly had ordered that emergency exits were to remain locked until midnight or 12.30am on disco nights. He told the Tribunal that this was confined to just a few of the exits, not all of them. His own doormen said that this isn't what happened in practice – and that all the doors were locked – and Keane agreed. 'The Tribunal is satisfied that Mr Butterly did not, either expressly or by implication, limit his directive in the manner suggested by him in his evidence, and that it was not understood by any of the members of his staff to be so limited.'

The report specifies how, by using sub-par professional expertise, the owners contributed to the scale of the disaster by allowing carpet tiles to be used as wall linings and in the 'inadequate consideration' given to using the main entrance foyer as an emergency exit.

It is strongly critical of Harold Gardner and William White, who prepared the architectural drawings for the building, writing that neither of them had 'the necessary skills or qualifications to undertake a project on this scale'. 'Some degree of responsibility must be attributed to them for undertaking work of this nature in the knowledge that they were not equipped to deal with it,' the report says. The report says that Eamon and Patrick Butterly were primarily responsible for the errors and omissions in the 'design, supervision and execution' of how the building was converted – particularly the carpet tiling on the walls and Exit 2 not meeting fire safety standards – but White and Gardner were 'also in part responsible'. These errors and omissions contributed significantly to the deaths and injuries, the report said.

The fire was always going to cause harm, but the report notes that some injuries and probably some lives could have been saved if the building had been properly evacuated. If this had actually happened, it is not possible to say that all the deaths would have been avoided, the report says, but the injuries would have 'unquestionably' been less and the death toll would 'almost certainly' have been reduced.

Instead, the report estimates that between 200 and 300 people stood in front of the West Alcove and watched the fire when it was first discovered. At the same time, many people who were dancing in front of the stage at that time, who may have had their backs to the West Alcove, didn't try to leave. 'There can be no doubt that many of the dead and injured were members of this group,' the report says.

It dedicates two whole pages to summing up the main – but not all – areas where the Stardust didn't comply with legislation, regulations and guidelines:

Planning Act:
- The requirements of the Chief Fire Officer were not ascertained during the planning permission process and no steps were taken to ensure that they were complied with. The specific requirement that the wall linings should have a better flame rating was not met.

Building By-laws:
- Work was started on converting the building before Dublin Corporation had granted permission.

Public Resort By-laws:
- There were at least 12 failures to comply with these by-laws, including: Chains and padlocks for emergency exit doors should have been kept on a special board for keys while the public were on the premises; employees were never given specific duties in event of a fire and fire drills were never heard; the licensee did not take 'due precautions' for the safety of the people

in the venue; and the corridors intended for exits were not kept entirely free from obstruction.

Fire Protection Standards:
- There were at least 12 failures to comply with these standards too. Among others, Exits were not kept clear and unobstructed; there was no fire plan at the building; and there were no hydraulic hose reels on the premises.

Draft Building Regulations:
- Some of the materials used in the conversion of the building were not suitable.

Dublin Corporation gets reprimanded by the report for its many mistakes during the planning process stage, but the report saves its harshest words for the lack of inspections carried out by the local authority once the venue was up and running. It lists all of the obvious things that would have been spotted if Dublin Corporation had ever bothered to come out and inspect the Stardust for fire safety issues: the locked doors, the carpet tiles on the walls, the absence of a fire plan, the lack of a staff member responsible for fire safety, the lack of an evacuation plan, the failure to hold fire drills, the absence of notices telling patrons what to do in case of a fire and the absence of somewhere to hang the padlocks and chains while the public were on the premises. This lack of inspection 'directly contributed to the deaths and injuries in the fire'.

The Department of the Environment received its share of blame in the report. The department had dilly-dallied for almost 20 years in introducing a modern code of building regulations with the force of law across the State to replace local bye-laws, which the report described as 'wholly unacceptable'. The lack of national regulations seriously increased the workload on the already understaffed Dublin Corporation. The Chief Fire Officer of Dublin Corporation told the Secretary General of the Department of the Environment this in 1971, pointing out that some of this fire safety and prevention work needed to be transferred elsewhere. This did not happen. 'The Department failed to treat the introduction of the regulations as the urgent matter which it clearly was,' the report says.

At the same time, it notes the pressure on the Fire Prevention Department of Dublin Corporation, which had to deal with an increasing number of applications from venues at the same time as their staff was declining. The number of applications referred to the Fire Prevention Department grew from 1,127 in 1976 to 1,800 just four years later.

It describes the tiny staff of the department, which declined at the same time as Dublin city went through the most rapid expansion in its history. This 'derisory' number of people – just five – working in such a crucial area was not just a local problem for Dublin but a 'national scandal', the report says, and it was the responsibility of the government, and specifically the Department of the Environment, to deal with it 'as a matter of urgency'.

*   *   *

It is fair to say that none of this, however, is generally what people remember about this report. Instead, the Keane Report is often remembered for what it says about the cause of the fire.

The report considered eyewitness accounts, forensic evidence and recreations of the fire by experts in considering what may have started the fire, and came up with six possible options. Four of them were accidental. A careless smoker could have tossed away a match or cigarette onto a seat in the West Alcove, which could have led to a fire if the seat had been ripped and the inner foam exposed. A waitress or floor girl could have put a smouldering bag of ashtray contents beside the main bar in order for it to be brought out with the rubbish. The fire could have started accidentally in the roof space. There was little combustible material in the roof space but the store room below it had toilet rolls, paper napkins, cleaning aerosols – perhaps a fire started here, spread to the roof space and then dropped down into the West Alcove. Or perhaps there was an electrical fault at the immersion heater in the main bar, just beside the West Alcove. The cabinet it was in had been completely destroyed by the fire and there was evidence of some bad wiring.

The other two reasons were deliberate. People on the roof could have started the fire. It is known that four (named) young people got onto the roof around 11.45pm that night and tried to open one of the glass skylights, before fleeing when they spotted a garda car. Could they have come back and started the fire? Or perhaps someone started it in the West Alcove, where the fire was first spotted? There had been a small number of people in and out of the West Alcove all evening. Did one of them do it?

The report puts forward suggestions and knocks them all down. When it comes to the immersion heater, the report says that it wouldn't give a 'satisfactory explanation for the rapid spread of fire from seat to seat' if it had started there.

THE LAST DISCO

The Butterlys had suggested that the fire might have been started so someone could rob money or alcohol or cigarettes, but the report notes that there's no evidence to back this up. There were some gangs of youths from Artane and Donnycarney – the Dragon Gang, the Animal Gang and the Soap Gang – who frequently attended and could sometimes cause trouble, but these were a tiny minority of the large attendances. There was occasionally some 'disorder' on disco nights which led to 'some animosity between some of the patrons and the doormen', but even with that kind of bad-temperedness, the report notes that 'the evidence of a motive for a deliberate act of arson on the premises remains tenuous'.

And then the report says this:

'The cause of the fire is not known and may never be known. There is no evidence of an accidental origin and equally no evidence that the fire was started deliberately.'

If the report had ended that chapter after those two sentences, then it would have been remembered very differently. But it continued.

'The examination conducted by the Tribunal of each of the hypotheses based on an accidental origin has produced serious and, it may be, insurmountable objections to every hypothesis ... In these circumstances, the Tribunal has come to the conclusion that the more probable explanation of the fire is that it was caused deliberately.'

Those final four words were to become the legacy of the Keane Tribunal. In saying that the fire had probably been caused deliberately, the Keane Report laid down the official narrative for what had happened on the night and changed the trajectory of how the Stardust disaster was seen.

It said that the cause was not known but decided anyway that it was probably arson. There was no way to know who this arsonist was, if there was more than one person involved, what the motive was and if there was any premeditation, the report says. The arsonist or arsonists had most likely slashed a number of seats in the West Alcove with a pen knife or something else sharp, and then used a match, or cigarette lighter, or lit some papers on or under the seats. There was no smell of petrol or paraffin at the scene, so this seemed most likely, the report says. 'It may be, and this again must remain no more than conjecture, that the object of the arsonists was to do no more than cause a fire in the alcove itself, for whatever motives; and that, in carrying out this reckless criminal enterprise, they had not intended to cause any injury or death, still less on the appalling scale that, in fact, resulted.'

In other words, it jumped dramatically and unsteadily from saying that the cause of the fire was not known to concluding that it was most likely a deliberate act.

In the days after its publication, the initial reaction focused on the failures of Dublin Corporation, Dublin Fire Brigade, the Department of the Environment and the owners, rather than on the arson finding, and how all of these agencies could or would be reformed as a result. One newspaper praised the Tribunal report for its 'clarity of thought and vision'.

For the survivors, the families of the victims and the people living in the area, though, the arson finding was the focus. It didn't make any sense. It was saying that someone among them had been careless and criminal and had inflicted this on them, but where was the evidence? The report itself hadn't been able to back this up and there were no signs of a criminal case being taken by gardaí. It was a knock-out punch: it blamed the people in the area, and it spoke to the worst prejudices that people had about this part of Dublin, but when they tried to argue this, it was seen as being overly defensive. The Tribunal had been run by experts and had heard all the evidence, so it must be correct. Why couldn't they just accept it and move on?

The arson finding had a number of impacts. The Butterlys had had to pay their own costs at the Tribunal, rather than having the State pay. Separately though, they had already filed a case against Dublin Corporation for malicious damage deliberately caused to their property, which could now begin to wind through the courts.

There were some positives in it: by highlighting how stretched Dublin Fire Brigade and other fire brigades around the country were, extra resources were put into modernising and expanding the fire service in the country. Dublin Fire Brigade and other agencies now practise for major incident plans several times a year, while fire crews on the way to a fire now have access to maps of affected buildings and the location of water sources. Dublin Fire Brigade inspects more than half – around 70% – of pubs and hotels and clubs that apply for licences each year, and visits all premises at least once every two years. Fire crews now aim to be driving out of the door of the station between 60 and 90 seconds after being alerted to a fire, rather than the three minutes that it took on the night of the Stardust fire.

Overall though, it is seen as a baffling outcome which was to put obstacles in front of the families for decades to come. 'The problem is its legacy,' said Darragh Mackin, a lawyer at Phoenix Law who specialises in human rights.

'It came to a conclusion that doesn't match the evidence. It leaves you scratching your head because you wonder how it came to that conclusion.'

He points out that the report being done immediately after the fire means that it collated a huge amount of information – statements from witnesses, agreed facts, details on how the fire spread – that would come in useful in the years ahead. 'Unfortunately, this is also its biggest weakness,' said Mackin. 'It happened at a time when many families and victims were still hospitalised or traumatised, and couldn't engage with it.'

It was also one of two Tribunal reports in the 1980s – the other being the Kerry Babies Tribunal several years later – which blamed the victims. The Hillsborough disaster would do the same thing towards the end of that decade. '[This] tells us what this is really about: social class and social power,' Fintan O'Toole wrote in the *Irish Times*. By perpetrating a false narrative, the State put its weight behind a theory that 'working class people are wild, reckless and the authors of their own calamities,' O'Toole wrote.

For Mackin, one of the big lessons is making sure that people affected by a disaster can participate in any kind of inquiry or judicial process after the fact and have their voices heard.

'When you take on an investigation like this in relation to a hugely traumatic event or a mass tragedy, it is so important to get it right – because if you get it wrong, it will only add salt to the wounds, as opposed to assisting in the grieving process.'

Chapter 7

IT WAS A NIGHT like any other in the Lantern Rooms.

Tim Hastings was there with a work colleague, arriving around 9pm. There were around a dozen people playing snooker under lit tables. Others were playing arcade games.

The Silver Swan next door was busy, with around 100 people there, chatting, having a drink, enjoying their evening, but that wasn't why Hastings was there. He was focused on something that the other punters were, seemingly, oblivious to.

Two of the emergency exit doors in the Lantern Rooms had heavy steel chains wrapped around the panic bars. The chain and a lock were plain to see for anyone heading to the toilets near the snooker room. The exit from the Silver Swan was unobstructed.

Hastings was a reporter with the *Irish Press*, and the colleague with him was a photographer. His paper's newsroom had received an anonymous tipoff from a man who had previously been in the Silver Swan pub and was surprised to see chains on the panic bars.

The paper subsequently ran the story under the headline 'Locks Again On Stardust Doors' on 13th September 1982. Not only was the complex where the Stardust once stood still open, but it was haunted by a familiar sight 18 months after the fire.

It was news to Eamon Butterly. Quoted as speaking in a shocked voice, the manager told the paper that he had issued instructions for no chains to be put on the doors and the exits were unobstructed when he was on the premises at 4.30pm that day. The story led to investigations by the gardaí and Dublin Corporation. The same paper reported on 15th February 1983 that the Director of Public Prosecutions was to recommend charges be brought.

Butterly and barman John Dignam appeared in court in April 1984, the *Evening Press* reported, and pleaded not guilty to charges of allowing the Lantern Rooms' doors to be locked.

Both men were acquitted. The *Irish Times* reported that Mr Justice Thomas Neylon directed the jury to find both men not guilty, that it seemed 'that there had been a misunderstanding between two staff members as to whether the doors had been unlocked, but there was no criminal intent'.

The misunderstanding was caused by the day in question being a Sunday. Up until 2000, it was common for pubs in Ireland to close for 'holy hour' between 2pm and 4pm. Dignam told the court that he went on his holy hour break, and when he returned, the front shutters were unlocked and other barmen were on the premises. He presumed the building hadn't even been locked up.

Butterly's businesses were back on their feet a little more than a year after the fire. Survivors and families did not experience the same swift recovery.

The Keane Tribunal was anything but the full stop in the story that many had hoped for. Its forensic detail both provided clarity and raised questions for the nation about what happened that night.

THE LAST DISCO

The Tribunal's verdict that the fire was probably caused deliberately was a hammer blow to locals. Now, the disaster was framed as if it was their own fault because it was someone in their own community who killed their loved ones. It fed into prejudices about these working-class areas, doubling down on a stigma that was already hard to shift. It did little, if anything, to quell the anger and loss that families already felt, and those feelings quickly hardened into something difficult to erode, something that hadn't softened five years later, or 10, or 40.

In those months and years after the fire, the lives of survivors went on in a way that was alien compared to their lives before Valentine's Day 1981. Social circles had been shattered. People maimed in the fire were now faced with adapting to the changes to their bodies. The unseen psychological trauma began to emerge too, and in a time when mental health issues were treated vastly differently than today. Survivors who were previously outgoing spoke of becoming more reclusive and crankier, with a new fear of crowded spaces. They had persistent nightmares, waking others in the household with their screams. Suddenly, jobs became more difficult to hold down. Many started smoking more. Some took to alcohol, some took to drugs.

Some took their own lives. A court in the mid-1980s would hear that there were more than two dozen suicide attempts.

'I wasn't in the right frame of mind after we lost Robert,' Eugene Kelly said. He had a breakdown and attempted to take his own life. 'My mind was all over the place. I couldn't accept his death.

'I was having many the nightmare because when I saw Robert's coroner's report . . . there was nothing left of him. There was nothing left of the chap.'

People who did not experience this type of intense grief suffered too. Hundreds were left comparably unscathed by the fire, but they still suffered from survivor's guilt and overlooked what they themselves were going through.

'I shook – literally, shook – physically for about two or three weeks,' Linda Bishop recalled.

'I thought everyone else was the same. We always thought that we were the lucky ones, and you didn't complain because looking at the families, so many people dead, in hospital, badly burned. So we just didn't complain, and you weren't looking for anything from anybody.'

Proper support was lacking, or the means or knowledge to access it. The finger-pointing of arson claims compounded these difficulties. Parents and friends felt the growing pain of the lack of autonomy over the funerals of their loved ones: their goodbyes were never going to be how they wanted them to be after the fire, but they were robbed of the chance to make them their own. Before long, people started to feel as though wider Ireland was moving away from trying to help them.

* * *

For the first couple of weeks, the nation mourned alongside the Stardust families. They wanted to help.

For a brief few days, a bus conductor and part-time social worker from the area was the face of this. Ultan Courtney, like many from the area, knew victims personally.

THE LAST DISCO

He tapped into the national outpouring of grief to assist the families impacted.

He set up a fund with the initial aim of providing cash assistance – burials, medical expenses, lost earnings – while also potentially using surplus funds to construct a youth centre on the northside as a 'living memorial'.

It was envisaged that this help would bridge the gap in the period before compensation claims were settled, Courtney was quoted as saying.

He was immediately inundated with offers of donations before the fund even had a bank account. Two anonymous Dublin businessmen offered to help with funeral expenses.

Taoiseach Charles Haughey phoned Courtney personally to lend his support to the fund, while The Chieftains and Johnny Logan offered to play concerts to raise more money.

The Lord Mayor of Dublin, Fergus O'Brien, was also on hand to help Courtney. He set up the Artane Disaster Fund, and the two initiatives were merged within a few weeks in the name of effectiveness.

Before the end of February 1981, the fund had already received £25,000 (the equivalent of more than €120,000 in 2024). By early March, it had tripled to £75,000, and O'Brien was even grabbing headlines for reportedly attempting to get The Who to play a gig in Tolka Park to raise more funds.

The first payments, totalling more than £60,000, were made before the end of March, by which time the total fund was now worth more than £150,000. The Minister for Health also committed to 'foot the bill' for hospital fees.

But tension was brewing beneath this, the positivity only surface-level, which led to the first elements of the long-running Stardust campaign coming together.

On the evening of 10th March, around 150 Stardust survivors, victims and families came together in Coolock. Representatives gave a press conference to the media the following day, the same day the 48th victim of the Stardust fire, Liam Dunne, died in hospital. He had regained consciousness but wasn't able to speak to family.

Vincent Hogan, who lost his brother Eugene in the fire, took on the role of acting secretary of the newly formed Stardust Relatives' and Injured Committee, representing around three-quarters of the victims.

The group wasted no time in giving the government both barrels, hitting out at 'politicians who turned up at the funerals and later forgot all about us'. The *Irish Times* reporter Frank McDonald's article on the press conference details that the government was 'clearly taken aback by the militant mood of the committee and the Taoiseach immediately agreed to meet them as soon as possible'.

Vincent outlined the range of issues that had sprung up in less than a month. There was frustration amongst victims and families that payments from the relief fund were slow to materialise. Organisers of the fund said checks and balances were being put in place first, but treatment was needed, and bills needed to be paid. Vincent told the press conference that one girl requesting assistance was asked whether she 'did not think the money should go to a more deserving family', and was also told any money paid to her would have to be repaid from any compensation she won at a later date. There was also no family on the fund's board of trustees, which included, amongst others, representatives from the main churches in Ireland and the Minister for Health, who would be assessing and approving claims. The government said it was helping with travel for hospital appointments, that it would approve medical card requests, and that it had set up a dedicated advice centre, but still, families said they were experiencing persistent issues with medical expenses and social welfare benefits.

The committee also wanted the scope of the Keane Tribunal to be broadened. Another major sticking point was the government's appointment of legal representation for families and survivors for the Tribunal two days before its first sitting and without any prior consultation, which the committee described as an infringement of their constitutional rights. There were concerns, too, about who would pay for this.

This was the genesis of a long-running movement that stood up to the State and called for better treatment. By Saturday, the same day Liam Dunne was laid to rest, Haughey had met with the committee. By the following week, the government announced that the family's chosen legal firm had been added to the tribunal panel. As we've seen, this arrangement fell apart.

The group kept the government on its toes, meeting with ministers and speaking to the media, putting forward the voice of survivors. This stepped up a gear when it emerged that the undamaged parts of the Stardust complex would reopen.

The *Irish Independent* reported on a statement issued by the Butterly family in June 1981, outlining plans for the Silver Swan to reopen on the 20th, followed by the Lantern Rooms. It would be a quick turnaround, given they were only due to get the keys to the premises back from gardaí a couple of weeks before the reopening. This flew in the face of a commitment from Haughey that the government would oppose any attempt to reopen the complex until after the Keane Tribunal. When asked about the family's opposition to the move, Eamon Butterly was quoted as saying: 'The trouble up to now is that they have never approached me or asked to talk the matter over.'

The families turned their anger into action. From the morning of the alleged reopening, families picketed the venue for 48 hours and called on trade unions to boycott any renovation work – but no reopening came. 'What reopening?' was essentially the reaction from Butterly when the *Irish Press* followed up. There were 'no immediate plans', he said, despite the earlier reported statement, but he said he was keeping 'an open mind'.

When he did reopen the Lantern Rooms, on 28th September, it took everyone by surprise. Not even Dublin Corporation had prior notice, although they were powerless to intervene, and the only action taken was to send a fire inspector to take a look at the premises. Families rushed to the scene and mounted a fresh picket, urging the public not to go inside. Butterly responded by seeking an injunction against the picket, granted in October and made permanent in December.

All the while, between his appearances before the Tribunal, Butterly was also trying to renew the Silver Swan's licence to sell alcohol. Relatives, who opposed the move alongside the State and local gardaí, packed the court hearings. It was revealed during the proceedings that the Silver Swan never actually had a licence in the first place, with Butterly pleading ignorance to the fact

THE LAST DISCO

that Scott's Food having a licence didn't mean that the Silver Swan was included. The request to renew the licence was granted subject to certain conditions – including an undertaking that a disco would never be held at the site again. The Lantern Rooms was also granted a limited licence in February 1982.

(Butterly later sold the Silver Swan to William Kenny, a businessman who ran a window installation company, had no prior experience in hospitality and had recently been on holidays with Butterly. 'Subterfuge' is how a solicitor for An Garda Síochána described the sale in court during a licence hearing. The President of the District Court said in November that it was 'not a bona fide sale' and ruled that Kenny was not fit to hold the licence.)

* * *

The avenues of recourse for the families were closing up. On top of the bitter aftertaste left by the Keane Tribunal, there was no sign of a criminal investigation into the circumstances that led to the deaths of their loved ones. There were inquests, but they were brief, held over five days in March 1982. Their function was not to determine the circumstances surrounding the deaths but to focus solely on the identification of victims and determining their cause of death. The jury returned a verdict in line with medical evidence for each of the 48 victims. There was no cross-examination of witnesses. The court ran through each case in a formulaic fashion, hearing about the victims' medical reports; what was known about their evening in the Stardust; and how they were identified using dental records, clothing or jewellery – like Margaret

Thornton's miraculous medal, Teresa McDonnell's eternity ring and Jimmy Buckley's wedding ring. The jury recommended that certain public safety laws be more strictly enforced.

The official arms of the State hadn't remedied the concerns of survivors and families, but there was one more option, and they didn't require the government's help – on paper, at least. Time and time again, victims' families will say that if they were from the southside suburb of Donnybrook, not the Coolock townland of Bonnybrook, the fallout wouldn't have turned into a decades-long saga; they would have been able to access the truth and closure they wanted a lot quicker. This class element means that compensation is a dirty word in the Stardust story, deeply intertwined with the stigma attached to people from this working-class area of Dublin.

Some people think they just want money. It is important to address that head-on. The vast majority of the public have honestly held sympathy for the Stardust families and survivors, but as journalists who have worked on this story for years are sometimes asked, in quiet tones, 'Is it really just money they're after?'

The public had some sense of a local community left shattered by what happened. But while everyone has lost loved ones, the quality of grief attached to this event is different, sharper, wider.

'When somebody has lost a child or children or a friend or friends in something like Stardust, then they're forever changed,' psychologist and author Niamh Fitzpatrick said. She has written extensively about grief following the death of her sister Captain Dara Fitzpatrick in the R116 Coast Guard helicopter crash. All four crew members died when

THE LAST DISCO

the aircraft struck an island off the west coast of Ireland in 2017. Issues with navigational aids were among the issues found to have led to the tragedy.

'The Stardust families are on a huge journey that drains the battery enormously, that journey of trying to come to terms with and learn to live with the loss and the trauma of that loss.'

Grief is not just a sad emotion, she explained. There's rage, loneliness, guilt, resentment, anxiety and more. It impacts people physically, emotionally, financially, psychologically, practically, cognitively – in every way.

When a disaster like the Stardust strikes, whole communities experience a ripple effect from the changed way people interact with each other. This includes the first responders, the hospital staff, people who worked in the club who were exposed first-hand. Simply living and working on Dublin's northside could mean you were affected. It spreads out and out. As the dynamics of parent-child relationships change, the effect becomes generational.

But how would money fix that? 'It is key in that because these people involved are doing their best to try to learn to live with their loss,' Fitzpatrick explained.

'If that loss is not seen, if it's not acknowledged, if it's not validated, if it's somehow dismissed, then that places an added weight on them on that journey when they're trying to grapple with their feelings and learn to live with their loss.

'Psychologically, you could swap out the word "compensation" for the word "acknowledgement". That's what it's about in these circumstances. No money can make up for the loved ones lost, for the lives, years, futures, peace of mind robbed.

'What the money can do is acknowledge that your loss exists, your pain exists, that wrong was done, that you were heard and that you were seen. What it does is that it allows the person to say, "Okay, now I can be free to feel the feelings of loss." Compensation, investigation, the truth, any of that coming out feeds into that bit around allowing the person then have no blocks in the way for them to be able to get on with the work of grieving – because it is work.'

From the beginning, families suspected they would be facing a long, uphill battle to get this acknowledgement. It didn't come from the Keane Tribunal; maybe it could come through the courts. A High Court case was a daunting prospect and would likely turn into a complex battle. It was the only route left available to them, but years went by without any progress.

It was a different situation for the owners of the Stardust. The Butterlys sought compensation worth a combined £3 million – £2 million for Patrick Butterly's Scott's Food Ltd, which owned the building, and £1 million for Eamon Butterly's Silver Swan Ltd, which leased it. This claim against Dublin Corporation (the defendant in this type of case when private property is damaged by an alleged criminal act) was lodged promptly after the fire, as the legal deadline for a malicious damages claim was one week after the event.

The case would not be heard until June 1983, and the District Court ruling took many by surprise when it was delivered. The judge, Sean O'Hanrahan, went further than the findings of the Keane Tribunal and ruled that the fire was started maliciously.

'Final proof of what I have maintained all along' is how Eamon Butterly described it to reporters afterwards.

The final settlement was less than the £3 million figure sought, which was the largest claim Dublin Corporation had ever faced. The judge ruled that Silver Swan was not entitled to compensation, and the council eventually got the figure down to £581,491, the equivalent of more than €2 million in 2024. The *Evening Herald* reported that Butterly was happy with this outcome. 'The finding that the fire was deliberate was the most important thing,' he said.

The families were incensed. The council was paying out a claim to the owners of the club where their loved ones died, but their own claims were still languishing on the court lists. These cases, potentially worth a combined total of £10 million (the equivalent of almost €50 million in 2024), were piling up but not a penny had been awarded yet. The majority had barely moved past their initial stages.

'We're getting treated like dirt since the fire,' Lucy Croker, whose 19-year-old daughter Jacqueline died in the disaster, told the *Irish Press*. '[Butterly is] in and out of the courts getting things sorted out, and we're getting left aside. I still haven't had the return of my daughter's rings. They're in some police station. And we haven't heard from the courts yet about when our claim will go through.'

'It appears to us that money revolves around Mr Butterly, but not around us,' Jimmy Kiernan of the committee said. 'Of course, it was never compensation we were after, only justice. But justice appears to have evaded us.'

The High Court had always been an option for a civil case, and it was how many were pursuing their claims. It offered the potential of substantial awards but with legal costs to shoulder and no guarantee of success.

A rare photograph of the Stardust's interior from before the fire. This is taken from close to the main bar, facing the stage.

This is all that was left of the ballroom the morning after the fire.

Right: An image taken the Monday after the fire, showing a chain and padlock wrapped around the panic bar of an exit door and assorted discarded belongings.

Below: An aerial view of the Stardust complex, showing the extent of the damage.

The foyer after the fire. The doorway seen is the main entrance, the cloakroom and cash office are on the left, and the stairway is on the right.

Huge crowds of people gather as the coffins of four young people who died in the fire leave the Church of St Luke the Evangelist in Kilmore on 18th February 1981.

Right: The scene inside the morgue on Store Street the morning after the fire.

Below: Justice Ronan Keane, who chaired the 1981 tribunal into the cause of the fire, pictured here in 2002.

Forty-eight doves are released over the Fountain of Youth at the Stardust Memorial Park to mark the 25th anniversary of the disaster.

A protest calling for a new inquiry blocks traffic in early March 2006.

The façade of the complex on the 25th anniversary, when the Skelly's Bar was rebranded as the Silver Swan, sparking massive anger from survivors.

Christine Keegan, Eugene Kelly (holding an image of his brother Robert) and Antoinette Keegan before a meeting in Leinster House in 2014.

The faces of all 48 victims at the Stardust Memorial Wall.

A photograph of the main bar – the immersion where the inquests deemed the fire likely started is seen in the far corner.

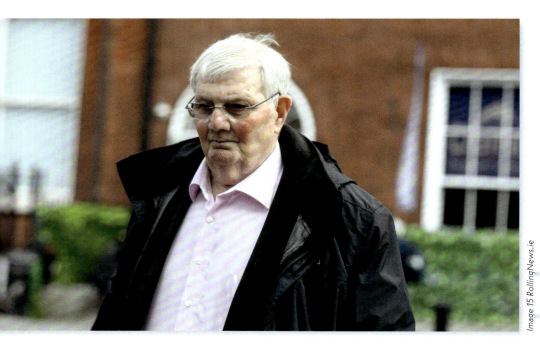

Eamon Butterly, former manager of the Stardust club, arrives at the Rotunda for his second day in the witness box at the inquests in 2023.

Supporters and family members of The 48 gather in the Garden of Remembrance, a short distance from the Pillar Room, after the verdict of unlawful killing was delivered at the inquests.

This process was underway even before the Keane Tribunal, with claims being lodged against the Butterlys and the companies involved but also against Dublin Corporation, the State and the Minister for the Environment for their perceived failings in the run-up to and after the disaster.

Taking a case like this in the High Court can be a protracted process at the best of times, but the Stardust cases dragged on and on. They were stalled for a range of reasons: the sheer number of individual claims; the number of defendants; the fact that each put up a defence (Dublin Corporation claimed contributory negligence, that the people themselves played a role in the injuries they sustained); there were issues with the discovery of documents; some writs weren't issued until after the Keane Tribunal, or until just before the statute of limitations expired in February 1984.

The *Irish Independent* reported that some 'lawyers said simply that the wheels of justice move slowly and that final reports on injuries are awaited from doctors before pushing the cases into the court lists'.

A test case that would define how these claims would be treated in court and clear the bottleneck never materialised. The State simply watched on and let the process pan out; victims and families essentially had to figure it out for themselves.

The disaster fund had provided some relief, but it wasn't enough. It stopped accepting donations at the end of 1981, by which time the total amount received had grown to more than £400,000. By September 1983, the decision was made to wind up the fund. A 'four-figure sum' remained, said to be ring-fenced for some survivors with complex needs, the rest having been distributed. At one point, £30,000 was to be used for a memorial to the victims, but the plan was shelved following disagreements over what form it would take. Instead, it was donated to Beaumont Hospital, which was under construction close to the Stardust.

By the fourth anniversary in 1985, there had been little, if any, movement in most cases – except for Danny Hughes, the DJ on the night of the fire, who was awarded £11,200 for lost equipment the previous November.

Publicans and hoteliers were occasionally in the news expressing their frustration over the new fire safety regulations put in place after the disaster. The bill could run to hundreds or thousands of pounds, and they could face having to make new alterations each year depending on who inspects the premises. One publican, while making it clear that no one wished to see a repeat of the Stardust, said that the new laws were a 'panic' measure.

Fire services across the country were taking a different view: there was little to stop a repeat of what happened. A slew of known fire traps across the country hadn't been closed down. The chairman of the Chief Fire Officers Association suggested that the issue was money for public buildings, and the government couldn't afford to bring their properties up to the standard required. A fire in an old hospital risked another major loss of life, he warned. He called on the government to act.

The Stardust story itself was slipping further and further down the news agenda.

But that all changed in May of that year.

* * *

John and Christine Keegan were the parents of Mary and Martina, who died in the fire, and Antoinette, who was left with severe burns.

'While progress was being made, my dad didn't think it was happening soon enough, as years were going by,' his son Damien said. 'Then one day, while we were all sitting at home in the sitting room, my da said, "Chrissie, I am going to set up a new committee. I am done with listening to all that is getting said, like 'John you cannot rock the boat, sit still, be quiet' and so on." The frustration got to my da.'

The previous committee, which John was part of, was quietly disbanded in June 1983 after Eamon Butterly's successful malicious damage case and, according to the *Sunday Independent*, 'simply decided there was nothing else they could do'. The article went on to describe them as 'one of the most successful pressure groups in the history of the State', given their access to politicians and ability to garner media coverage, but with fire regulations still lacking, the Silver Swan reopened, and no significant memorial to the dead, 'they failed to do anything more than ripple the surface of Irish life'.

At a meeting at the start of May 1985, in the Camelot Hotel, Coolock, the Stardust Victims' Committee emerged with John Keegan as its chairperson.

He and Butterly had history.

Antoinette remembers the night. It was 23rd October 1983. Her father was out. She and her mother presumed he was up to the graveyard where Mary and Martina were buried, as he would often drive up at 1am or 2am and sit in the car, shining his headlights on the gravestones. But he wasn't there that night. John had instead gone to the buildings where the Stardust had been. In his boot he had a heavy chain, commonly used at the time to deter would-be car thieves by wrapping it around the steering wheel.

John walked around the complex, smashing the windows of the buildings and a lorry. Butterly came out, inviting him in to have a drink and talk.

'Go into that crematorium where my two daughters were cremated? I won't go in there,' John said, then struck Butterly across the head using the chain. The Keegans received a call that he had been arrested and was in Coolock Garda Station. John appeared in court the next day charged with assault and later received a one-year suspended sentence on the condition that he kept the peace for two years and 'the window breaking stopped'.

The new committee hit the ground running. Protests through the centre of Dublin city were held in May 1985, calling for the Stardust complex to be closed, better enforcement of fire regulations and – crucially – a court to be set up to handle the compensation claims. One demonstration blocked traffic for 45 minutes. In June, the committee attended a Dáil sitting on the invitation of Charlie Haughey, now in opposition, while he made the case for their right to have their cases heard quickly. Minister for Justice Michael Noonan said he would examine the cases but wouldn't give any commitments. Noonan highlighted that 219 writs had been issued, which is the first step of lodging the type of High Court claims that the families were in the middle of. The second step is when a statement of claim is submitted, containing more details provided by the plaintiff. However, just 108 had been issued. The State lodged a defence in 79 cases. Noonan was shouted down by the victims from the public gallery. 'They died for nothing,' one screamed.

Amid all this, Christy Moore was in court over the Stardust. The Irish folk singer, who would become a regular at vigils and protests for the Stardust victims over the decades, had written a song about the tragedy called 'They Never Came Home'. After enjoying a hit album with *Ride On* a year before, the song about the Stardust was set to feature on his new album *Ordinary Man* in 1985. The album was only out a few days when Moore's record label received a legal letter on behalf of the nightclub's owners. It claimed Moore was in contempt of court for a line referencing matters that were still 'before the courts'. The song told the story of what had happened, including the lines 'All around the city the bad news it spread / There's a fire in the Stardust there's 48 dead / Hundreds of children are injured and maimed / And all just because the fire exits were chained.' Although no punishment was imposed, the record had to be withdrawn, as the High Court ruled the song couldn't be promoted, distributed or sold in Irish shops. It wouldn't be included on the reissued version of *Ordinary Man*, with the whole saga coming at an enormous cost to Moore, his manager and the record company.

Moore was worried about the impact the case against him would have, particularly on the families. He needn't have worried. 'A really powerful memory for me is when the court case happened,' he told the Free State podcast with Joe Brolly and Dion Fanning in April 2024. 'I was feeling a bit paranoid because the song was getting all this publicity. What would all the families think about this fucking song? But I turned around, and they were all there. They were all there in the court to support me.'

This kept the story in the headlines and helped drive forward the growing momentum of the committee. The *Irish Times* took interest, and carried a detailed report on 20th August, delving into the myriad of firms representing various survivors and potential causes of the delays in legal cases. Some smaller firms were reluctant to be the first to see a case come to trial: Harry Ward, representing two victims, said the situation was 'full of horrible complexities' that he would struggle to explain to solicitors, let alone clients. 'You wouldn't want to be the first to bite the cherry' is how he framed it. Liam Lysaght, who represented the majority of claimants, was given particular attention in the article. In February, he angered campaigners after he sought £1,000 in fees from each client, even going as far as to secure a loan on their behalf that would be repaid from any damages awarded.

The *Irish Times* reported that most of his cases started in mid-1982, with statements of claims being lodged by November, but it wasn't until late 1984 that Lysaght sought for the defendants to enter a defence.

'I don't believe in speed for the sake of speed,' he told the paper. 'There may be those who say I was too cautious, but the careful legal practitioner gets a complete picture before he starts shooting off proceedings. My clients appear to be happy. I hold no brief for public disquiet. We work behind closed doors, quietly.'

Then, suddenly, there was progress: the government announced on 25th September 1985 that a new scheme would be launched to compensate victims to break the deadlock, not through the courts, but by using another tribunal to access each claim. It followed a meeting with the Attorney General the week before, and amid plans for a large protest in November. In one interview, John Keegan told the *Evening Press* that the committee had met with Taoiseach Garret FitzGerald and warned that if there wasn't any action, the committee planned 'to expose the hypocrisy' by taking their case to Europe.

Within the government itself, there was a clear appetite from the Taoiseach to leave the matter to others. A memo written by an official in his department from October 1985, released to the public decades later, read: 'Essentially, I think that the whole issue, which will involve a lot of detailed work, and could be highly controversial, should be kept as far from this department as possible.'

The Stardust Victims' Committee seemed cautiously optimistic that progress was finally being made. John warned that it would be foolish to rush into it. Committee members were still eager for a test case to establish liability, the *Irish Independent* reported, and some were concerned the new Tribunal would be an attempt to side-step that possibility. They wanted someone to be held responsible.

Antoinette explained the predicament many were in: 'There was no income coming in, families weren't working, parents were out of work over the loss of a child, there was a lot of struggling going on, and bills were piling up.

'People wanted to try to get something sorted, and what they gave us was like waving a carrot – take it or leave it.'

* * *

By November 1985, the Stardust Victims' Compensation Tribunal was up and running. It sat in St David's National School around the corner from the Stardust complex.

There was a core team of three: Donal Barrington, a High Court judge; Hugh O'Flaherty, a barrister; and Noel T. Smith, a solicitor. The team received 953 applications and sat for 49 days between November 1985 and December 1986.

The compensation scheme, on the face of it, was simple. The Tribunal would assess each claim. A successful claimant could receive an *ex gratia* payment – one that doesn't admit wrongdoing on behalf of the person paying it – from the State, including the cost of legal representation before the Tribunal, and any costs incurred in their own High Court cases, minus any social welfare or sick leave entitlements.

Each claimant would submit an application detailing their connection to the disaster and its impact on their life. This could include a medical report on the injuries sustained or a letter from an employer detailing loss of earnings. The team also had access to the statements people made to gardaí in the immediate aftermath of the fire. This all proved useful, as some people were understandably 'emotionally upset at the recall of the memories of that horrific happening' and found it difficult to speak.

The hearings were then conducted in private in a 'non-adversarial' manner, with no cross-examination. Hearsay and opinion were accepted as evidence. The Tribunal saw it as crucial to hold hearings in person, explaining that it was 'conscious of the importance of viewing the scars of all physically injured applicants'.

What these physical scars looked like varied. There were burns, ranging from minor to those that resulted in 'crippling disabilities and very significant cosmetic disfigurement'. One case was described as 'a miracle of medical science'.

There were injuries sustained after falling or in crushes. Damage to the lungs was common, sometimes comparable to a lifetime of smoking cigarettes, one doctor said. There were cases where the damage only became apparent after exercise or due to frequent chest infections.

The Tribunal also documented cases where people's voices had become noticeably lower, and 'a very small number of victims could still only speak at a whisper'. One other symptom appears unexpectedly in the final report: skin rashes on a large number of victims.

'These claims caused the Tribunal some difficulty as no dermatologist was prepared to state positively that exposure to the Stardust fire could lead to a skin rash or to psoriasis,' it reads. 'Nevertheless, these complaints were so numerous that the Tribunal became convinced that there was a causal connection between them and the fire.' The rash sometimes developed whenever the victim was under stress. In two cases, it happened while they were giving evidence.

There was also the psychological trauma. The Tribunal singled out one woman's submission, encapsulating what the wider community faced.

'At the age of sixteen, I suppose I was like most of my friends at the time; completely wild, outgoing and very hopeful for the future,' she said. After the fire – from which she escaped physically unscathed – she became quieter, more reserved. 'Quick-tempered and easily agitated with people not only about the fire but about anything I felt was private and personal to me – I wasn't like that before the fire.'

Her employment suffered. She lost her temper with colleagues and customers. She would refuse to sit in a pub unless she knew where the exits were. 'I don't think I will ever lose the fear of being caught in a fire again.'

'No matter how much time goes by, I will never forget the fire or the people who died in it. I certainly won't forget the effect it had on me as a teenager.'

These symptoms of post-traumatic stress were common and fell across a spectrum. People felt claustrophobic in dance halls, pubs or even on the bus. There were nightmares. Bedwetting was common. People moved out of their family home because they would wake up screaming so frequently.

One man had his hat stolen off his head in jest by a girl just before panic broke out in the Stardust. He was praised for his bravery afterwards, helping to rescue the injured and recover the bodies of the dead. 'For years afterwards, he was haunted by a dream in which he saw a stretcher covered in black plastic with one charred arm dangling down beneath the plastic. The hand was clutching the burnt remains of his hat.'

Those with access to a family doctor had better outcomes than those who did not, but for many, the Tribunal was the first time they had been examined and treated by doctors, as solicitors were sometimes able to refer their client to professionals knowing that the Tribunal would pay the cost.

'In a number of cases where the Tribunal feared that the symptoms of which the applicant complained might be more significant than he or his solicitor realised, the Tribunal adjourned the hearing with a suggestion that the applicant be examined by a general practitioner or by a specialist in a particular area at the Tribunal's expense,' the report reads.

A total of 823 claims were paid out, with a total value of £10,458,115 (around €50 million in 2024). The vast majority (666) received a payment of between £1,001 and £20,000. Roughly one in three received between £5,001 and £10,000. Five were awarded between £100,000 and £200,000.

This Tribunal's team were praised in the media for the 'informal and human manner in which they conducted the proceedings', but the Stardust families do not speak of it in such glowing terms these days.

'We were brought into this room, one by one, and there was a big table,' Catherine Darling remembers. 'You sat at the end of the table, and they started asking you loads of questions.'

'How are you now?'

'We were crying and stuff like that. We were saying, "Well, all our friends are dead."'

'Yeah, but how are you now? Are you back to work?'

'Well, we had to go back to work because you have to earn a living.'

'And are you alright now?'

'You're just looking at them going, "What the fuck are you talking about?"'

'Okay, right, so that'll be 5,000 for you now. Are you alright with that? That's 5,000. Right, next!'

A payment of £5,000 is equivalent to almost €25,000 today.

'Shut up money' is how it was described by one survivor, as there was a significant caveat attached to accepting it: discontinue any pending legal proceedings and agree not to launch any new proceedings in respect of the injury or loss. You were, of course, free to decline the payment and either bring the case to court or continue an existing case.

'You were told, if you didn't accept this compensation and you go to court, you could lose your home,' Antoinette Keegan said. 'Families lost their loved ones, they lost their children, and this is what they were putting up to us?

'People had no option but to take it. What do you do? You can't do anything. Our hands were tied and the government knew what they were doing.'

Maurice Frazer, who lost his sister Thelma in the fire, said that 'when you look back at it, it was absolutely nothing'. 'You were basically forced. You were put under immense pressure. My dad wanted to go sue, but then again, he could lose it all, and with so many kids at home.'

'[The money] was neither here nor there, at the end of the day,' Lorraine McDonnell said. 'We were supposed to just accept it and walk away. We're just working-class people.'

It was presented to Errol Buckley as a choice: take the money, which would come in handy as a young man, or wait another five years to take a case. That was an option if you could get a decent solicitor and wanted to pursue that path – but it wasn't of any interest to Errol. 'It wasn't about money or anything, at the end of the day,' he said. 'Nothing's going to bring my brother back.'

* * *

The situation became a lot more complicated for families of those who died in the Stardust and who could also apply to the Tribunal. These were the people whose lives were shattered in the hours after the fire, and many were struggling to pick up the pieces. Some 195 people made submissions who were not in attendance at the Stardust.

While other factors were at play here, the majority are believed to be people who had lost children or siblings.

These claims posed a problem for the Tribunal. It was able to award a maximum of £7,500 under legislation from 1961 for 'mental distress', and it did so in the case of each parent whose child died in the Stardust, along with the potential for further payments on a case-by-case basis. But there were also claims of 'nervous shock or mental trauma', something that encapsulated more of the mental anguish that many were experiencing, something beyond distress. It was also beyond what was set out in the relevant law.

The Tribunal found a solution not in the Irish statute books but in English tort law and a well-known case known as McLoughlin vs O'Brian, in which the plaintiff's family were travelling in a car when it was hit by a lorry. She was driven by a neighbour to the hospital where her family were being treated. There, she saw the extent of the injuries suffered by her husband and daughter, then soon learnt that another daughter travelling in the vehicle had died.

She brought a case against the driver and owner of the lorry over the range of psychiatric illnesses caused by the shock she experienced at the hospital. Even if she wasn't there to witness it first-hand, was her case still valid? Was she owed a duty of care?

Several courts said no until she took it to the House of Lords, the highest court of appeal in the United Kingdom at the time. It ruled that yes, the case was valid, but with three limitations: the person must be a close relative, the shock must have been experienced physically close or quickly after the incident, and the person must have learned about the incident or aftermath directly through 'sight or hearing'.

THE LAST DISCO

This judgement was used as the basis to award 68 Tribunal claims, sometimes to the tune of tens of thousands, and refuse 63 (the remainder withdrew their applications).

Christine Keegan's case was approved. John's was refused: the Tribunal didn't believe his experience of the fire, losing two children while another was seriously injured, was worth more than the basic payment of £7,500 for the distress caused by the loss of each child.

John's submission was detailed, with 'very extensive written, medical evidence and the oral evidence of a psychiatrist who had submitted a written report' that detailed the depth of grief he was experiencing. McLoughlin vs O'Brian was called on again, this time the fine print: 'The first hurdle which a plaintiff claiming damages of the kind in question must surmount is to establish that he is suffering, not merely grief, distress or any other normal, emotion, but a positive psychiatric illness.'

The Tribunal faced what was described in its final report as an 'invidious task': deciding where profound grief ends and illness begins. A parent's grief upon hearing about the death of their child could be 'so intense that it passed the border between grief and illness'. The Tribunal highlighted how, although just 48 people died in the fire, 50 deaths were accessed, including two parents who died from the shock, whose dependants' claims were successful. One of these was Bridie Coyne. She was waiting for news of her three children who had been in the Stardust that night. Her two daughters had escaped, but she suffered a heart attack when she learned that her son had been injured.

In the eyes of the Tribunal, what John was experiencing was mere grief and wasn't enough to merit the State offering to make amends beyond a basic payment.

The £7,500 was nothing compared to what could have been awarded in the High Court, but that wasn't the point. It was now beginning to become clear that, in the eyes of some, the Tribunal – and by extension, the State – didn't properly comprehend what they were going through. There were as many as 150 other similar cases where parents were left in a situation where their 'mere grief' was seen as nothing more than just a spell of mourning.

John took his anger to the High Court in April, his failed submission becoming essentially a test case for the dozens of others in the same situation. The *Irish Independent* reported on a sitting in June that heard of the father's struggle with alcoholism, 'sitting out on the edge of his bed at night', and his assault on Eamon Butterly. The Tribunal was ordered to justify its decision to reject the claim.

It rumbled on until the end of July, when the High Court bounced the ball back into the Tribunal's court: it was their jurisdiction, even if they got it wrong.

John and his solicitor kept pushing. Many felt the State had already dragged them through the dirt so many times, and it wasn't going to happen again. They took the case to a higher court.

On 16th December 1986, the appeal was dismissed by the Supreme Court. A key element was judging whether the Tribunal acted 'unfairly or irrationally'. The court didn't believe so, citing that, although his nervous shock application had been turned down, John had been awarded the £15,000, plus an additional £12,300 covering other elements such as loss of earnings. There were also some differences between Christine's successful case and John's rejected one. Both involved oral testimony, which the

Tribunal did not document, so the nuances were unavailable to the court.

That was Tuesday.

The following Monday, John was laid to rest beside his two daughters.

He had been diagnosed with cancer in the summer of that year and by October, was told it was only a matter of time. He passed away on 18th December, two days after the Supreme Court ruling, aged 49.

Chapter 8

YOU CAN WALK TO it from the Stardust in less than half an hour, or it's a five-minute drive.

Head up Kilmore Road to the Northside Shopping Centre, and turn right at Dunnes up Barryscourt Road.

You'll come to a public park with the River Santry cutting through the middle. There's a water feature there called the Fountain of Youth. In the centre is a bronze statue of a young couple embraced in dance. It's so full of energy, as if they'll burst again into dance as soon as you look away. Surrounding the fountain is a circle of 48 pillars.

The long-awaited lasting memorial, Stardust Memorial Park, was opened to the public on 18th September 1993. Families were promised it in 1986, and Haughey turned the sod in 1991, but delays and cash issues led to families threatening to picket the Dáil to demand progress.

'This is sacred ground to us,' Christine Keegan told reporters at its opening.

Christine was never in the background of the Stardust story, but following her husband's death in 1986, she took up the mantle as head of the Stardust Victims' Committee.

You would be forgiven for thinking that the committee considered its work done once the park was open. If you flick through the papers from that decade, you won't see much about the Stardust.

THE LAST DISCO

Articles around the 10th anniversary detail the anger of fire officers and the government opposition benches that the Keane Tribunal's recommendations had not been fully implemented. For example, the 'chaotic' control room at Tara Street Fire Station was still in place a decade on.

By 1999, you still find similar articles. At its annual conference, the Chief Fire Officers Association chairman Michael Fitzsimons said flawed legislation meant they were powerless to implement fire safety notices. This was at the height of the Celtic Tiger, when new buildings were popping up across the country, and he said they were 'toothless pussycats'.

On the 20th anniversary, Fitzsimons spoke to *Irish Times* reporter Kitty Holland and said that the Keane Tribunal's recommendations still had not been fully implemented. There was still no national training centre for firefighters. Fire services were still not under the 'control and direction' of central government. Fitzsimons also said that, while some of the powers that fire authorities held were 'draconian' in that they could lead to almost stronger-than-required prosecution, powers to address issues such as overcrowding or keeping exits clear were still lacking.

The park also comes up again and again: silk floral tributes laid at the memorial park were broken into pieces or thrown into the fountain's water on the 13th anniversary in 1994. By 1997, drug use plagued the park to the extent that some relatives were said to be fearful of visiting the memorial. In 2001, a private developer dumped silt in the park's pond.

Just a few weeks into the new millennium, on 24th January, you might have spotted in the *Evening Herald*

172

death notices that Patrick Butterly had passed away the previous day.

Almost two decades had passed since the fire, with so little progress made in the previous 15 years. It was getting to Christine Keegan.

'I want to get this sorted. I want to find out why my two daughters aren't here – I'll never give up,' she told her daughter Antoinette. The family attributes stress caused by the fight for compensation as a factor in her husband John's death, but that wasn't going to deter Christine.

Antoinette stepped up to help rather than leaving her mother to fight this battle alone, still under the banner of the Stardust Victims' Committee. The intention was to highlight the inadequacy of the Compensational Tribunal and rally calls for a new inquiry.

The mother and daughter had a strong team by their side. Eugene Kelly wasn't giving up fighting for answers about what happened to his brother. Neither was Gertrude Barrett, who still held her son Michael close to her heart to give her the courage to keep going. What happened to William, George and Marcella McDermott was never going to be something their mother Bridget could forget. Tommy Broughan, Labour TD for the area and who had also served as a councillor in Artane and Donaghmede, was on hand to give the political weight they needed.

'If it had happened over on the southside, I maintain it would have been sorted out long ago,' Eugene said. 'But we're only working class. What would we know? As far as I'm concerned, we may be working-class people but we're very strong, and we're going nowhere till we get our justice.'

In 2002, a new name entered the process. Geraldine Foy, described as an independent researcher, came on board to help the families. Critics questioned her lack of qualifications in areas of expertise relevant to the disaster. The Dáil heard that she was 'compensated by the tenacity she demonstrated in going over the documents and transcripts right back to the travesty that was the Keane Report'.

The government met with representatives from the committee. Taoiseach Bertie Ahern made it clear that a new inquiry in itself wasn't the issue, it was the requirement for new evidence that would stand up legally.

The committee submitted a report to the Department of Justice in 2004, but officials disagreed that the evidence presented was sufficient.

'We're not going to give up,' Antoinette said. 'We're going to keep going.'

When 2006 rolled around, the 25th anniversary of the disaster put the story back in the headlines, and this presented an opportunity for the families involved to make their case. They were asked to share their experiences of the past two decades. How raw it still was. How little they still knew. They shared that they had been writing to Bertie Ahern for four years requesting a meeting, receiving the same response every time: 'I'll meet you as soon as I can.' The repeated snubs led to him being asked not to attend the anniversary mass.

They could also share their hurt and anger at RTÉ's plans for a two-part docu-drama about Stardust. The broadcaster kept the production a closely guarded secret, right down to the cast list. Families only found out once filming had wrapped. Listeners flooded the Liveline switchboard about it, with Joe Duffy describing a move by RTÉ – who maintained they approached groups representing the Stardust families – to not discuss it publicly as 'bizarre'. Jimmy Fitzpatrick told the programme that he understood his story appeared in the series but had heard nothing from Montrose.

While the creative arm of RTÉ was causing uproar, the editorial division was building a case for the families. News and current affairs programme *Prime Time* spoke to a world-leading fire expert who called the original investigations into question. Dr Michael Delichatsios said that new evidence about the storeroom gave more credibility to the possibility that the fire started there and wasn't deliberate. Tony Gillick, a former chief fire officer for Dublin Fire Brigade, and Robin Knox, a fire safety consultant, also shared their reservations on the Keane Report.

But at the site of the Stardust, where ownership was split equally between Eamon Butterly and his brother Colm, the 25th anniversary was being marked in a very different way. The Silver Swan had been operating under the name Skelly's, but it was suddenly rebranded under its original name – and rumour spread that the opening night was to be Valentine's Day. Families gathered at the site to protest, but the reopening didn't take place immediately. Amid the pickets, families also objected to an attempt to transfer the licence from Eamon Butterly to businessman Jason Gamble. There were accusations that this was to hide the true ownership of the premises, but Gamble maintained he had no connection to the Butterlys and that the transaction was purely business. It was ultimately successful. The licence was transferred to Gamble, and protests were called off once an agreement was reached to rename the pub Skelly's and erect a memorial.

Meanwhile, the committee kept the pressure on Taoiseach Bertie Ahern. Although a meeting with families wasn't forthcoming, he got one regardless one evening while out in the Beaumont House pub. Gertrude Barrett was also there, fundraising for the Stardust campaign. She approached him.

'Good evening, I am collecting for my son,' she said. 'What is it for – your son?' he replied, unable to see the details on her coin bucket.

'Do you remember the Stardust fire? My son was one of the 48 cremated in that fire.'

Barrett told the *Evening Heard*: 'He walked away from me and stood over by a pillar. When I was walking out, all the people said to me, "He's over there. Did you see him?" I said, "Oh yes. He doesn't want a drink now; he needs one."'

The government maintained it would only entertain the idea of any renewed investigation if families put forward new evidence. It was difficult to get anything concrete. The committee relied on theories, but the experts felt it was enough to merit a fresh look at the Keane Report. Was the Tribunal aware of the amount of flammable material in the storeroom above the dancefloor? Would that have lent more credibility to the possibility that the fire started in the roof space? Were all the maps the Tribunal had to hand accurate?

Foy expanded her dossier into a document titled 'Nothing But the Truth: The Case for a New Inquiry'. Knox, Gillick and Delichatsios were all involved too, along with pathologist Dr Derek Carson.

The files outlined what the Keane Tribunal had potentially overlooked and that the campaigners saw this as warranting a new investigation into the fire. The committee submitted the document to the government that summer – in the first meeting with Ahern, solicitor Greg O'Neill said the Taoiseach and Minister for Justice Michael McDowell were 'taken aback' by what they heard. 'Nothing But the Truth' convinced them to lay the groundwork for a new investigation, essentially a scoping exercise.

It was a slow process, as the families expected at this stage. By April 2007, the government still had not said who would lead the investigation. Families gave the government a 48-hour ultimatum to announce a name, and the following day, barrister John Gallagher emerged to lead the process. He led months of negotiations between the government and the committee to draw up the terms of this new inquiry.

Gallagher wouldn't instigate a new investigation but would pore over the evidence outlined in 'Nothing But the Truth'. Families were relieved by Gallagher's apparent openness to engage with the information. Confidential meetings were held at the start of 2008 to get the ball rolling.

By the end of March, as hearings began in earnest, it had all ground to a shuddering halt. The committee accused the government of not being open about Gallagher's past: he had represented gardaí during the 1982 inquests into the fire. The families, 'angry and disgusted', pulled their support after discovering this.

Throughout this time, work had been ongoing to finally put a name to each of the five victims whose remains couldn't be identified after the fire – Eamon Loughman, Paul Wade, Michael Ffrench, Richard Bennett and Murty Kavanagh. Work began on exhuming their remains on 30th January 2007, following a request from families the previous summer. Following sustained pressure, the government agreed to pay for the costs involved, including reburial.

'We could finally go to visit Michael,' his father said. 'The grave would be ours to do what we want with. It would be a big relief. It has been difficult not knowing for 26 years where your son is buried. I know it sounds ridiculous, but because we're not 100% sure I often wonder if he lost his memory and might walk in tomorrow.'

DNA samples were sent to the United Kingdom for testing, and it wasn't long before the results came back in April: all five had been conclusively identified.

The families laid the five people to rest that summer in low-key ceremonies. Murty's brother told the *Irish Examiner* that it brought a sense of closure, 'but we don't feel that justice has been served'.

However, the scoping exercise still hung in the balance, even if the government was eager to see it continue. The *Irish Independent* reported that one of Ahern's last acts as Taoiseach, before resigning in June in the wake of the Mahon Tribunal, was to write to the families, saying efforts would be made to appoint a new chair of the process.

Eventually, Paul Coffey, also a senior counsel, emerged to take over, but it took a Leinster House sit-in protest by Antoinette Keegan and Gertrude Barrett to force the government to announce the name on 10th July.

In September, the inquiry heard oral evidence over three days. Coffey used this unsworn testimony and the submitted materials to form his report. The senior counsel didn't view it as the open-and-shut case the committee took it to be, but it did give cause to the belief that the fire may have originated in the roof space.

It pointed to the fact that eyewitnesses recalled that, as the ceiling collapsed, there was a gush of black smoke.

And what about the two bouncers who felt 'unbearable heat' coming from above them while fighting the flames during the early stages? And the fact that one expert from the Fire Research Station said this would be possible from gases accumulating, but that it would need to be from a blaze of 'a significant size'?

There was 'the Blair photograph', taken by a local resident, which appeared to show flames high above the roof at 1.35am, barely minutes after it was first observed inside the club. However, the reports of other locals seeing it earlier again were dismissed.

There was also new evidence presented on the roof collapse. Tony Gillick, a fire expert, pointed out that the length of time it would take to melt the steel supports in the ceiling was far longer than the length of time the fire was observed. The senior counsel deemed this 'new' evidence, as Gillick was the first expert to say that the ceiling collapse couldn't be accounted for by the fire in the West Alcove.

But other matters didn't convince him. A suggestion that the fire started in the lamp room amounted to no more than a theory, he said. 'Even if I am incorrect in this, the evidence given to the Tribunal would suggest that the hypothesis, if not incredible, is at least implausible.'

A former waitress said large quantities of oil were kept in the store room. Coffey deemed her credible but said it only demonstrated that there was combustible material in the roofspace, as the Tribunal had already found, albeit of a greater volume.

A contractor who installed fire protection around columns in the ballroom noticed that an insulation known as Polyzote – a type of polystyrene with a very low flashpoint – had been used and suggested that this could have been the particles dripping from the ceiling. But a shirt belonging to a bouncer onto which these particles dripped was 'no longer available', and that was as far as his evidence went.

The final report was published at the end of January, but not before committee members held yet another protest at the seat of government, this time waiting outside the Department of the Taoiseach for three days, demanding access to it.

There was cause for celebration and cause for continued frustration.

Based on the evidence presented to him, Coffey felt that the verdict of the Keane Tribunal should be struck from the public record.

'I am satisfied that the Committee has established a *prima facie* case that the Tribunal's conclusion as to the cause of the fire cannot be demonstrated to be objectively justifiable,' he said.

'In so concluding and in the absence of any evidence that the fire was started deliberately, the Tribunal has placed on the public record a finding of probable criminal wrongdoing which is *prima facie* speculative and fraught with evidential and logical difficulties,' the report reads. 'This is profoundly unsatisfactory to the survivors and the bereaved who, through their Committee argue that such was the scale of the disaster that it has become a matter of communal if not national history to an extent that engages a public interest in ensuring that the public record of what happened is factually accurate and established by evidence.'

This was monumental progress. The decades of finger-pointing were finally over. The State had erred in its conclusion on the fire, and would set the record straight.

Photographer Julien Behal captured the emotional scenes in the courtyard of Government Buildings. Committee members embracing, crying tears of joy. An image of Bridget McDermott, who lost three children in the fire, weeping into her hands, appeared on newsstands the next day. Beside her, Eugene Kelly kicking his leg in the air in celebration.

'We were right,' Bridget told the *Irish Times*. 'We knew from the very beginning but it will never bring back any of the 48 children and not mine, William, Marcella and George, whom I still miss very much. But at least I can say to them now they will get justice.'

On 3rd February 2009, Minister for Justice Dermot Ahern addressed the Dáil: 'The Government wishes to acknowledge that, as a matter of fact, the actual cause of the catastrophic fire at the Stardust on 14th February 1981 is unknown,' he told the chamber. 'None of the victims of the Stardust disaster or the persons present at the Stardust on the night of the fire can be held responsible for the fire. We simply cannot say how the fire was caused and nobody present on the night can be held responsible for its cause.'

This didn't mean it needed to be investigated further. The new evidence fell short of Coffey's threshold for establishing the cause of the fire; it, at most, echoed the Tribunal's finding that the cause of the fire is unknown.

The families wanted this properly investigated, that this new evidence and hypotheses would be interrogated and used as part of a new inquiry to determine what caused the fire once and for all. To just bring it all to an end, to give closure and to give the truth.

'It seems to me that at a remove of nearly three decades from the date of the fire and in the absence of any identified evidence which can establish the cause of the fire wheresoever it arose, the public interest would not be served in establishing a further inquiry solely for that purpose,' Ahern said.

Antoinette Keegan was initially buoyed by the probable arson verdict being struck out.

'We thought this is great, this is fantastic. But nothing happened. I rang [the Department of the Taoiseach] and asked if they would press the owners for the compensation awarded. "Oh God, no," they said. So, literally, what was the point?'

As John Keegan threatened in 1985, they took the case to Europe. Five parents who had lost children – Bridget McDermott, Elizabeth Bissett, Edward and Patricia Kennedy, and Christine Keegan – argued in two submissions to the European Court of Human Rights that, due to 'deficiencies in the investigation into the deaths of their children', 'those responsible had not therefore been punished'.

Ultimately, the court decided in 2012 that its six-month rule to bring a case applied not to Coffey's report but – at the very latest – to the 1991 Compensation Tribunal. There was also nothing in their submission to suggest the possibility of criminal prosecution. Their submission was declared inadmissible.

* * *

The early and mid-2010s were marked by false start after false start for the Stardust campaigners.

There was an investigation by gardaí into alleged perjury at the 1981 Tribunal – but the Director of Public Prosecutions ultimately decided there wasn't a case to be answered.

The financial crash wasn't kind to the Butterly family. AIB appointed receivers and sold off the former home of the Stardust, now called Butterly Business Park, to be redeveloped.

An earlier draft of the Coffey Report emerged, which solicitors for the committee claimed contained changes that would have favoured a new inquiry. There was seemingly no record of why the changes were made. The Department of Justice denied any attempt to influence the report's outcome and that Coffey had requested to make amendments for clarity.

Swans at the Stardust Memorial Park were taken into the care of wildlife experts after a diesel spill in 2013.

The Stardust committee kept focusing on the same elements. The original investigation was flawed. The fire started in the roof space. New elements, too, began to emerge. An alleged unrecorded 999 call about a fire on the roof came in at the same time the fire was seen on the seats inside the club, and there was a possible flaw in the plans of the complex that gardaí relied on.

There were protests here and there to try to spark some action. Another sit-in, this time in Government Buildings with Antoinette Keegan and Eugene Kelly, demanding to see Taoiseach Enda Kenny.

Minister for Justice Alan Shatter said no new inquiry was warranted. His successor, Frances Fitzgerald, was willing at least to review any new evidence.

The persistent pressure eventually led to another review of the evidence, primarily due to a bill tabled by

THE LAST DISCO

Independent TD Tommy Broughan, and pressure brought at cabinet level by Independents 4 Change super junior minister Finian McGrath.

Retired judge Pat McCartan was appointed then, reportedly, almost stepped down because the committee was withholding the report until the government agreed to cover research fees.

McCartan looked at the evidence – and eviscerated it.

'The dossier was rambling, argumentative, disorganised and at times incoherent,' McCartan said. 'It was only at the end, on page 358, that there was any statement of what the new evidence was. Even there it is very difficult to understand what items of evidence this Assessment was being asked to examine.'

Foy, in particular, came in for particular criticism:

'She described herself in the dossier as a horticulturalist. She advised the Assessment that she received a diploma qualification in horticulture from an institute in Termonfeckin, Co. Louth. She acknowledges in the dossier that she is not a fire expert. She does not have any medical, engineering or other scientific qualification that would make her an expert and allow her to give a professional view on matters relevant to the cause, spread or impact of the Stardust fire.

'While such qualifications are not necessary to uncover new evidence, they are vital if someone is purporting to give an opinion on the cause of a fire, the spread of a fire or the cause of death of an individual as a result of fire.'

McCartan also included a quote from Foy on how she became involved in the committee: 'The families I met for the very first time on the 21/2/2002. I became aware of

184

their situation just by chance. I had no insight or interest in the case. But on a Thursday prior to that date I was in the dentist's surgery and he had a copy of the Northside people [*sic*] paper. I started to read it as I waited to be seen and came across a picture of a lady in a red jacket planting a tree. As a horticulturalist I was engrossed in the article and read that the tree was being planted and the women in the picture prays [*sic*] for someone to help them make sense of the Keane tribunal report. That evening I was visiting friends and asked them about the Stardust case. I discussed the article. They handed me a small make up mirror and told me the person in the mirror would be the best in the world to help the families. Two days after I rang the paper to pass my phone number onto the families.'

Opposition politicians later defended Foy's work, with Richard Boyd Barrett telling the Dáil: 'If Geraldine Foy is not an expert, then neither are [McCartan and Coffey].'

McCartan found nothing in it he considered warranting a new inquiry. The Minister for Justice was now Charlie Flanagan, who relayed this finding to the Dáil.

'The government has fulfilled its commitment in relation to assessing the new evidence,' he said, and, to the families, that 'I understand that each of you will never forget this terrible tragedy and will carry heart-breaking loss and memories with you for the rest of your lives.'

'He doesn't know what pain is,' Eugene Kelly said. 'He said he understands what we're going through. He doesn't. He doesn't understand the pain we're going through. He's got to be there. He's got to be living it every day. I wake up in the morning and the first thing I think of is Robert. I'm working on jobs and I'm thinking of Robert. I'm going to bed and I'm thinking of Robert. That won't go away until I get justice for him.

'Why should we give up now? We're not going anywhere.'

Chapter 9

THE STARDUST FAMILIES NEEDED to change tack.

Decades had now passed and they were no closer to moving forward. They had hassled and harried politicians. Petitioned them. Implored them. They'd marched. They'd protested. They'd theorised. They'd put forward their case. They'd been made promises. And each time, the answer was the same: No new evidence, too much time has passed, not worth looking at again.

The media continued to cover it, but it was the same story being told again and again and it often failed to capture the imagination as time passed. Repeating the same story doesn't sell papers.

After facing this so many times, the question could be asked: why did they keep going? It would be easy enough to make an argument of 'it's been nearly 40 years, is it not time to move on?' or words to that effect.

Speaking to the families before the new inquests were granted, it was clear why many of them could not readily accept this position.

Eugene Kelly certainly couldn't let it go. He kept his brother Robert's jacket, embroidered with all manner of designs, in the wardrobe for decades. He needed to know what happened to him.

'I think what's actually happened at the moment is it's dragging out and out,' he said in May 2019. 'We never got justice to move on. You can't get counselling until you get closure. You can't move on until you get closure.'

'We were the underdogs because we lived on the northside,' Maurice McHugh said.

His wife Phyllis agreed: 'I said it probably would be different if it was the other side of the Liffey.'

She cited the example of the horrific 2015 Berkeley balcony collapse in California, in which six young Irish students died. Several lawsuits followed against the firm that managed the building, and these were successfully fought and settled in the years following the tragedy.

'The parents of those kids sued them. It's not about money. We don't need money, but we do need closure. And I have to say to you, we do need closure.'

'Before we kick the bucket ourselves,' Maurice said. 'It'd be nice to have the closure.'

'You go up to [the graveyard in] Sutton there and you see the kids' names, and then you see the mammy and daddy's name in the same grave as them,' Phyllis added.

Lorraine McDonnell described the Stardust fire as bringing an 'earthquake' into the home, and said it had remained there for decades.

'That hasn't gone away yet,' she said. 'I don't know if we can ever get closure, but I'd like to have closure.'

Antoinette Keegan was never going to give up. She was relentless in her efforts to get the justice the families felt was denied for so many years.

'I won't stop for the simple reason that I know what happened that night,' she said. 'I know what the truth is. I'm not going to give up because my poor father died.

And my two sisters both died. They deserve justice and 46 others deserve justice. It's going to happen. It's going to happen.'

Selina McDermott said that the families and friends of The 48 who died owed it to their loved ones to keep going.

'You feel disheartened, you feel tired,' she said. 'You know sometimes I feel between work and trying to live a normal life and then family . . . juggling the whole lot can be tiring.

'But then again, you have to keep thinking. We're the only ones that they have left to get themselves justice.

'Why can't they just open a new inquiry? Give us what we want, give the people justice and, you know, then let it rest. Let it lie. Let these families get on with their lives.'

Even at that point, others not active in the campaigning may have felt that no new investigations into the fire would happen at such a late stage. Or may have accepted it. But when the chance came again, at last, it had to be seized.

With the involvement of Belfast-based legal firm Phoenix Law and Sinn Féin MEP, and later senator, Lynn Boylan came a complete change of tack.

Phoenix Law was formed in 2018 by a group of lawyers who, they say, 'have a shared determination to improve human rights and accountability on the island of Ireland and beyond'. It's been involved in high-profile cases in the North, including the Ballymurphy inquest and the Glenanne Gang inquest, alongside other legacy events. They were also involved in a court bid claiming their clients had been unlawfully discriminated against in the infamous 'gay cake' row in Northern Ireland.

Whereas the call had always been for new inquiries into what happened at the Stardust, it was Phoenix Law's Darragh Mackin who spearheaded a new campaign. It was a brave approach that hadn't been tried before: request that new inquests be held into all 48 deaths at the Stardust.

An inquest is a detailed examination of the circumstances surrounding a person's death. They are held in cases of a sudden, unexplained or violent death, usually within a year or two. They are presided over by the local coroner, who can decide whether or not to have a jury. Most cases don't. Most inquests are generally small, usually dealing with one death, occasionally with two or more. It would be extremely unusual to hold inquests on such a scale as for those who died in the Stardust – but this was the route chosen.

The legal team believed that any fresh inquests into the deaths at the Stardust would have to look into what had caused the fire and the situation on the ground in the club that night, rather than the cursory inquests which had taken place afterwards, which had merely given the medical cause of death.

Boylan was one of the many politicians contacted by the families over the years, and was one of the few who delivered real progress. She became heavily involved in the case and helped to guide them along a new path with Phoenix Law. She explained: 'This is a working-class community that were tired of the label of arsonists, and they never got justice.

'One of the things you find with Ireland is that we have a very poor system in terms of access to justice. That is something that was acknowledged by the Council of Europe when I brought the families to Strasbourg. The fact that the families have to go away and find all this extra evidence themselves. They don't have any financial recourse to do that.

'So these are just ordinary families who've been thrown together by this horrific tragedy. That all accumulates to how do you run a proper campaign? What is the best legal avenue for you to pursue? I think that's where Darragh Mackin was such a sea change. It was his idea that you don't call for new inquiries because inquiries are always constrained by the terms of reference.'

Instead of an inquiry – and even going back to 1981, the terms of reference for the Keane Tribunal were scrutinised as not going far enough – it was an inquest they would seek instead.

'And that's worked for Hillsborough as well,' Boylan said. 'It's you get an inquest, you establish the facts, and from that evidence it sort of leaves the door open for an inquiry with the proper terms of reference.

'It's a way of wedging the door open for justice.'

In a bid to demonstrate the level of public support for these inquests, the families started a postcard campaign. Stalls were put up around the country at public locations and people were asked to sign their postcards urging the holding of the inquests.

'We had the public support,' Antoinette Keegan said. 'We travelled the north, south, east and west of Ireland and got 48,000 signatures through the campaign.'

'It's about how you galvanise the public,' Boylan said. 'The public want to help. There's a huge amount of people out there who know about the Stardust and they want to help. It was about making a simple way for people to show their support.

'That was something tangible they felt they could do. When we started those stalls, one man drove from Kildare to Ballyfermot because he'd heard on the radio that morning that we were going to be there.'

In November 2018, they dropped 48,000 postcards – itself a number of great significance given the 48 who had died – into the office of the Attorney General, imploring him to hold fresh inquests. It was an emotional day for the families. A real milestone in their long fight.

They were accompanied to the office of the government's legal advisor by Christy Moore, playing the song he wrote about the tragedy as they walked.

'The argument for doing it in the public interest is overwhelming,' Darragh Mackin said. 'The postcard campaign demonstrates that, but the argument on its own is very, very strong.'

In his submission to the Attorney General, he cited the Hillsborough inquests, which found in 2016 that the 96 Liverpool fans who died at the stadium in 1989 were unlawfully killed.

Phoenix Law argued this demonstrated how fresh inquests can shed light on events that took place many years ago, even where detailed investigations had already taken place.

'The original inquests only recorded the medical cause of death and offered "uninformative" conclusions,' the law firm wrote. 'In a disaster of this magnitude, a more informative conclusion was required in order to meet the public interest.'

Furthermore, the central conclusion of the original inquiry into the fire from the Keane Tribunal – that the probable cause of the fire was arson – was quashed in 2009 by the government.

Phoenix Law's submission also hinted at fresh evidence from eyewitnesses and assessments by fire experts which could shed light on issues not dealt with at previous inquiries.

As with every time the Stardust families had set their stall out to the State, they were forced to wait. And wait a long time. An excruciating wait through the spring and summer. By June 2019, Antoinette Keegan was adamant that it was going to happen. She had to believe it. She couldn't believe anything else.

'I'm confident because if it doesn't happen in this county or in this constituency or the Republic, we'll take it to another source and we'll get it one way or the other,' she said. 'Because with all the evidence that we have given to the Attorney General, the Attorney General has to apply the law. He has to apply it and we have to get our loved ones vindicated and validated. That right to life has to be applied.

'We all are determined. We're going to do it. We're not going to stop and we will get justice. It's going to happen. It is going to happen.'

It was ticking on towards a year since the postcards were delivered to Attorney General Séamus Woulfe before he finally had an answer for them.

And it was the answer they'd yearned for.

In a statement on the evening of 25th September 2019, the Office of the Attorney General said he had 'formed the opinion that fresh inquests into the Stardust deaths are advisable'.

'This is because he considered that in the original inquests there was an insufficiency of inquiry as to how the deaths occurred, namely, a failure to sufficiently consider those of the surrounding circumstances that concern the cause of the fire.

'The Attorney General is thus satisfied that the holding of fresh inquests is, on balance, in the public interest and in the interests of justice.'

At an emotional press conference the following day, there was relief, hope and tears at the news.

Darragh Mackin said: 'Over the years, the families have been, unfortunately, spectators in their fight for justice. But today, they enter the ring in their own fight.'

Photographers captured the poignant moment of Bridget McDermott, now in her eighties, wiping away the tears at the news, the deaths of her three children never forgotten.

At last – at long last – the Irish State had agreed to take a look at this again. A proper look. Entering 2020, the families could be forgiven for thinking that a chance at closure was in sight at long last.

That feeling was palpable at the vigil in February 2020 to mark the 39th anniversary of the fire in Artane.

Former RTÉ journalist Charlie Bird, one of the first journalists on the scene that night, spoke with his usual force and resonance to the crowd. Despite having covered so much in his career, the Stardust and the families stuck with him, and he stuck with them.

'I went to many places,' he said. 'I covered tsunamis, earthquakes, and the one thing I learned that you learn as a journalist, sometimes numbers trip off your tongue. "Last night, five people were killed in a car crash", "20 people", "one hundred people were killed in an earthquake, in a plane crash".

'But remember, every one of those names, every one of those people has a name. They are real people. They have family, they have friends. And that ripple effect spreads out.'

Veteran journalist Eamon Dunphy spoke, becoming visibly choked up at points. 'We'll do everything we can to keep your case on the agenda,' he said. 'You've not had your justice. And I know that. And they know that . . . So thank you very much. You've shown great dignity. It's very moving, as you can see.'

Antoinette, there with her mother Christine, told the crowd: 'The public spoke, and the Attorney General listened.'

But it's never that easy. It never had been with the Stardust. After the new inquests were granted in September 2019, it would be three and a half years before they actually got under way.

A major and unavoidable disruptor was the pandemic. With life turned upside down almost overnight in March 2020, things were never going to run smoothly.

It would be over a year after the inquests were first ordered that the court would sit for the first time.

Sadly, Christine Keegan wouldn't be there to see it. She died peacefully on 14th July 2020. A woman who lost two children to a terrible tragedy and never gave up the fight, she was among the few who'd become synonymous with the Stardust and the campaigning thereafter. Hailing her as a 'hero' and a 'tireless' fighter, her notice on RIP.ie acknowledged them. 'She is predeceased by her loving daughters Mary and Martina who died in the Stardust disaster,' it said.

* * *

The location of the Dublin District Coroner's Court could hardly be lost on the families. Ostensibly, it's in a very accessible spot in Dublin's city centre.

Coming from Artane, the bus could have you there in half an hour. It's around the corner from Dublin's Connolly train station and opposite Busáras.

But it's on Store Street. Where they had come all those years ago to identify their loved ones. The exact same site.

Stepping inside it at the very first pre-inquest hearing on Wednesday, 16th October 2020, it was clear it wouldn't be suitable for an inquest of this size.

The legal teams and journalists managed to squeeze in, but that was about it. It was also still early in Ireland's Covid journey, with no indication yet of when life might return to normal, and so social distancing was enforced.

The families arrived outside but were turned away. They had to go home or elsewhere to watch it online.

Inside the courtroom, Coroner Dr Myra Cullinane set out her stall. She would not be bound by any previous inquiries into the disaster.

'I hope we can go forward in a positive manner and not look back at what has gone before,' she said.

She also signalled that pen portraits – where people could get up and be given the time and space to talk about their loved ones – would form a key part of the inquests, giving the families of each of the victims a 'meaningful engagement' in proceedings.

'I will provide time for each family to describe their loved one who died . . . [to] bring human detail to those lives lost,' she said.

Darragh Mackin didn't feel like mincing his words. He told the court that these fresh inquests would draw a 'line in the sand' on previous inquiries and said it would be argued that there was a 'state-sponsored effort to cover up' what happened in the Stardust.

The mood of the families that day was hopeful. A year after the inquests were set up, this was a step in the right direction.

All the logistics and planning required meant that they would have to wait longer for this 'meaningful engagement' than they had anticipated. How the inquests would work and where they would be held needed to be ironed out. The second pre-inquest hearing took place just a month later, giving a sense of momentum to proceedings.

The importance of speed and efficiency with these inquests was reinforced even further with a fresh tragedy.

Eugene Kelly's drive to get justice for his brother Robert was still clear to anyone who spoke to him at the pre-inquest hearing – undimmed despite the passing of the years. Finally, it was starting to seem like that might happen.

But Eugene would never see the inquests. He died suddenly, a week after the first pre-hearing.

Eugene had been a core part of the Stardust campaign. In a tribute to him, Antoinette Keegan said he'd 'fought side by side' with them through the years.

'Eugene Kelly, you came into my family's life,' she said. 'You stood tall and stood by our ma. Never once did you ever let her down. It's just so sad today. I swear to my God in heaven, you will never be forgotten and we will get truth and justice.'

Eugene's untimely death, aged just 62, along with the death of Christine Keegan a few months earlier, reinforced the crucial need for progress.

The location remained a stumbling block. At the second pre-inquest hearing, Dr Cullinane said she'd been advised by the Department of Justice that holding the inquests in Dublin Castle as planned was 'no longer possible'.

An alternative was found in the RDS. Deep in Dublin's southside, it was a considerable distance from where many of the families were still based, but it would have ample space to fit in the many attendees expected. The coroner had more to say on how the inquests would run.

Dr Cullinane said that the inquests 'will enquire into the broader circumstances surrounding the deaths' and that she would give 'consideration to wider issues beyond the pathological cause of death'.

'The scope will extend to ascertaining the cause of the fire, if possible,' the coroner said, adding that the court may consider factors such as the condition of the premises before the fire and forensic analysis of the scene following the events.

This was crucial clarity. 'Ascertaining the cause of the fire, if possible' would go right to the heart of what the families had called for in seeking the new inquests.

At this point, the idea that it would take two and a half years for the inquests to actually get under way would have appeared pessimistic at best. But it did take that long.

Question marks also hung over how all this would be paid for. The Department of Justice had set aside €8 million from Budget 2021 to cover costs related to the inquests. Despite other Tribunals and inquiries run by the State seeing their costs stretch into the tens of millions, this was still not an insignificant sum.

One of the delays to the inquests was caused by an issue around access to legal aid, an essential element for the families to pay their legal teams. Because this was an inquest on a scale not before seen in this country, the normal rules couldn't apply. Phoenix Law submitted proposals to the Department of Justice to ensure the cost could be minimised as much as possible. In early 2021, it appeared as if it was resolved, but Darragh Mackin returned to court saying they had essentially been 'in a game of snakes and ladders' for six months.

Having set aside the money for it and arranged a venue, it appeared the Department of Justice was similarly baffled by the delays. Perhaps it was due to the unprecedented nature of inquests of this scale. In any event, it said then that it had asked the Attorney General to arrange for 'urgent' drafting of measures to fix the issue.

While this was going on, the coroner and her team had been busy.

Dr Cullinane told a hearing in March that her team had lined up experts in fire investigation, forensic pathology and forensic toxicology. Always keen to reference the families throughout, she acknowledged the impact of the delay on proceedings. She said the deaths of a number of members of the bereaved families had occurred and extended the condolences of the court to those families.

It dragged on, and on, and on, right into 2022, and reached the stage where the initial contract with the RDS expired, despite the venue not being used by the inquests, bar a handful of pre-hearings.

At one such hearing before the RDS lease expired, the vastly experienced senior counsel Michael O'Higgins set out the stall for the families on what the inquest should achieve.

'There have been a number of previous inquiries. Most, if not all, appear to have deficits some have retrospectively found to be substantially flawed,' he said.

'Other inquiries have been unsatisfactory. There is a heavy onus on everyone participating in this process to do everything within our grasp to get this as right as is humanly possible.'

O'Higgins stressed it was about the families and was an opportunity for them to 'try to find out the answers to questions which remain unanswered for many years'.

But delay would be heaped on delay, compounded in 2022 with a High Court case taken by Eamon Butterly that put the start date back significantly. It could also have seen the inquests radically changed in terms of their scope and what they could achieve.

Butterly and his legal team had clearly taken exception to the language used by Phoenix Law and the likes of O'Higgins at the pre-inquest hearings.

Particularly, they felt that the coroner had to provide clarity on what verdicts would be open to the jury at the inquests.

A jury can return multiple verdicts at inquests. This can range from accidental death or death by misadventure, to an open verdict or a verdict of unlawful killing.

At a hearing early in 2022, representatives for Butterly took aim at the potential for an unlawful killing verdict and what impact that could have on him, in particular.

The families' barrister, Seán Guerin SC, said there was no suggestion that a person should bear civil or criminal liability in these proceedings.

Guerin said the 'greatest misunderstanding' was one of 'perspective'.

'These inquests are not about Mr Butterly,' he said. 'The verdicts won't be either. The inquests are about the victims and how they died.'

On 16th February, Dr Cullinane rejected the bid for 'unlawful killing' to be excluded as a possible verdict at the inquests. 'To rule out any verdict prior to the hearing of any evidence would be manifestly to invert the prescribed process,' she said. 'It is not appropriate for a coroner to rule out any verdict, on the grounds that it is not possible to know definitively what evidence may be called or what findings may be made on foot of that evidence.'

Having failed in this bid to the coroner, Butterly's solicitors then filed papers to the High Court. These proceedings were also aimed at preventing the new inquests from 'making him a target' for an unlawful killing verdict.

The legal team for the families again came to the fore to fight their corner in the High Court.

When Mr Justice Charles Meenan granted Butterly permission to bring the court bid, Seán Guerin told the court that the decision to launch such proceedings at 'a very late stage' just weeks before the new inquests were likely to start, was also 'bordering on the unthinkable'.

Butterly's lawyers said the 'proposed targets of the claim of unlawful killing' put forward by lawyers for families of the deceased consisted of four named individuals and a company of which Eamon Butterly was the 'only living natural person' left.

It meant he would be 'clearly named for the killing by implication if he and other persons in this group were to be found guilty of unlawful killing in the course of these inquests', his lawyers argued.

The substantive hearing in the judicial review didn't take place until July 2022.

At this point, barristers for the coroner told the High Court that she never suggested a verdict of unlawful killing could or should be returned.

The coroner's job is to investigate the facts of the deaths, 'and that is all she is doing,' Simon Mills SC said.

It wasn't until November that the High Court ruled on the judicial review, and the result was that Eamon Butterly had failed in his court challenge to the new inquests.

Judge Meenan said he was satisfied that the coroner's ruling the previous February was correct in law, that a verdict of unlawful killing could not be ruled out at that stage. There was wiggle room in his ruling that left the door open to be challenged. But that could be worried about later. There was lost time to make up for.

*　*　*

Nearly a year was spent bringing us back to square one: the inquests could proceed, and it was up to the coroner to direct a jury on what options would be available to them.

In the meantime, the Department of Justice passed new legislation to allow for the jury to be properly paid for their time. Given that the inquests would surely take many months, the same provisions would have to be made for the jury, as would be the case in a criminal trial. This had never been done before. Juries are not often called to serve on inquests and are usually randomly selected by the gardaí, a situation referred to by Darragh Mackin as 'bananas'.

It was only in 2023 that the final hurdles were cleared, a long time away from the inquests first being ordered in 2019.

On the 42nd anniversary of the fire, a vigil was again held where the Stardust was located in Artane, with a renewed sense of hope amidst the ongoing frustration.

Charlie Bird had become a fixture at these events for his support of the families, and he spoke again at this event. This time, he used speech-generation software, as he had been diagnosed with motor neurone disease in 2021.

'Everyone in this country should hang their heads in shame that after over 40 years we still have not found the truth of what happened on that night,' he said. 'Hopefully you will finally get the answers when the inquest into the deaths gets under way this coming April.'

A few days beforehand, the final venue for the inquests proper was selected: the Pillar Room of Dublin's Rotunda Hospital. This is a prime city-centre location without the baggage of Store Street and closer to the families on the northside than the RDS.

The Pillar Room was of adequate size and suitable heritage. It was here that Irish revolutionary Constance Markievicz lay in state after her death in 1927. Although she was denied a State funeral, thousands passed through the Pillar Room to pay their respects before her burial in Glasnevin Cemetery.

* * *

The Stardust families have often felt like they were bashing their heads against the walls erected by the State, and by whatever other circumstances, trying to get to the answers they were seeking.

THE LAST DISCO

After everything that came before, as they took their seats along with their legal team in the Pillar Room, there was the sense that the odds were very much even this time around. Especially given the calibre of the legal team on their side.

Parties at an inquest are entitled to legal representation, and the team representing the families was a stellar one.

Anyone who is a regular watcher or reader of Irish news may recognise the name Michael O'Higgins, who had spoken for the families at the pre-inquests. His name has appeared in news reports again and again over the years in the highest profile of cases. His oration and questions posed to witnesses often come in a booming, eloquent manner. He frequently lays out scenarios to witnesses and closes with an 'if you follow me'. The tone of his voice rises when he's pushing someone on a particularly important point.

Like O'Higgins, Belfast-based Des Fahy KC was a journalist turned barrister who would adopt a 'dog with a bone' style of questioning, pulling at the threads of witness testimony with the persistence and discernment of the very best.

The name Seán Guerin SC will be equally familiar to those who follow the news from Irish courts from numerous high-profile cases over the years. He's quietly forceful, and meticulous and perceptive to a fault. He was the prosecuting counsel in perhaps the most infamous criminal trial in Irish history: the murder of Elaine O'Hara by sadistic killer Graham Dwyer.

Brenda Campbell KC had over 20 years of experience, specialising in historic inquests and police shootings. Clear-eyed and sharp throughout, at the same time as the Stardust inquests were getting under way, she was also representing the Northern Ireland Covid-19 Bereaved Families for Justice at the UK's Covid Inquiry.

Bernard Condon SC has been around the block too. He had sat on the defence teams in landmark trials such as the 'Mr Moonlight' murder and the Regency Hotel gangland killings. In a talk to students studying for the bar in 2021, he laid out his ABCs of advocacy in court – 'accuracy, brevity and clarity'. He would bring plenty of that to proceedings, particularly the B element.

Alongside them were a team of solicitors and other barristers, who would require a whole set of rows to themselves in the Pillar Rooms when proceedings properly got under way.

All 'interested parties' could and would be represented at the inquests. As well as the families and Butterly, there was separate legal counsel for An Garda Síochána, Dublin City Council – formerly Dublin Corporation, under whose remit Dublin Fire Brigade fell under – and a team for the coroner herself to advise on proceedings as they happened.

Nearly a dozen tables were set up for the army of barristers and solicitors who would be taking part in these inquests. They would vacate them on the very first day, however, to let the families take centre stage.

When the inquests sat then on 25th April 2023, families gathered first in the Garden of Remembrance just a short distance away before filing into the Pillar Room to take their seats in front of the coroner and the jury for the first time. With the call of 'all rise' from the registrar, Dr Myra Cullinane came into the room, followed by the jury, to begin her opening address.

The time had finally come. The beginning of the end of this longest of roads that first began off the Malahide

Road onto the Kilmore Road and into that place over 42 years prior.

And this road would be walked down with the families at its centre. Given the chance to finally reclaim their loved ones from the darkness that had taken them so long ago.

Chapter 10

GERTRUDE BARRETT SAT IN the public gallery throughout the inquests. She was there every day, frequently taking notes during the witness evidence. She had the arguably unenviable task of being the first family member to step up and address the Stardust inquests on its first day on 25th April 2023. She stood up before the jury, before the coroner, before the legal teams and before the families and friends of the other victims, and talked about her son Michael. She did it with dignity, with gravitas and with an emotion that still sounded so raw so many years on.

'Good morning all, and welcome,' she began. 'My name is Gertrude Barrett, the mother of the late Michael Barrett.'

Her 17-year-old boy was an apprentice plumber and the eldest of four, as well as a complete music fanatic, she told the court. He loved the Dublin GAA team and Liverpool FC. He was helping out as an assistant DJ at the Valentine's disco, and was the only person who was working on the night who died. Before turning to that night, she painted a vivid picture of the kind of person he was, and the kind of man he could have become.

'He was a great son, a kind son; we had a very close mother-son relationship,' she said. 'Michael had wisdom beyond his years. If he said everything would be alright, then the chances are that it would be alright. For him, nothing was ever too much and nowhere was ever too far. He was keen to make life and the future easier, better and brighter for himself and his family. He had an aura and a presence that brought belief, calm and confidence.

'For such a short life, Michael left an impression on people he met, be it for a minute, a day or a week. We have come to know this down through the years, from the many stories people have shared with us about the times they met Michael. Michael was always smiling and had an infectious laugh; another thing people would say about him is "I still remember his smile and his laugh". Michael was quite popular and well-liked. He knew lots of people, and lots of people knew him. However, he was most comfortable with and among his small, tight-knit, close circle of friends. He was a very loyal friend too.'

Gertrude said that Michael had very clear hopes and dreams for the future, and was optimistic for the future he could create. He was going 'to make it', she said.

But then everything changed. 'Up to and including the 13th of February, we were a happy family unit, with four children, doing regular things, living a regular life, doing what you do with a family of four aged 17 years and under,' she said. 'Life was good, and all was well. But little did I know that Friday the 13th of February 1981 would be the last day of life as we knew it and that the following day our lives would change catastrophically forever.'

On the morning of the 14th, they 'woke up to trauma and were catapulted into unimaginable grief and sorrow'. When she went to Coolock Garda Station, she was told to go down the Malahide Road and get the bus into Store

Street. To the morgue. One of the first families to arrive, the Barretts would witness the staggered arrival of other parents looking for their children.

'As the morning and the day went on, the scale of the fire was becoming obvious, from the sheer volume of grief, the tears, the crying, the unknown, the confusion, the mayhem, the chaos, just everything with it. It was horrendous, utter horror, a living nightmare. The experience will stay with me for life and my daughter too, who was with me. No one explained to us what we were about to face. From the enormity of the situation, the ferocity of the fire, the number of deaths, identification of bodies, outcomes or what to expect. No one to help you comprehend, understand or grasp what lay ahead.'

Gertrude described the 'roll call' where gardaí would call out a list of names. She didn't know if it was a good or bad thing that Michael's name wasn't called out. It would be four days before it was confirmed he had died. She was told his body would be released to an undertakers on the following Thursday.

'I asked if I could see him and if I could have his clothes,' she said. 'I was told "remember him the way he was" and "you can come in any time in the next six weeks to get his clothes".'

Michael Barrett was buried on Friday 20th February, a week after he went out for the last time. The funeral was an 'impersonal and rushed' affair. They were 'told' what was happening. They weren't given a choice. It was all taken out of their hands.

'I will never get over losing Michael in such an appalling way,' Gertrude told the court. 'Never. I am forever haunted by the thoughts of his final moments. What were his last words? Did he call out for help? How frightened was he? Did he know he was going to die?

'Like a tornado, the Stardust fire ripped through the core of our beings, wreaking havoc and utter devastation in its wake, leaving nothing untouched, be it our home, our lives, our relationships, our education, our future, our outlook on life. Our everything. Nothing was ever the same again.

'We, his family, have and will continue to wonder what life might have been like had there been no Stardust fire.'

Speaking then of a 'life ended before it even had a chance to begin,' she concluded: 'Rest in peace, Michael. We miss you and everything about you every day.'

Gerty Barrett received a standing ovation in the courtroom and was embraced by Selina McDermott as she stepped off the podium. Tears flowed freely from all sides of the court. In being so incredibly honest and detailed in describing Michael and the impact of his loss, she set the tone for what would happen over the subsequent few weeks in the Pillar Room. For the first time at an inquest in Ireland, each family would have the chance to deliver these pen portraits, which would tell the story of their loved ones and shine a light on the real lives of the people collectively known as The 48.

Gertrude's pen portrait was technically the second thing that had happened that morning. Before the pen portraits had even begun, coroner Dr Myra Cullinane had outlined clearly to the 15-person jury what lay ahead of them and what she expected of them.

'To the jury, good morning,' she said. 'You were all empanelled and have already been sworn in. And you're aware of the facts of the tragic inquests we're about to commence. Although, we're not starting the formal legal proceedings today. You won't be hearing any of the evidence from the witnesses today. Instead, we're commencing the inquests with this very important introductory phase: the presentation of pen portraits, by each bereaved family. Members of the jury, given the centrality of the deceased and their families to these inquests, I had decided we should commence with this distinct phase. It allows the families to publicly commemorate those who died. A pen portrait is a description of each of the deceased by those who loved them and knew them best. Painting a picture of them in life as an individual, their personality, their hopes and dreams. It gives an opportunity to describe the immediate and longer-term effects of this tragedy.

'It helps you to picture the young people as they were at the time of the fire. It is their lives that must be vindicated. In this way, both you and the public more widely will understand the very human loss they've experienced.'

While pen portraits were new for Ireland, they had been used recently in similar situations both on this island and across the Irish Sea.

* * *

Ireland may never have seen inquests on this scale before, but in Northern Ireland, inquests had just begun to be seen as a useful tool to establish the truth about atrocities that had happened in the recent past. The landmark inquests into the Ballymurphy killings in west Belfast in August 1971, which Phoenix Law had been involved with, had particular parallels for the Stardust families. After an inquest which began in November 2018, it eventually found that 10 people killed in the wake of an army operation in Ballymurphy were 'entirely innocent'.

Families of the Ballymurphy victims said in the aftermath that they always knew their loved ones were innocent and there was absolutely no justification for their killing. 'Now the world knows,' they said following the verdict in May 2021. Darragh Mackin, who had represented one of the families at the inquests, echoed the kind of language he would use when talking about the Stardust victims and their families when speaking about it afterwards.

'Today's ruling is the long-awaited vindication of the families of Ballymurphy,' he said. 'There is no equivocation – all of the families killed at Ballymurphy were entirely innocent. The British government should sit up and take note. Today's ruling epitomises the importance of ensuring truth and accountability for the legacy of the past. Despite their best efforts, any attempt to draw a line in the sand of accountability and impunity is misconceived and seeks to promote no purpose other than to hide from the truth.

'The victims of Ballymurphy have now, almost 50 years later, established the truth. The truth is their families were entirely innocent [and] were killed unjustifiably.'

Vindication. Truth. Accountability. Entirely innocent. These words are as applicable to what the Stardust families were seeking as to those at Ballymurphy.

The bonds between the families of Bloody Sunday victims and Stardust victims run strong. The Bogside massacre in Derry, when British soldiers shot and killed 14 unarmed civilians, provoked outrage at the time, but inquiries by the British government were deemed a 'whitewash'. It was only after sustained campaigning and a 12-year-long inquiry that the killings were eventually declared 'unjustified and unjustifiable', prompting then Prime Minister David Cameron to issue an apology. Given the Derry girls in the Stardust that night, where Susan Morgan was among those who lost her life, support from the Bloody Sunday families had been sustained for the Stardust campaigners over the years. They attended Stardust vigils and protests and pledged their support.

The other obvious comparison was Hillsborough. The incredibly long journey to get to the new inquests for the 96 (a 97th victim of Hillsborough died in 2021) who died in the stadium tragedy in Sheffield bears more than a passing resemblance to the bid for inquests into the Artane fire. At the time, the Liverpool fans who attended that game were smeared by *The Sun* newspaper just days after the tragedy with a headline of 'The Truth' and a story claiming that fans had picked the pockets of victims, had urinated on police officers and beat up one police officer attempting to resuscitate a casualty. The undertones of this kind of coverage were clear. These loutish football fans from the working-class city of Liverpool had brought it on themselves. The parallels with the arson verdict that hung over the Stardust families were clear.

There was an instant connection between Stardust and Hillsborough. You will hear 'You'll Never Walk Alone' sung at Stardust protests. They felt they were denied the truth of what had happened at the time. They were told to go away because it's much easier to tell a working-class community to go away than ones from the leafy suburbs on Dublin's southside. And then it's the length of time to get this far, banging their heads against a brick wall until it comes down. The families of Hillsborough would set a template that Stardust would follow to get to the truth.

After all the uncertainty and innuendo, the truth could act as an end in and of itself. It's the least that the families and the victims are owed.

When the jury returned their verdicts in the Hillsborough inquests after two years of proceedings, they found unanimously that the fans did not contribute to the dangerous situation that developed in that stadium in Sheffield on the day. By a majority verdict, they found that the 96 were unlawfully killed. Representatives for the families said on the day that the verdicts 'completely vindicate the families' long fight for justice'. Stepping into the courtroom for the first pen portrait on 25th April 2023, families of the Stardust victims were hoping for a similar outcome.

* * *

Samantha Curran was also in attendance for every day of the inquests, arriving each morning without fail. She spoke about her mother Helena Mangan, who died in the Stardust. She was just four years old at the time of her mother's death. Samantha described her first day of school just a few months after the Stardust, seeing the children cry for their mothers and hoping her own would walk through the door and tell her how brave she was.

Helena was a second mammy to her younger siblings and doted on Samantha, who has had to pass so many milestones without her. It wasn't easy being a single mother in the late 1970s and 1980s, but she held her head high. She was proud to be a mammy, and Samantha was proud to be her daughter.

'I so wish she could've been there to guide me in the right directions,' she said. 'I miss her so much I feel a huge piece of me is missing. Now I need answers as to what happened to my mammy and why she never came home.'

* * *

'They were very emotional and, sometimes, it was the little things mentioned about a person – anecdotes about their day-to-day life – that were the most upsetting. I felt so sorry for the family members who were reading the tributes, because it must have been so painful and difficult for them. I had tears in my eyes on many occasions.'

For two years, *Liverpool Echo* reporter Eleanor Barlow covered the fresh inquests for those who died in the Hillsborough disaster. At the very beginning of the proceedings, each of the families of those who died in such horrific circumstances were given the chance to deliver pen portraits for their loved ones. Those emotional scenes in court paved the way for two long years of evidence which would ultimately end with a jury concluding that all of those who'd died in that stadium in Sheffield were unlawfully killed, with multiple failings by the police and ambulance service contributing to their deaths.

It was another echo of how the Stardust was linked to Hillsborough, with the legal teams already having cited Hillsborough extensively in their successful bid to be granted fresh inquests. Now, this process for the Stardust victims would begin in exactly the same way. Barlow's words would prove as accurate for the pen portraits of the 48 victims of the Stardust fire as for those who died at Hillsborough. Over the course of three weeks, families bravely stepped up to talk about their worst memories.

But it was more than that. It was a way to bring their loved one back and into the room. One by one, they described what they were like, what they hoped to do, what kind of a brother or sister or son or daughter they were. While the age of victims of Hillsborough ranged from 10 to 67 years, the Stardust victims were all within a much closer age range, all barely beginning their lives, with plenty to look forward to. It was in this context that mothers and sisters, fathers and brothers, nieces and nephews, friends and family, followed the example of Gertrude Barrett and stepped up to talk about that person. They did it with great dignity and great humanity, with great regret and great sadness.

Each story told was its own tapestry of a life not lived and the impact it had on the loved ones left behind. Some of the names were recognisable to anyone who had followed the Stardust story in the media over the years, but a lot weren't. These were the ones whose families hadn't been in the media spotlight, who hadn't led the campaigns, but, nonetheless, they all came forward when the time came.

* * *

Errol Buckley's words for his brother Jimmy were read out in court by his son.

'On Friday, February 13th 1981, Jimmy's daughter Julie-Ann celebrated her first birthday,' he said. 'After having a tea party for her, Jimmy came with me along with my other brother Albert and Jimmy's wife Christine to support me, as I was dancing in the Valentine's disco competition in the Stardust.'

After winning the competition, Errol recalled Jimmy jumping up onto the stage, giving him a hug, and telling him how proud he was of him. These were the last words Jimmy spoke to him.

'The days that followed were a haze,' he said. 'Attending the funeral, after the funeral. Guilt was eating away at me. If I hadn't been dancing that night, Jimmy wouldn't have been there. Jimmy would never get to see his beautiful daughter grow up. It all got too much for me. I ran away to England and later on to America, but the nightmares I suffered with stayed with me, no matter where I went.'

* * *

'These will be the biggest inquests that the State has ever held,' Sinn Féin's Lynn Boylan said after the inquests had been granted. Her comment would turn out to be something of an understatement. The Pillar Room on the grounds of the Rotunda Hospital, smack bang in the middle of Dublin city centre, would become the venue for reliving that horrible night and its aftermath over 40 years on. It would see over 120 days of often gut-wrenching, harrowing evidence from more than 300 witnesses.

As time ticked on towards the first hearings in April 2023, to when the jury would be empanelled, it was clear what was at stake. 'The rules around inquests are that an inquest is supposed to not just determine the cause of death, but also what were the circumstances that led to that cause,' Boylan said. 'That had never happened for the families. They were told that their loved ones died of smoke inhalation, but where did the smoke come from?

What were the circumstances that led to them being in that particular place and dying in that way?'

But there were risks inherent in this process too, from the very start. Inquests have a very defined scope under the legislation. There are things they can do. And there are things they are absolutely not permitted to do. Eamon Butterly had already tried to prevent the verdict of unlawful killing from being open to the jury before the inquests even began, strongly arguing that inquests cannot apportion blame or exonerate people. They are limited in their scope, despite the vital function they have.

As the pen portraits concluded and the inquests were about to turn to their first witness evidence, Dr Cullinane told the jury: 'The question you might pose is why are we holding these inquests now?' She told them the Stardust fire had one of the highest death tolls from any one event in the history of the State, and remains so today.

'The loss of life has left an indelible mark on the suburb of Artane and the surrounding areas where the majority of victims lived,' she said, before referencing the Keane, Coffey and McCartan reports and the decades of campaigning by families and survivors to bring us to this point now.

'Whereas I will direct you in matters of law, the facts are a matter for you solely,' the coroner said. 'You are the arbiters of the facts you will hear in evidence. Therefore you hear the evidence in an attempt to reveal the truth in a public forum. You decide what happened.'

And, in a refrain we would hear time and time again in the court, she clarified for them at the very start of the evidence that nobody can be blamed or exonerated or excused at an inquest. No verdict can decide or appear to decide criminal or civil liability. 'It's important to approach these inquests with an open mind and base your considerations only on the evidence you hear. I wish to thank you in advance for the important task you're about to undertake. Your service as a juror is one of utmost importance. I'm immensely grateful to you for answering your summons.'

* * *

Susan Behan was the sister of John Colgan, known as Johnny. She said she was speaking on behalf of her mother and father, who'd both recently passed away, and her sister Patricia, who couldn't be there on the day.

Susan talked of him as a 'charmer' and a 'truly special person'. His favourite song was 'Lovely Day' by Bill Withers. It 'summed up his outlook on life'. He worked with his dad as a painter and decorator but had previously worked in St John of Gods, where he would sing and play his guitar for the patients. 'They loved him,' she said. Susan was pregnant at the time of the fire and due to give birth in less than a month. Johnny couldn't wait to be an uncle.

'I treasure those last few moments, but it still hurts as if it was yesterday when I think about it,' she said. 'Losing Johnny in the Stardust was indescribable. The effect of losing him continues to this day. It dictates how I think, how I view certain things and how I worry about my own dear children.'

* * *

The Pillar Room was a carefully chosen venue. It was large and accessible, but that still didn't mean that everyone who wanted to be there could be there, be it for health, geographic or work reasons. Many of the siblings of those who died would still be of working age, and you couldn't take weeks or months off at a time to attend. Family members who'd since emigrated couldn't be here to watch in person.

While not particularly innovative in 2024, the solution was highly unusual for the Irish legal system: livestream it. Cameras are rarely, if ever, permitted in courtrooms here. Two Supreme Court rulings were broadcast in 2017, and pandemic restrictions prompted a greatly increased use of remote proceedings. Article 34 of the Constitution requires that justice in the courts should be administered in public, which has been seen as a guiding principle but not something that has required innovation over the years.

The stream was hosted on Zoom. Anyone could head to stardustfireinquests.ie, click the link, and watch live. In addition to those attending in person, there could be anywhere from a couple of dozen to more than 100 watching online, and there was certainly a spike in viewing figures when Eamon Butterly gave his evidence. It was a multi-camera set-up; the stream could cut between the witness box to the coroner, to the legal teams to the jury. At times it was intensely sobering viewing, as people took to the stand and relayed their memories of the worst day of their lives. But there were also plenty of inane shots when the camera focused for too long on counsel shuffling papers or the coroner twiddling a pen while waiting for the court to get in order.

Some gaffes, too, such as when a high-profile witness gave evidence remotely and left their microphone on when the court had risen.

The stream was also visible in the Pillar Room itself on seven large screens dotted around the room. Sometimes, it would switch to graphics, or the photos gardaí took in the aftermath of the blaze as they diligently recorded the scene. Some are available publicly and appear in the Keane Report, some were kept private, but all were made available to the inquests. The scenes at all of the emergency exit doors. The fire damage and the debris and devastation in the main ballroom. The skip that people fell over on the way out. The van that blocked the door. Suspect wiring. Examples of the seating.

* * *

Siobhán Kearney spoke about her brother, Liam Dunne. On the morning after the fire, she found him after a 'horrible' search in the Mater Hospital while her parents were looking for him elsewhere. One of Liam's brothers had walked by him several times, not recognising him. His face was all swollen, and he had bandages on his hands and arms. 'That evening, Liam was taken for an operation because the blood flow in his hands was bad,' she said. 'He was moved to the ICU that night and was given 24 hours to live.' But he held on. His family went to visit him every day. On 10th March, Siobhán had spent hours making tapes so Liam and Jimmy Fitzpatrick, also badly injured in the fire, could listen to them. But Liam would never get the chance to hear them.

Liam Dunne was the last of the Stardust victims to die, just before midday on 11th March.

'I also died,' Siobhán said. 'I was 16, and the pain of that sadness has never left me. That month ripped our family apart. To watch my lovely mum cry and just stare. No talking, just tears. My older brothers were away serving

THE LAST DISCO

their country. On their return, our family tried to support each other, but like most, trying to understand the grief and pain and sadness left us silent. My brother's passing has resulted in changing all of us as people, because living with such a young death at a young age causes a pain you carry with you through life every day.'

* * *

One graphic was shown almost daily in the court. It was a floor plan of the Stardust complex. It was old – hand-drawn, in black and white – and used to show where a witness first saw the fire, or to indicate which exit they used to escape. Sometimes, it displayed the crudely recorded locations of where bodies were found. The court also watched aerial footage of the scene, filmed from a helicopter circling the burnt-out wreckage of the disco.

It left the jury with a clear idea of both the layout of the Stardust and what it looked like after the fire. But few photos were available to the court that captured what the Stardust looked like prior to the events of 14th February 1981. Those that exist show the intensely red interior of the ballroom – red sets, red walls, red curtains around the stage. Tables and chairs arc around the dancefloor in front of the stage. A disco ball hangs from the white ceiling. As a way of helping them visualise what it was like, a 3D digital rendering was shown to the jury before the first witness evidence was heard after the pen portraits. Dr Cullinane, as she would do at numerous junctures throughout the inquests, gave a kind of content warning before showing the visualisation. Some of those watching in the public gallery or online would've been there on the night. 'It might be distressing to see the materials,' the coroner said, perhaps understating it. She said people were free to exit the Pillar Room if they wished to do so. This incredibly detailed recreation was given mainly from the point of view of someone walking through it like a first-person view in a computer game. The details were striking. The cigarette machine. The taps on the bars. The microphone stand on the stage. The dance floor. The plates welded to the windows in the bathrooms.

Mark Tottenham talked through the different aspects of the venue the first time it was played for the jury. He went into granular detail, such as how one of the doors at Exit 5 opened just 90 degrees because it was blocked by a shed. On the second time it was shown, it was in total silence.

This bright and airy-looking venue could not have stood out more in contrast with the photos of the devastation of the Stardust after the fire: the black-grey debris everywhere, the interior a mess of metal wire, scorch marks on the external walls, broken windows, the roof totally caved in. The jury would hear so much about this place over the next year, but having seen this so early on in the process left them with a searing clarity both of what the Stardust was, and what it would become.

* * *

Bridget McDermott came in flanked by her family on the day of the pen portraits for her three children, William, George and Marcella. A woman in her eighties who couldn't accept that there were no answers for how her children died. 'Probable arson' was never good enough. She had to know what happened.

It was Selina McDermott, delivering the pen portrait for her beloved older sister Marcella, who created the most haunting image. One that anyone listening could vividly imagine. Imagine the horror of seeing the coffins of three of your children laid out side by side in a church. The coffins bearing 'gentle giant' Willie, Georgie the joker and the music-mad Marcella. Selina described her mother seeing the three coffins laid out, banging on them and pleading to be allowed to see her children. That wasn't an option given to them. 'She kept saying, "why did He take three?"' Selina said. 'How do you wake up from a nightmare like this? She'd still leave a key in the front door for years in the hope one of them would walk through it.'

Their family life became difficult. They were all dealing with grief, and with blame. It became unbearable, and little help was offered from outside.

Their father was a fireman who was off duty that night. He frequently said he could've saved them if he'd been there. Aware of the kind of injuries they'd have sustained, he would say: 'I know the death they had'. 'This haunted him for the short years he had left in his life,' his family said.

Bridget McDermott stepped up after everyone else had spoken. Supported by her daughters, she said: 'They went that night and they never came home to me. I miss them and I love them. And god bless them.'

* * *

The scope of the inquests was to determine more about how these people died beyond a doctor's report, but the coroner had also set out a carefully decided range of questions that the jury must reach answers on: Where and how did the fire start? How did the fire progress? What was the response in the Stardust to the outbreak of the fire? The circumstances that may have led to the fire and other contributory factors. The design and condition of the building and whether it contributed to the fire.

The evidence of hundreds of witnesses would help the jury form their answers. 'It doesn't mean they will all be present,' Dr Cullinane said. 'These events occurred in 1981. Many of the witnesses have since died. Others may be ill or unavailable. When their evidence is deemed important to assist you in making their finding, it will be read into the record. But when a witness cannot be questioned, consider the weight you attach to that evidence.'

There would also be occasions when 'matters of law' would be argued and bashed out in court. The jury would have to leave the room on such occasions. The coroner told them that there were 'uncontested facts' they could take as read, but the other facts would be for the jury to decide.

'There can be no doubt that [where and how the fire started] is a matter that needs to be re-investigated in these inquests,' Dr Cullinane said. 'The cause and location of the original fire are not matters that are accepted as having been settled, whether in the Keane Tribunal report or otherwise. It is therefore appropriate to investigate in detail the question of how the fire progressed from its original location.'

Given the scale of the task at hand, Dr Cullinane left the then 15-person jury under no illusions over how long this could all take. 'These are likely to be lengthy inquests,' she said. 'They are likely to run until the end of the year. As we run through, we may have a better understanding of how long it will take.' As it would eventually transpire, the inquests ran beyond her prediction. It would be some time after Gertrude Barrett's address to court before these proceedings were finally brought to a close.

*   *   *

The pen portraits for the Keegans were delivered by their siblings Lorraine and Damien.

Lorraine said Martina was a stunningly beautiful girl who had ambitions of being a model. 'She had everything going for her: very attractive, a beautiful figure, natural blonde hair and a fantastic personality,' she said. 'We honestly know that there wasn't one fella in Coolock or its surrounding areas who didn't fancy Martina.'

She spoke at length about their family and how happy they had been before the Stardust. 'That day changed the family and we have never been the same since,' Lorraine said. 'Our happy family days were gone. Our happy family home was gone.'

Of Mary, Damien spoke of her as a loving, compassionate and sociable girl who was shy at heart. As the oldest sister, she looked after them and was almost like a teacher at home. After the Stardust, he said the children would wake to the sounds of their parents crying.

He said: 'I would sit on our doorstep and wait for my sister to come home every day for months after Mary was killed. I was only three and a half and couldn't understand why Mary never came home or walked up the path again.'

That same day, Antoinette delivered the pen portrait for Robert Kelly, the brother of the late Eugene who had campaigned alongside her for so long, alongside Eugene's daughter Mandy. 'If Eugene were alive, it would have meant so much to him to speak here today about his brother Robert, whom he loved so much,' Antoinette said.

'Robert had been saving all his money to go on a holiday to Spain, and I always recall Eugene saying that his mother had always said, "Poor Robert was saving for his holiday, but little did he know he was saving for his funeral".'

* * *

Dr Cullinane has been a Dublin District Coroner since 2016, having transferred from the Cork City District. She is a medical doctor and a barrister at law. Educated at Trinity College and the King's Inns, she has been a fellow of the Royal College of Physicians in Ireland and a member of the faculty of legal and forensic medicine of the Royal College of Physicians in the UK. She also gives lectures on medical and coronial law to legal and healthcare professionals. Given the scale of the task that would be required with these inquests, this was someone more than qualified for the task.

She was supported by a legal team of her own who would attend every day, and whose role would be to guide the coroner in matters of law and question witnesses when they appeared at the inquests. There was also Phoenix Law, a separate team from Brabazon Solicitors representing the Kennedy family, and legal counsel for An Garda Síochána and Dublin City Council. Eamon Butterly was also represented at the inquests as an interested party by Dómhnaill O'Scanaill from O'Scanaill & Company Solicitors, who had acted on his behalf at the judicial review before the inquests started. However, unlike the rest of the teams, Butterly's legal team would only rarely be in attendance in person for the evidence. Having said that, the opportunity to view proceedings online to facilitate those not able to make it to court every day was an option regularly taken by O'Scanaill & Company, keeping a watching brief on proceedings throughout.

And so, having occupied centre stage at the outset of the inquests, the families stood up en masse from the tables in the centre of the Pillar Room and took seats in the public gallery to make way for the legal professionals. Well over a dozen of them would play a crucial part in what was to come. The families of victims now had to trust them to put their case forward to the jury at every turn. The vastly experienced senior counsels were said to have dropped their fees to allow the free Legal Aid to cover their costs and not burden the families with huge bills.

The inquests would indeed be the last great opportunity for answers about the Stardust, and in Dr Myra Cullinane they had Dublin's senior coroner overseeing inquests like no other. Inquests in Ireland typically last a day or two. Never much longer than that. Certainly not longer than a week. These inquests would go on for a whole year.

* * *

An accurate way to sum up what the families set out to achieve came in the pen portrait delivered by the family of Marie Kennedy. Her sister Michelle told the inquests that it was so difficult to write for many reasons, with the good memories often as painful as the bad. She spoke about Marie's love of Leo Sayer, ABBA and the Bee Gees, of how glorious she looked in her Aran jumper and silver jewellery, of how mischievous she was. How she was 'young and sweet, only 17'. The description invoked images of a girl going to the disco-dancing competition that night, hoping she'd hear her favourite tunes and dance with her friends.

'I was going to write a whole section about the night Marie died,' Michelle said. 'About how our parents found her in Jervis Street Hospital and our mam recognised her by her feet; how our dad and grandad went to officially identify her the next day and came out forever changed; how her loss destroyed our family. But in the end, I decided not to. Marie has been lost in the smoke and devastation of the Stardust for too long. The decades-long fight for answers has taken far too much from us already.

'So today, we are taking her back and remembering her life. We are reclaiming her from the darkness and despair and bringing her back into the sunlight where she belongs. She's our sister, daughter, sister-in-law, niece, aunt, great-aunt, cousin and friend. She's our Marie.'

Chapter 11

'I REMEMBER THE 13TH of February 1981.' It's such a simple phrase, but it carried a haunting resonance in the large hall of the Pillar Room throughout the Stardust inquests as it was heard again and again.

'I remember the 13th of February 1981' is how many of the statements originally given to An Garda Síochána as part of their investigation into the fire at the time began. Gardaí at the time managed to gather 1,400 statements and spoke to large numbers of the attendees and staff there on the night. Many were teenagers, mourning their friends or family members, and now had to attend a garda station and repeat what they had experienced to an officer. The investigating officers would write it down, and they'd have a chance to read over and sign the statement at the end.

Some of these statements were taken mere days after this tragedy. Some had to go straight to a garda station after attending a funeral, or even after days and days of funeral after funeral. There is a grim irony that these young people would've begun their statement to gardaí just a few days later by saying 'I remember the 13th of February 1981' when this would've been the most traumatic event many of them would have ever faced. The horror would have been fresh in their mind. Over 42 years on, however, the phrase took on a new meaning. 'I remember the 13th of

February 1981' was like a code phrase to signify the night their life changed.

Prior to a witness fielding questions from the legal teams at the inquests, their original statement to the gardaí would be read out to give context to what they had reported seeing back then. If there was anything there they didn't agree with or remembered differently, they'd have the chance to address it. They would take the stand, swear to tell the truth, the whole truth and nothing but the truth. Given the option to either read their original statement themselves or have the registrar do it for them, most went for the latter option.

The registrar on the day would clear his or her throat before beginning the statement 'I remember the 13th of February 1981'.

In the case of patrons, what would follow was descriptions of what they did on the night leading up to going to the Stardust, the mundanity of life pouring out when these young people found themselves in a garda interview room after suffering such trauma. It wasn't difficult to see the contrast. Men and women in their fifties and sixties hearing or reading aloud what they had to say over 40 years ago. It was something they may never have spoken about before to anybody. For some, it brought them right back, weeping as their words were read back to them. Coroner Dr Myra Cullinane would sometimes intervene, asking if they needed a break.

They were being asked to recall and give important evidence on an event that took place more than 42 years ago. The barristers would stress that it's been a very long time since then, that their questions weren't a memory test, and that instead it was about getting details from

THE LAST DISCO

them. But the inquests got a lot more than just these details. It gave an insight into how the memory of these horrible events lingers in someone's life over all this time.

Patricia O'Connor – just 16 at the time – remembered that Caroline Carey wasn't meant to go to the Stardust that night because she was grounded. Patricia and a friend went to the Carey house and asked Caroline's mother if she could come out that night. Her mother relented, on the condition that she came home after the dance competition. They were all 'so excited' to head out that night.

Her descriptions of what happened were incredibly vivid. When she first became aware of the fire, she only had time to stand up and tried to lift up her coat and bag before the lights went out. 'Out of the corner of my eye, I could just see and hear something shooting across,' she said. 'It was seconds. I'm not going to say it was flames because I didn't see flames. I heard it more than seeing it.'

Patricia described something like tar or oil dripping on her, 'big enough to burn the whole of my arms, the whole of my back, my chest, my neck'. 'You could feel it, taste it,' she said. She could recall people screaming for their mammies and daddies to help them open the doors. 'That's what I heard. That's what I still hear.'

Caroline, who was around four months pregnant at the time, never came home. Patricia said she couldn't walk up that road for 10 years afterwards. 'We promised her mammy that she'd come home,' she said.

All of the evidence could, in an instant, become harrowing – tough to listen to for those in the public gallery, but unimaginably tough to recount when faced with a jury and an army of barristers and solicitors. Across the dozens of days of evidence from the patrons of the

Stardust, it was impossible to know in advance how affecting and emotional a particular day might be.

Even despite everything the inquests had heard so far, and after so many had come and gone from the witness box, it could still retain the power to stop you in your tracks, to cause a sharp intake of breath from the public gallery, to bring a tear to your eye.

There was the 17-year-old hairdresser pulled out of one of the exits who, in shock, went to work the next morning, still coughing from inhaling the thick black smoke.

The girl who fell over a chair near one of the exits and saw the 'ripples' of fire shoot across the ceiling like a wave. She was on the floor being trampled and thought, 'That's it, I'm gone now'.

The man who saw his best friend dance with a girl just 10 minutes before it all kicked off. 'It was a place we could get a drink, have a bit of freedom,' he said. 'We thought we were big men.' Both his friend and the girl would die in the fire.

The man who wakes up every day thinking of what he witnessed just after he'd gotten out the exit door. 'I have to face every day for 42 years looking at Exit 4 and seeing this girl [inside] burning,' he said.

You could see what getting up on the stand took out of people, often very visibly. The tremendous courage it took shouldn't be underestimated. But it took its toll.

It took its toll on Joseph Cummiskey. He was one of the first patrons to give evidence at the inquests. Having been given his original statement to gardaí to read over a week or so prior, he became acquainted again with the details of what he had said back then. At the time, he described to gardaí how he thought it was a smoke bomb when he first smelled fumes. Luckily, he saw the fire at an early stage and told the people around him to get out.

'I was just outside the door when the lights went out,' Joseph said. He ran around to the main entrance and saw a man hanging out the window on top of the canopy, shouting for help. He heard the people trapped inside the bathrooms screaming. He found a hammer and tried to get in through the steel-plated windows, but it was no use. The entire roof of the building was ablaze; inside was a ball of flame. Joseph next ran around to Exit 4. People were still streaming out, some on fire.

When fielding questions from barrister Mark Tottenham, Joseph became emotional on the stand. Dr Cullinane intervened to say she was aware that giving this evidence was 'very hard', as Joseph knew so many of those who lost their lives.

As he had done in that statement all those years ago, he was again asked to describe trying to break the toilet windows. The steel plates placed across those windows made it a futile attempt.

'You could hear the screams,' he told the jury. 'There was nothing I could have done.' Joseph wouldn't be the only person to find it difficult in the witness box. Armed with just a hammer trying to smash a steel plate, there was nothing anyone could have done at that point. But by taking the stand to give evidence decades later, there was something he and all those other patrons there on the night could do. By giving the details of that horrific night to the jury, they were explaining what happened to them and to their friends who never made it out.

The exits were pored over at great length. Witness after witness described the crush at the main entrance, the locks on Exit 3, the chains around the panic bars of Exits 4 and 5. So many common experiences from initially seeing the small fire to the chaos that would follow. The small acts of heroism or attempts to help those still inside. The families would say afterwards how grateful they were for each and every one of them who got up to tell their story. Without them, and particularly their detailed accounts of trying to flee the Stardust that night, the end result of all of this may have been different.

* * *

As the inquests entered December 2023, the evidence had switched from the patrons to the emergency responders, the men who rushed to the Stardust when the call came through just after 1.40am.

All much older men now, they took their seats side by side. Some of them chatted away while waiting for court to begin, perhaps the first time they'd seen each other in years. Others stayed pensive, reading over the statements they'd soon hear read out to the court and the horrific details they'd be asked to share again.

The court was now approaching 100 days of evidence, but still, time and time again, Dr Cullinane was careful to warn the jury of the difficult testimony they were about to hear.

'Most of the evidence will contain distressing and potentially graphic detail,' she said before former firefighter William Redmond's testimony was read out. 'Be aware of that.'

Redmond was not there to give evidence in person, having passed away just a year prior. The social media pages representing the Stardust campaign had paid tribute

THE LAST DISCO

at the time, describing him as 'one of the many heroes who saved many lives' by repeatedly entering the nightclub during rescue attempts.

His statement was read into the record. As usual, the registrar's clear, dispassionate tones delivered the words of those who could not be there themselves. Redmond had described the 'mass of flames' he saw on his arrival and the ceiling 'falling down in big sheets' into the 'inferno' inside. He also described the recovery operation afterwards, as the fire brigade and gardaí swept through the club searching for remains. At one point, he saw two bodies huddled close together, lying beside each other. 'It looked like they were holding hands,' he said.

When witnesses were unable to give evidence themselves, they couldn't be questioned further about what they had seen or asked for more details. When they were in court, however, this could lead to further harrowing details emerging.

Like when retired fireman James Tormey described how he and his colleagues rushed into the Stardust on the night, before the rescue operation became a recovery operation. Tormey described finding the torso behind the door of Exit 5. 'My feeling was that the poor individual was two or three steps away from safety,' he said. He believed it was a man, only because he found a gent's watch nearby.

Noel Keegan's graphic recollections of the night were heard on the 89th day of the inquests. The retired fireman had recalled seeing bodies 'still on fire' and 'burnt to a cinder'. He also remembered six bodies piled on top of each other in the toilets between Exits 5 and 6.

'I would hope some there were alive, but I don't know,' Keegan said. As the legal teams did whenever many of these first responders spoke, barrister Des Fahy thanked him on behalf of the families of victims for what he and his colleagues did on the night.

Noel Hosback also spoke to the inquests. He is the fireman who bravely found a way into the club through a small window and rescued people trapped in the bathrooms, one by one, sharing his breathing apparatus with them. Sitting in court that day was Deirdre Dames, one of those he brought to safety, one of the many people who wouldn't be here today if it wasn't for the bravery of firemen like Hosback. After the sitting, they shared a hug in the foyer of the Pillar Room.

The Keane Tribunal determined that firemen rescued as many as 15 people on the night, and this embrace between Deirdre and Hosback all those years later reinforced the power of those acts of bravery.

The courage shown on the night by these men was commended time and again by the families and their legal teams at these inquests. One retired fireman remarked on the stand at one point that 'no one had ever attended a brigade call' before. This was uncharted territory for them, but they stepped up regardless. The details they could provide could not but add to the understanding the jury had developed of the situation there that night, but they still had a long way to go, and a lot more to learn before they could reach their verdicts. How had we reached a situation in the first place where people could be trapped inside? The answers would lie in testimony given much earlier in the Pillar Room.

*   *   *

Bernard Condon SC was fixated on 'the lie'. With a witness on the stand for his third day, Condon said this witness's lie had caused 'an enormous shadow or fog to fall on the investigation'. 'I don't think it has ever lifted,' he said.

Michael Kavanagh, a doorman working in the Stardust on the night, took to the witness box when the Stardust inquests resumed after the summer break. Courts in Ireland don't usually sit in August, so the Stardust inquests had followed suit, starting again in September.

There was an elephant in the room during Kavanagh's testimony, and the coroner's counsel, Simon Mills SC, addressed it before Condon got to pose the questions: Why had Kavanagh made a statement to gardaí about unlocking the emergency exit doors when he hadn't done so?

'I can't even remember making a statement,' he said. 'A lot of what happened then was a blur. I was all over the place.'

During the course of his evidence, the court heard that Kavanagh's girlfriend at the time was Paula Byrne. She was missing, and he had gone to several different hospitals in the early hours of Valentine's Day to look for her – he wasn't aware yet that she had died in the fire. At some stage that night before speaking to the media, he found himself back in his friend Michael O'Toole's house, sitting in the kitchen. His friend's father James was there too. According to James O'Toole, Kavanagh told them: 'The poor bastards in there must have died like rats. They couldn't get out. The doors were chained.' Michael O'Toole made similar statements to gardaí, saying that Kavanagh had said the doors were padlocked and that 'we were told to keep the doors locked'.

On the Monday after the fire, Michael Kavanagh appeared on RTÉ's *Today Tonight* programme. James O'Toole couldn't believe what he was hearing, watching as Kavanagh told the nation that he had unlocked the doors. It made him go to the gardaí the following day and make a statement.

'If Michael and his father Jimmy said it, I must have said it,' Kavanagh told the inquests. Although owning the fact that he had lied, a definitive answer on why he'd done so was not so forthcoming. He said it was through stupidity that he'd done it. He'd been caught up in something not of his own making.

Condon put it to him that the management might have pressed him to say that he'd opened the doors, leaving Kavanagh with a decision to make. He could 'go along with' what they wanted him to say or he could 'tell the truth that he didn't open the doors and risk being scapegoated'. Kavanagh again said he had no such recollection of such a conversation.

Things came to a head that Wednesday evening after the fire, 18th February, when Leo Doyle and Patrick J. Murphy – both doormen – came to visit the Kavanagh household. The court heard that the pair told Kavanagh's parents that, 'for the love of God', he had to retract his previous statement that he'd opened the doors. Condon suggested it was because they were worried Kavanagh wouldn't 'stick to the story'.

It was only after a 'reality check' from his own father that Kavanagh would go to gardaí and retract the original statement where he said he'd unlocked the emergency doors. 'It triggered something off on me,' he said. 'I was the one they were trying to pin the whole thing on. I was being lambasted. I felt they were trying to make a scapegoat out of me at the time.'

It was put to him that, once it appeared his story of unlocking the doors wouldn't hold up, he had to 'clear the way' for someone else to open the doors. Kavanagh said he didn't clear the way for anything. When asked if he was put up to it to tell the lie to advance the interests of other parties, he said no. Before finishing with him, Condon told Kavanagh that he'd led people on a 'merry dance' with all this.

He said Kavanagh had 'one last chance' to explain why he had given this dishonest account that was 'very helpful' to the Butterlys and the other doormen. But he didn't say why, leaving the jury the task of penetrating that 'fog' themselves when they came to consider the evidence around those emergency exit doors.

* * *

Michael Kavanagh was not the first staff member to give evidence at the Stardust inquests. Throughout the summer and into the autumn of 2023, the small army of glasswashers, barmen, waitresses, lounge boys and – of course – doormen that worked in the Stardust on the night of the fire passed through the Pillar Room. With these witnesses, an important question asked of every one of them was if they'd been given fire training or directions on what to do in an emergency. The answer in every case was no, they hadn't been.

Many of them saw the fire and could describe how it progressed. They could recall seeing exit doors chained. But it was this specific policy surrounding the emergency exits at the Stardust that would see the doormen put under scrutiny at these inquests.

John Furley was one of them. Michael O'Higgins, the barrister representing some of the families, told him that some of the earlier witnesses had been 'low on the food chain' at the Stardust. Furley, he said, was at neither the bottom nor the top despite previously being head doorman. He was just 23 years old and, like several of the other doormen, it wasn't his full-time job. His day job was working as an apprentice plumber.

O'Higgins put to Furley that there was a 'chasm' between his evidence and the account given by several others regarding a particular exit door on the night. This was Exit 5, the one partially blocked by a skip used for empty bottles. Multiple witnesses said they had difficulty getting out of these doors as the fire spread. Some of them also recalled seeing a doorman kicking at a door and padlock to get it open. Witnesses recognised him as living on the same road that a friend of theirs had lived on. They said it was John Furley. 'I wasn't kicking the door,' he said. 'The account I gave was the truth.' Furley's account was that he had seen five or six fellas banging on Exit 5, trying to get out, but he was able to push the bars to open the doors. The witnesses identifying him as kicking down the door were 'wrong', he told the court.

O'Higgins said that Furley's original statements to the gardaí were a means of letting those who ran the Stardust 'off the hook' for padlocks and chains on the doors and was 'blaming the patrons for not being able to get out'.

Furley would remark to the inquests that he didn't know if Eamon Butterly was 'very vexed' by the idea of people getting into the Stardust for free but said Butterly 'didn't like to be bested'. But Furley wouldn't complete his evidence. After a brief adjournment, the coroner came back

THE LAST DISCO

to say she was standing the witness down on medical grounds. The same happened with another doorman, Gabriel O'Neill. As he lives outside this jurisdiction he could not be compelled to return. Dr Cullinane would later tell the jury to treat this evidence as 'part-heard'.

* * *

Phelim Kinahan was the floor manager in the Stardust, and he gave evidence remotely at the inquests, dialling in using Zoom. This would lead to a startling moment still relatively early on in the inquests.

The court had risen for its usual hour-long lunch break. Kinahan had just spoken about not remembering the doors being locked at the Stardust, and that the policy had been to drape the chains over the bars to give the impression of being locked. Kinahan had told the court he was telling the truth to the best of his ability. Whenever the court wasn't sitting, the screens in the Pillar Room would switch from the live video feed to a static holding image. It was the same for people watching online – but with a crucial difference. Kinahan's microphone wasn't muted. A phone rang, and Kinahan appeared to take a brief call. The voice of a woman, who seems to be in the room with him, can be heard. 'How much longer will this go on for?', the voice says. The line was slightly garbled, but she appeared to reference something about whether or not the doors were locked. 'Either the fucking doors were locked, or they weren't locked.' Kinahan replied that it was nothing to do with him, 'so I'm not saying that'. Then, a third voice. The rest was heated but unintelligible. Families and friends of the deceased who had left the call open could hear this

242

unfold, as well as members of the public and journalists watching in. It led to a frantic hour in the Pillar Room as Phoenix Law strove to find out exactly what had been said, legal teams calling anyone who they thought might have been listening or could see their name listed on the call's attendees, and decide how to put it to the witness.

Kinahan appeared to be caught unawares when Des Fahy, barrister for some of the families, raised it with him when court resumed, referring to it as a discrete matter. Fahy described what happened and asked Kinahan if he understood what Fahy was asking him. 'Not really,' Kinahan said, but added that it was his daughter-in-law in the room. It was put to him what he had been heard saying just a short time ago. 'I don't remember that,' he replied. Des Fahy KC put it to him that there was a 'running theme' to Kinahan's evidence and how, in 1981, when he spoke to the guards and spoke to the Keane Tribunal, Kinahan was 'an Eamon Butterly man'. And when he gave evidence to the jury at these inquests 42 years later, he remained an Eamon Butterly man. Kinahan replied: 'I think so.'

And then there was Leo Doyle's evidence. Doyle was the deputy head doorman at the Stardust on the night of the fire. By his own admission, no one else wanted the job; doormen weren't sticking around very long, and morale was on the floor. Regarding the justification for locking the doors at all, Des Fahy put to him that the idea of patrons letting their friends in for free was a false justification and that some doormen were 'on the take', letting people into the Stardust and pocketing the takings for themselves.

Again, Doyle was steadfast for quite a while in his assertion that the doors were unlocked on the night at the time of the fire. However, he told the jury on numerous occasions that he believed Michael Kavanagh opened the doors. This didn't happen. Bernard Condon, fond of the odd rhetorical flourish in his questioning, asked Doyle if he'd ever heard the phrase 'oh what a tangled web [we] weave when first we practice to deceive'? Doyle said he had not.

Romantic-era poet Walter Scott may not have described his verse in such a way, but Condon told the witness that it means 'if you're going to tell lies, you have to have a good memory'. He went on: 'It means that when lies are being told, left, right and centre, it becomes almost impossible to know the start from the end of them. And that's the position I'm suggesting you are in today.' Again, Doyle rejected this.

The barrister put to him that he had advanced two different conspiracies at two different times – one that Thomas Kennan had unlocked the doors and the other that it was Michael Kavanagh, but he denied this.

Doyle faced long questioning about his role at the Stardust, but it was some of his final words that would cause the biggest shock. After a brief break, he returned to the witness box and said he wanted to apologise to the coroner because he believed he had made 'a boo boo'.

'I maybe now believe that the doors were locked,' he said. 'They may have been locked. I just don't know.'

A boo boo, indeed.

There were some key takeaways from the jury's perspective on the evidence of the doormen. One was the clear divide between what some of them said about the exits and the experiences of patrons. Thomas Kennan's evidence, which was read in, was that he opened all the emergency exits on the night. This flies in the face of the witness evidence regarding Exits 3, 4 and 5 in particular. They struggled to get out. Lads had to kick the doors in. Kennan's statement to gardaí on the day of the fire also made no reference to him having unlocked the doors. It was a week later – after Michael Kavanagh's recanting – that he told the guards it was he who had unlocked the doors.

Another was the changing of the doormen's accounts. If the doors were easy to open and had been unlocked before the fire, why had some doormen initially said words to that effect before changing their story? Why lie about it in the first place at all? Was there something to hide?

All along, the families sat in court or watched online listening. They all listened intently. These doormen were at the centre of the state of the exits, and the bereaved had to listen to them speaking about what was an indescribably raw part of this story for them. But they knew it was vital. The fog of the past few decades was finally lifting.

Chapter 12

IF PHOTOGRAPHY HAD BEEN allowed inside the Pillar Room at Dublin's Rotunda Hospital, the veteran snappers waiting outside the grounds would have fallen over themselves to get the shot. It was lunchtime on the second day of Eamon Butterly's evidence at the inquests. Families had packed into the public gallery and watched, and listened, and scoffed and cried out in frustration. But, when the court broke at 12.30pm and many left the confines of the room, Butterly took a seat next to his solicitor and buried himself in that day's edition of the *Irish Times*.

That edition just so happened to have a large close-up photo of his face on the front page. A good photographer could have gotten the perfect shot of Eamon Butterly reading the paper with his own face all over the front page.

His eyes may have been drawn to page 4, where a report from Kitty Holland bore the headline, 'Butterly insists he told doormen not to lock emergency exits'.

He was nonchalant, his usual demeanour when giving evidence, seemingly unperturbed by the events around him. Looking every inch his 78 years, but still sharp and able to think on his feet, he was going to be *the* key witness. The one the families wanted to hear from the most. What would he have to say after all this time? Would he say he felt sorry for any reason? Would he be totally unapologetic? Would he be able to withstand the legal teams and their plethora of questions? Would the handling of his testimony before the inquests precipitate another judicial review in the High Court that could risk the process derailing again?

The search for answers had lasted more than 40 years, and now the man who ran the venue where so many young people had died was in the witness box for the first time since the Keane Tribunal in 1981. At last, the families would be able to ask him the important questions they long sought answers to, and through some of the finest barristers on the island of Ireland.

As Lisa Lawlor, who lost both her parents – Maureen and Francis – in the fire, remarked: 'I knew the name Butterly before I could walk'. And yet despite everyone knowing so much about him, 'I don't even know what he looks like' was a common refrain from some of the family members in the courtroom. He hadn't even been photographed for many years. A lot of them wouldn't have attended the Keane Tribunal all those years ago. An old file photo from the *Irish Times* back then showed Eamon next to his father Patrick. The families and survivors would have attended protests and demonstrations down through the years, but most would never have caught a glimpse of the man himself.

The Pillar Room would usually open half an hour before proceedings were due to begin on any given day, but they were open even earlier on the day of Eamon Butterly's first appearance. The team running the inquests had planned for a big crowd. The court had made just four seats available for journalists, clearly not enough for the level of interest. Dozens packed in early, awaiting Butterly's arrival.

The media were still jostling for seats when word began to filter around: 'he's here'. Some had believed he might not show. But there he was, wearing a black suit, white shirt and dark glasses.

As they did with all the other witnesses, a member of the inquests' team explained the process and how it would work. Butterly engaged in a few last-minute discussions with his solicitor before the registrar said 'all rise', the coroner took her seat and Butterly was invited to come over to the witness box.

At last, he was there. Swearing to tell the truth, the whole truth and nothing but the truth. And so it began.

* * *

The practice for each witness had been the same throughout the inquests. First, the statements – some witnesses had made several – made to the gardaí in the aftermath of the fire were read out to them.

Then, the barristers acting for the coroner were first up with questions. Between them, Simon Mills SC and Mark Tottenham BL had over 40 years of experience in court. Another barrister on the team was Gemma McLoughlin-Burke BL, who was called to the Bar in 2018.

The function of the coroner's legal team was very different from the other legal teams representing clients at the inquests. Phoenix Law and its crew of venerable legal minds were coming at it from the clear perspective of the families. What they believed happened. What they believed went wrong. How they believed their loved ones were failed.

There were also other interested parties acting on behalf of their clients at all times, even if they were not as vocal a presence in the courtroom. One example was Phylis Cobb, a waitress in the Stardust, who told the inquests there was something in her original statement to gardaí that she had never said. John Fitzgerald, a barrister representing An Garda Síochána, put it to the waitress that she'd have been given a chance to read her statement and then signed it before she left the garda station all those years ago. She agreed she had. Not a single word, statement or claim would slip by the legal teams.

Mills, Tottenham and McLoughlin-Burke, along with Amy Walsh BL and solicitor Conor Minogue, had a different role. In legal speak, they act for the coroner, whose job it is to lead an inquest, a 'fact-finding exercise' into the circumstances of someone's death. The legal team comes in when a witness is giving evidence to extract as many facts as possible from them. The more they can glean from a witness's account and recollection, the better a position a jury will be in to come to conclusions at the end.

Much of the tougher questioning of witnesses before Butterly were the domain of Condon, O'Higgins, Fahy, Campbell and Guerin – all of whom were acting for the families. The doormen especially faced tough questioning from Phoenix Law's barristers as they were probed on what they knew about locked doors, mock locking and draping chains.

The coroner's team questioned Butterly rigorously, with Tottenham first and McLoughlin-Burke following after. Word filtering around the Pillar Rooms was that McLoughlin-Burke, in particular, knew the details inside out, so she got the chance to ask Butterly about

THE LAST DISCO

the night of the fire rather than her more experienced colleagues.

Tottenham began his questioning on the afternoon of 21st September. He told Butterly that he was going to ask 'mainly about the background and design of the Stardust'. 'These inquests were called on the application of the families of the deceased to inquire into the circumstances of their deaths,' Tottenham said. 'It's to assist the jury in understanding how these deaths came about.'

He added that he was 'very grateful' to Butterly for being there and said he wanted him to answer to the 'best of [his] recollection'. Tottenham first asked Butterly if the content of his statements read out to the court was to the best of his recollection. He said it was. A few comments in that statement drew sharp intakes of breath from the public gallery, some raised eyebrows.

Three of his statements to gardaí were read out in court. The first two were made shortly after the fire. The third, and by far the most substantive in terms of the length and breadth of the topics covered, was made to gardaí in October 1981, eight months after the fire.

This statement wasn't made in an interview room with gardaí asking questions. It was a question-and-answer format, given to his solicitor, and prepared with his solicitor before being returned to the gardaí.

At one point, the questioning focused on the chains and locks on the doors. Butterly was asked if any consideration had been given to people who may have been fleeing the venue in an emergency such as a fire when partially blinded by smoke, who then saw a lock and chain draped over the panic bars on an emergency exit that they intended to use to get out.

250

At the time, he said that in such a situation, all a person had to do was push the bars, and they would open immediately. 'There was a sign on all of them saying "push bar to open",' he said. As would later be put to him, it was by no means that easy for many who tried to escape the Stardust on the night of the fire.

Butterly was also asked to describe what exactly his role was at the venue. 'In terms of management of Stardust, were you mainly in charge?' Tottenham asked him.

'I was in charge of the managers who managed the whole complex,' Butterly said. 'I was the manager of the managers,' he repeated again.

Tottenham asked: 'All the staff answered to you?'

Butterly replied: 'Yes, and they'd have the whole place to run. [Brian] Peel would run the place.'

He also suggested that Patrick Butterly, his father, essentially ran the whole show. 'My father would make the important decisions, and we would carry out his instructions. He was the boss, really, you know,' he said. And there was one of the main cruxes of what Butterly's account would be.

Although the manager of the Stardust, Eamon Butterly insisted that he wasn't the one who called the shots really. That was his dad. And then he had a general manager in Brian Peel and head doorman in Thomas Kennan who ran the place and who'd make decisions too. Then there was Harold Gardner, the draughtsman who drew up the plans to renovate the building into what became the Stardust, who Butterly said he deferred to on occasions during that process.

Tottenham wrapped up fairly quickly before giving way to McLoughlin-Burke, who was forceful and often withering through her questioning and in responding to the answers she was getting from Butterly.

It was this thread of what exactly his role was at the Stardust that she pulled on vigorously in her questioning of Eamon Butterly. With confirmation from the witness, she listed off a variety of elements: Butterly didn't hire or fire staff, didn't manage staff issues and wasn't told about problems in the nightclub.

He walked around the premises on the nights of various events but didn't keep an eye on whether patrons were underage and didn't make sure exits were unobstructed.

'So, Mr Butterly, what was your job in the Stardust?' Ms McLoughlin-Burke asked.

'My job was to look after the management of the place, through the managers that we had. That was my job. But I still went around and looked at . . .'

'Looked at things?'

'Yeah.'

'And had cups of tea.'

'I would go upstairs for a cup of tea, yeah,' Butterly replied.

And this was just day one.

*   *   *

The coronial system that governs inquests is not as adversarial as one would find in other courts. Obviously, the legal team representing the families wanted to confront Eamon Butterly with tough questions, given that it was his role to manage the Stardust. But there were limits as to what they could ask in an inquest. Questions that were predicated with the words 'blame', 'responsibility' or 'fault' were often seized upon by the coroner, Dr Myra Cullinane, who asked that the question be rephrased or the matter dropped entirely. This was a coroner who was very aware of her role and the limits of what the legislation allowed her to inquire into. Straying from that risked a potential legal challenge to the entire inquests.

Occasionally, Butterly's solicitor Dómhnaill O'Scanaill would take exception to the line of questioning taken. But only occasionally. The coroner would often look at him when a question was posed by one of the Phoenix team, expecting an objection that didn't always come. But, while not objecting frequently, he did make a point on several occasions to interrupt and request the jury be removed while he made a submission. At a tense moment, when Des Fahy put it to Butterly that he was 'deflecting' responsibility onto others for the planning of what to do in an emergency – a claim Butterly denied – O'Scanaill intervened. At these junctures, the jury had to leave the room.

'In my respectful submission,' he began, 'the cross-questioning has drifted beyond the line of pure inquisitorial into one of seeking to establish some sort of liability or responsibility.' Fahy said he hadn't used the words 'liability' or 'fault', and was merely trying to identify responsibility for the policy of having the doors locked in the Stardust at certain times of the evening. The coroner stopped the pair, and said that the use of the word 'responsibility' did have suggestions of liability and that the question could be rephrased.

Butterly's evidence was seen as some of the most crucial to the entire process, with each question posed to him by legal counsel being carefully considered. Each had an objective from Phoenix Law's perspective. The state of

THE LAST DISCO

the doors, the policy around locking and mock locking, and the conversion of the building into the Stardust were all under scrutiny. Butterly's opening gambit was an assertion that it was his head doorman Thomas Kennan's idea to keep the doors locked in the venue, and that he had actually fought against this.

McLoughlin-Burke asked Butterly what efforts he had made to ensure emergency exit doors were not locked while patrons were inside. 'I told [Kennan] that the doors shouldn't be locked,' he said. 'I never saw the doors locked.'

Butterly had previously told gardaí the policy was to keep some of the exit doors locked on disco nights until between 11.30pm and midnight, McLoughlin-Burke reminded the Stardust manager. Butterly replied that as soon as he found out about this practice he had told Kennan to stop it.

He maintained this stance for several days. He told the court that it wasn't his idea to lock the doors of the nightclub – actually, he was the one who tried to stop this practice.

Senior counsel Michael O'Higgins went back to 1981. When asked by the Keane Tribunal who made the decision to lock the doors to stop people getting in for free, his reply was more definitive: 'I made the decision myself.'

'You're owning it 100% there, aren't you?' asked O'Higgins. 'I am, yeah,' replied Butterly. If Butterly had 'owned the decision 100%' then, why, O'Higgins asked, was he now now telling the inquest jury the exact opposite?

'I made the decision with Mr Kennan and [deputy head doorman] Mr Doyle,' said Butterly. Suddenly, it was a shared decision. O'Higgins asked him if he believed the evidence he had given the Tribunal and evidence he had given the inquests was the same, to which Butterly replied: 'I've given the evidence to the best of my ability.'

The fog was creeping in again as Butterly's answers went one way, then another, prompting coroner Dr Myra Cullinane to step in and state it clearly and directly to Butterly: what he said in 1981 and the evidence he'd given so far at her court didn't tally. Why?

'In 1981, the decision was made between the three of us, so I went along with Mr Kennan. That's what I believed last Thursday,' he said, adding: 'It is contradictory all right, yeah [. . .] I believed what I said here, and now you've shown me what I said in the Tribunal, I have to believe that as well.'

O'Higgins claimed there was a 'vagueness' in Butterly's account of the practices surrounding the locking of the doors, and the practice of draping chains around the doors to give the appearance of being locked. He said this 'vagueness' was because Butterly was 'making it up'.

'I'm not making anything up,' Butterly replied.

Nevertheless, this was an example where what Butterly was telling the jury now could be called into question. And it was his own words from back then being put to him that undid his account. From the perspective of the families' legal team, it was an exercise in casting doubt, asking, 'What about this can we believe and take as fact if he was saying different things then and now?'

Butterly made frequent references to his father throughout his evidence. It was his father who Dublin Corporation wrote to after the Specials concert. It was his father who sought planning permission. It was his father who enlisted the services of William White, who wasn't an architect, to draw up the plans for the Stardust. He

THE LAST DISCO

would point out the role his father played at all of these points. Many of them were crucial, such as the aftermath of the Specials concert, when Dublin Corporation said they would appear at the Stardust's next licensing hearing if the problems weren't rectified. He had already referred to his father as 'the boss'. Although the manager of the Stardust, Eamon Butterly would defer to Patrick Butterly at several stages when questioned about the goings-on at the Stardust.

Another topic that came up again and again was the carpet tiles. Eamon Butterly consistently said that if Dublin Corporation had said they shouldn't be used on the walls, they could have told him and he would have taken them down immediately. The Corporation could have said so but didn't, he said. This is what he had told Keane back in 1981.

Michael O'Higgins put it to Butterly that his method of answering on these matters was instructive, as 'when you think there's trouble, you try and blame someone else'.

Butterly replied that wasn't the case and the coroner again interjected to say the inquests were not about apportioning blame but rather that they constituted an inquisitorial forum. O'Higgins said he understood but added that 'we live in the real world' and that if we're establishing facts, we can't ignore the surrounding circumstances.

Another telling exchange came when Butterly was scrutinised over the state of the exit doors on the night. While maintaining that he knew the doors were open at the time of the fire because Thomas Kennan told him so, O'Higgins asked a number of questions about the mock locking, where the chains were draped around the panic bars of the emergency exits. Butterly said that 'mock locking is not locking' and that it 'went on for a while' at the venue. He said it started with the doormen themselves and that 'they did it everywhere'. A crucial element here is whether mock locking impacted how the door functioned. The Keane Tribunal examined this in the clearest way possible: an emergency door was mock locked, and people had to try to open it. Butterly was among those people, and O'Higgins asked him to recall what the result was. Butterly told him: 'If you pressed the bar down the doors would open'. Quick as a flash, O'Higgins shot back, 'No, no, no, Mr Butterly, you actually pressed the bar in the Tribunal and it didn't budge an inch'.

O'Higgins's final question to Butterly was if there was anything he would have done differently. 'I would never got involved in converting that factory to a nightclub [in the late 1970s],' he said. 'I would have knocked it down and built a new one.'

O'Higgins repeated: 'That's the one thing you'd do differently?' and he replied: 'I would, yeah.' It was one of several instances where his answer drew sighs and scoffs of derision and consternation from the families in attendance.

Unlike Leo Doyle, Eamon Butterly would not make any 'boo boo' at the end of his evidence. He was steadfast and absolute in his evidence that the doors were unlocked at the time of the fire, even when conceding the evidence of others who had difficulty getting out through those doors. On the carpet tiles, Keane had said that Butterly's explanation regarding Dublin Corporation was a 'wholly unacceptable approach'. Indeed, in 2023, Butterly would be accused of taking an 'arrogant' approach, which he

THE LAST DISCO

rejected. The similarities between his account of the carpet tiles purchase and that given by Declan Conway – the man who sold him the tiles – were also pointed out. Butterly denied his account was so similar because he'd seen Conway's statement in advance.

For a factor that would cause so much pain for so many years, Butterly's reasoning for using the carpet tiles stood out as its own grim vista so many years on. Those carpet tiles had such a significant role in the loss of life in the Stardust that night. He would concede later that the price of the tiles did 'influence' his decision to purchase them, although it wasn't the first thought on his mind.

It was an innocuous-sounding question from Dáithí MacCárthaigh BL, representing the family of the late Marie Kennedy, that was the most telling. He put it to Butterly that it was an unusual thing to do, to put carpet tiles on a wall.

'It looked well,' Butterly said. 'It was different for the time.'

* * *

After everything they had heard, the video played to the jury was eerily familiar. It was clearly from the 1980s, with the grainy quality of a VHS tape.

It shows a tiered seating area of thin couches covered in red plastic. A fire is set on some seating in the back right. It takes hold slowly, but before long, the surrounding seats also start to decompose. Thick, heavy smoke begins to gather at the top of the room. Blink, and you might miss what happens next: all of the seats in the alcove start to smoulder, and suddenly, an ashtray at the front well,

258

metres from the fire itself, starts to smoulder. Spurts of flame are seen on other seats. The heat in the room quickly grows more and more intense as a flashover starts to develop.

Suddenly, the cameraman is pulled back, and the scene cuts to a wide shot. Intense flames are now pouring out of the alcove, and the cameraman is seen desperately trying to get away. Men in white boiler suits and hard hats step back from the scene, looking at each other in shock, while firemen don breathing apparatus to put out the flames. The fire has taken off with horrifying speed, scale and intensity. 'The experts were astonished at the speed of the fire as the experiment went out of control,' the narrator says, speaking in a clipped British accent, fitting for the time.

The footage was an experiment conducted at the Fire Research Station (FRS), based at Borehamwood in the United Kingdom. The Stardust's West Alcove had been recreated almost exactly, down to the same upholstery, to study how such a small fire turned into an inferno. The only difference is that this was set up as a rig in the middle of a warehouse, where the flames and smoke had space to disperse.

This was a 1980s video known as 'Anatomy of a Fire'. It's of its time, featuring a woefully inappropriate synth soundtrack, but it remained of use to the fire experts speaking to the courtroom. Under the scope of the inquests' fact-finding remit, the cause of the fire was going to be investigated yet again, with the evidence carefully examined and explained to the jury by those trained in the area.

The coroner's choice for this job was Jensen Hughes, a fire engineering consultancy headquartered in the US that specialises in forensic investigations of fire scenes on behalf of the judiciary worldwide. Dr Will Hutchinson, a senior forensic scientist and expert witness in hundreds of cases, would be their lead representative. Flanking him were fire experts retained by the families of victims. The court was told that they would intervene in situations where they diverged from Hutchinson's assessment, but this would happen very little.

From the outset, Hutchinson made it clear that focusing on one answer will not help you to analyse a fire scene. You need to examine eyewitness accounts, photographs of the scene, descriptions of fire damage, and more, combing them all until you can slowly eliminate explanations that aren't considered possible. The hypotheses you're left with can then be tested against real-world experience before you reach your conclusions – while always remaining open to more than one answer. 'We have to keep an open mind and consider everything,' he told the inquests. He approached the matter with such detail that the jury was even given an explanation of what exactly fire is.

Examining a fire that happened 43 years ago is no easy feat. As clear as Dr Hutchinson was about the things he could provide a definitive opinion on, he was equally clear about the things he couldn't be sure about. A lot of this was down to how the scene of the fire at the Stardust was treated. It was cleared in just four days, a process that would take weeks today. 'There's no way, in that time, everything can be preserved and recorded,' he said. Evidence was not handled with care and was lost, meaning no further evaluation is possible beyond any limited initial tests. All this missing information meant he was left with scenarios limited to probable, possible or unlikely.

It was Dr Hutchinson who showed the jury 'Anatomy of a Fire'. He said that, in the test, after just under two minutes, all of the combustible material in the area was 'involved', meaning alight and reacting to the fire. He noted the thick smoke it produced. In the video, it filtered out of the rig and into the hangar. In the Stardust, this smoke had nowhere to go after filling the space under the suspended ceiling.

The now-infamous carpet tiles were also factored into the Borehamwood experiment. The jury heard how researchers found the seats alone couldn't generate the heat necessary to cause their surroundings to combust spontaneously. Dr Hutchinson explained that the tiles were a critical factor; once put into the picture, the heat transfer was such that surrounding seats combusted, and the fire spread rapidly. Initial certification tests were also found to have only considered the tile when placed horizontally. When vertical, like in the Stardust, the fire dynamics changed completely.

But tiles alone don't cause a fire. To explore what did, Dr Hutchinson had to approach a hypothesis that families found deeply uncomfortable: was it started deliberately? All avenues had to be explored. For these inquests, the now-struck-out verdict of the Keane Tribunal had to be considered.

This was a shock to the families. How could we go back to arson now, 15 years after it was dismissed? It was by process of elimination that Dr Hutchinson got there. And it was a question of 'ifs'. If the fire started in the West Alcove, then the probable explanation was that it

THE LAST DISCO

was started deliberately. He said it was unlikely to have started here due to an electrical fault. It was unlikely to have been accidental due to a cigarette or match being left on seats, as they wouldn't have ignited in such a way as to cause the devastation that followed. Testing all the hypotheses elsewhere, he suggested that the fire being started deliberately in the West Alcove as being one of the most likely scenarios.

However, another theory from Keane that had been discarded at the time suddenly gained more weight. The fire was first spotted on the right-hand side of the West Alcove. On the other side of the right-hand wall is the main bar. To be more exact, the fire was spotted on the upper-right-hand side, close to the wall. A hot press in an elevated wooden cabinet was on the other side of that wall. The rest of the bar was largely undamaged, while the hot press cabinet itself had localised fire damage. Dr Hutchinson wasn't presenting any new evidence here, but it was now being seen in a new light. He showed the jury images of the 'poorly made' electrical connections to the hot press included in the Keane Report. There was corrosion around the connection to the immersion heater. This could then build up 'resistive heating', leading to an electrical fault. A fire could have started and travelled upwards through a missing tile in the corner of the bar as if it was a 'chimney'. Those working in the bar would have been unaware – although it is well-documented that staff smelt something burning earlier in the evening – as the fire would have only been noticed when it dropped down from the roof space into the West Alcove. Incidentally, a photograph taken a week later highlighted how ceiling tiles over the hot press appeared to have been 'reinstated' above the hot press after the fire. The fire expert wasn't able to say why this had happened.

Dr Hutchinson concluded his presentation to the jury, saying that either the fire being started deliberately or an electrical fault in the hot press were the most likely causes of the Stardust fire. And it was from here that Seán Guerin SC stepped up for the families he was representing. We had reached a critical moment. We had a fire expert of great pedigree offering two likely scenarios for the cause of the Stardust fire. One of them so happened to be one considered anathema to the families, a stain that had plagued them for decades. It could not be countenanced that we could get this far and arson could be considered seriously again.

At great length, he posed questions to Dr Hutchinson. The jury heard a great deal about electrical arcing, which can cause a flash or sparks. It heard about the materials in the roof space. It heard about the evidence from locals who lived near the Stardust, like Alan Buffini, Anthony Pasquetti and Michael O'Toole, who reported seeing the fire coming from the roof of the Stardust before the patrons inside had seen that fire in the West Alcove. The Blair photograph, taken at 1.35am, showing flames above the roof at a time just before it was spotted inside the club, was another addition to this evidence from what was seen outside.

It would culminate in Dr Hutchinson agreeing that there was 'absolutely no evidence' that anyone in the Stardust deliberately set a fire in the West Alcove on the night. He then agreed that there was a 'detailed evidential basis' that could explain how the fire was started in the hot press, how it was observed outside and then inside shortly after in the West Alcove by the dripping of molten burning material. After all these years, the possibilities for what caused the Stardust fire had finally narrowed and narrowed considerably.

There was more to Jensen Hughes's presentation to the inquests beyond the evidence of Dr Hutchinson. Mark Ross, a former London Fire Brigade member of 28 years, told the inquests that there was nothing the emergency services that rushed to the scene could have done to prevent the deaths of the victims. Ross said it was an 'unprecedented' scene that would have been difficult to plan for.

'I don't think anything done before or during that incident would've changed the outcome,' he said. 'Can I be certain? No, but I think it's highly unlikely. You could liken it to something like Grenfell, turning up to that.' Here was the Stardust being placed alongside another horrific tragedy, that of the Grenfell Tower fire that saw 72 killed in London in 2017.

Another fire expert from Jensen Hughes, Martin Davidson, would shed more light. He told the jury that the building itself wasn't at fault. It had an adequate number of exits, and its design, save for the main entrance, would compare favourably with a modern, compliant building. In this regard, there was no reason why everything had to go so wrong that night.

But there were the breached regulations. Of the 26 bye-laws deemed relevant to the Stardust, Davidson said 16 had not been complied with. For example, the exit doors were not always available to the public, and a fire drill had never been held on the premises. He laid them all out for the jury.

The scale at which the carpet tiles contributed to the fire was put in stark terms: once the roller blinds were lifted in the West Alcove, the fire was building with such ferocity that temperatures became untenable for human life within 52 seconds. Raising the blinds was a crucial moment for everyone who witnessed the fire, but Dr Hutchinson had said he didn't believe that lifting the blinds caused the fire to spread so quickly.

This sort of timeframe was crucial. Davidson demonstrated this with a visualisation of people trying to escape the Stardust, with each person presented as a dot, and what would happen if certain exits were chosen. At some doors, the expert said, there may have been a delay of anywhere between 34 seconds and 92 seconds in evacuating everyone from the building.

The next line spelt it out even more baldly: 'The obstruction of the exits would have contributed to the loss of life.' It went on to say that the time required for escape was longer than the time available for escape.

All these elements were adding up, these timings becoming so crucial. Because of this catalogue of failures, the difference between life and death in the Stardust boiled down to mere seconds. If the evacuation had been conducted well with clear exits and trained staff, things might have gone much differently.

Davidson was the last witness to appear before the inquests to talk about what had happened that night. 'We are concluded with all of the evidence that deals with those facts,' Dr Cullinane told the jury. 'It is on those facts you will be making your deliberations. You've heard all the evidence you have to rely on in that regard.'

* * *

It wouldn't be simple. It never was with the Stardust. At the 11th hour, before the jury would go to consider their verdicts, high-stakes legal chess would be played out in the Pillar Room. This was because Eamon Butterly, at this late stage, wanted to try again to get unlawful killing removed as an option for the jury when the coroner asked for submissions on the possible verdicts. He had failed in his judicial review bid in 2022. Now, his legal team was asking the coroner again to rule it out.

'I think there's a real danger that the integrity of these events that are unique in the history of the State could be affected adversely to the point that would undermine all of the work done by your team over the last almost five years now,' his solicitor Dómhnaill O'Scanaill said. 'The only way that can be achieved and to protect the integrity and good name and freedom from any judgements being made either of a civil or criminal nature is to withdraw from the jury the possible verdict of unlawful killing. I'd urge you would do so.' Unsurprisingly, Phoenix Law pushed hard against it and wanted unlawful killing to remain an option for the jury. But, perhaps surprisingly, this call to remove unlawful killing from the table was backed by Dublin City Council, the modern iteration of Dublin Corporation, as they also said they could be a target of such a verdict. The Dublin City Council legal team went so far as to suggest referring the matter to the High Court for the coroner to be advised on a point of law.

Dr Myra Cullinane would take a week to make up her mind. On unlawful killing, she said she would allow it as an option open to the jury. The sense of relief was palpable in the courtroom on that day, 1st March, but the Butterly legal team would have one last card to play.

And that was another bid to go to the High Court, two years on from the last one before the inquests had even gotten underway.

Seán Guerin told Eamon Butterly's barrister that it was 'beneath' him to make the claim he was making. It was 22nd March, right as the coroner had finished summarising the case before the jury, when Paul O'Higgins entered the court with a new bid to take unlawful killing off the table. It was partly based on a typographical error in the transcript, Guerin said, calling it an 'attempt to profit' from a tiny error. 'It's an attempt to undermine the entire inquest process itself, and it shouldn't be allowed.'

The court was back in the throes of this once more. It would take several days for a decision to be reached, and again, the coroner rejected the submission. This didn't satisfy Butterly's legal team. They wanted to take it further this time.

It was now 27th March, Spy Wednesday, and the Four Courts were deserted. Painters and decorators were working on the corridors and outside the room where the Supreme Court sits, taking advantage of the lack of people around for the Easter break. There were only a few cases listed for the day, but one stood out: an attempt by Butterly to launch another judicial review. This is a mechanism where you can apply to the High Court to challenge the decision-making processes of administrative bodies and lower courts.

This had the potential to derail the inquests by creating an unprecedented situation for the Irish courts. A judicial review can take months, as shown by Butterly's previous attempt, which occupied a chunk of 2022. Could they keep the jury empanelled, out of their regular jobs and

THE LAST DISCO

lives after all this time, for yet another few months? All the while, the families would also be kept waiting.

This sitting was the first step, where a court decides if you can be granted 'leave' to take the review in the first place. Mr Justice Tony O'Connor would sit until 8pm hearing the arguments for and, with Phoenix Law in court, against. There were endless references to sections 30 and 31 of the Coroners Act, of how inquests cannot apportion blame or rule on civil or criminal liability. On the other hand, Phoenix Law said this process had already gone on a year. The coroner had ruled on whether unlawful killing could be on the table several times already, and the High Court had ruled on it in 2022.

Mr Justice O'Connor worked through the night to make sure this could be decided in a timely manner. As Guerin had emphasised, so much was riding on it. This had the potential to change everything. If the jury were discharged – as you couldn't expect them to keep waiting around – the inquests would have to be re-run all over again. Another year of poring over the same evidence. The evidence Keane had heard all those years ago. The families had felt so close to the end of this process, to having that fog lifted, but now that uncertainty could descend all over again.

Legal teams and journalists filed into the High Court again on Holy Thursday. Sometimes, in delivering a judgement, a judge can keep their audience on tenterhooks, dropping hints of the way the wind is blowing as they explain their reasoning. Mr Justice O'Connor didn't. Very early on, he clarified that he was refusing the bid from Eamon Butterly. 'I am satisfied the coroner is acutely conscious of the line that cannot be crossed by the jury,' he said.

268

O'Higgins tried to argue, and was allowed to do so at length, but was shut down. 'I don't mean to be passive-aggressive,' Mr Justice O'Connor said. 'What do you want me to do? I've made my decision. What is it now you want me to do?' O'Higgins dropped it – but not before saying he was anxious to get a copy of the transcript from the marathon legal argument, perhaps hinting at future legal avenues to come. But it was done. Darragh Mackin would later say that this wasn't so much a worry as a frustration. But try telling that to the families who had sleepless nights along with Mr Justice O'Connor as he made his decision. When the Phoenix Law team returned to the Pillar Room in the city centre, the families stood up to applaud them. The very last hurdle had been cleared. It would all be in the jury's hands now.

Chapter 13

THERE WAS A SENSE of quiet disbelief at each stage of the inquests. The mere fact that, after so long, such a major new investigation had even been launched. The moment the first pen portraits were read out, survivors giving evidence – this was really happening.

The fact that so many witnesses were summonsed and emerged from the shadows to talk about the night and the events leading up to it. The fact that Eamon Butterly took to the stand.

That all really happened. The inquests had survived each hurdle or scare thrown at it. Now, the home stretch. The jury started out as 15 people even though just 12 were required by law. This was to safeguard against people having to drop out – two had, and 13 remained. On April 3rd, the coroner drew numbers at random, and the juror whose number wasn't picked was thanked for his time and told that he would not be part of the deliberation process. The coroner gave the panel their final address. This was really happening.

Their deliberations would not take place in open court. The jury would retire and consider in private what they had heard over the previous months. In the weeks leading up to their deliberations, they heard a summary of the evidence to date to ensure it was fresh in their mind. They could request extra details or clarifications throughout their deliberations. The only roles that the court and coroner played were when the jury sought guidance or had queries on the questions being posed to them.

Dr Cullinane issued them with a clear direction. 'This is where the focus is on you,' she said. 'To sit on the jury brings with it great responsibility. You must approach your task in an objective manner based on the law and the facts you have heard in evidence. You must be dispassionate and clinical in your approach.'

The inquests themselves were clinical, dissecting the events of the fire in a meticulous manner, but they were far from dispassionate. From the start, the young lives that had been taken away from their families and community were at the centre of the process. But it's not something that a jury allows to cloud their judgement.

Each death would be considered separately, although a single overarching verdict could be delivered if all 48 were the same, and the jury also had to confirm the date the person was identified, express if they were satisfied with the identification, and state the cause, date and place of death.

A separate, extensive questionnaire was also to be completed, featuring questions ranging from whether the cause of the fire could be determined to whether the exit doors were locked. The questionnaire ended with an opportunity for the jury to provide recommendations on how to prevent similar deaths in the future.

The aim was to reach a unanimous decision, that each member of the jury would be in agreement on the final verdict. That subsequently proved to be a sticking point.

The panel did not have a binary choice of guilty or not guilty. There was no accused whom they had to judge, so

THE LAST DISCO

their findings were more in-depth and nuanced than in a criminal trial.

An inquest can reach a range of verdicts. These can include natural causes, suicide or industrial disease, for example. But just five were available to this jury: accidental death, misadventure, an open verdict, a narrative verdict and unlawful killing.

The first three are easiest explained using the example of a single-car collision in which a person dies. A verdict of accidental death could be returned if they simply lost control; it was unforeseen, and there were no other factors at play. Misadventure could be considered if the driver was speeding; the person died due to a risk they were taking. Unlawful killing could be returned if the crash was caused by a fault that the car's manufacturer was aware of prior to the accident and had failed to address; someone was aware of potential harm and failed to take action.

An open verdict simply means that there is no clear indication of what caused the death. A narrative verdict is given when the circumstances that led to the person's death don't fit neatly into the other categories, and the jury can outline the reasons why that is.

Unlawful killing, having proved so controversial throughout, was the one on which the coroner gave her most detailed advice. She advised the jury that to return this verdict, they must apply a more rigorous test than the others: 'beyond reasonable doubt'.

'You must find that there has been a failure by a person or persons to a very high degree to observe such a course of action as experience shows to be necessary if substantial injury to others is to be avoided,' Dr Cullinane said, at all times emphasising that no person can be named as being responsible for the deaths. It was a fact-finding mission. No one was on trial.

There was huge caution attached to this potential finding. It carried the most weight in terms of potential civil or criminal cases that could be pursued in the future. At an early stage of deliberations, the jury asked the coroner if their findings could be used in potential future cases but were told they could not consider that and instead had to focus on the task assigned to them, namely reaching a conclusion on how the 48 were killed.

In closing arguments, the case for unlawful killing was put forward strongly by the family's legal representation, honing in on the practice of locking the doors.

Michael O'Higgins told the court that Eamon Butterly's credibility was 'shredded beyond redemption' over the conflict between the answers he gave on this in 1981 compared to 2023. He described the 'long road' to get here and gave a powerful sense of this road and who had trodden it. 'But first, I'd like to reflect on not just why we're here but why we are here 43 years later,' he said. 'How is that? The answer, ladies and gentlemen, is quite simple. Women. Mothers, daughters, siblings. Women possessed of indomitable spirit.'

'The locking of doors and what flowed from that runs through the culture of the Stardust like the rainbow colours through a stick of rock,' Des Fahy said. 'You've all the evidence you need.'

'Your duty now is to consider the verdicts, that evidence that these 48 victims deserve. Those verdicts, we say, are that each and every one of them was unlawfully killed. These 48 people lost their dignity because of the cruel and inhumane way in which they died. You can start the process of giving them that dignity back.'

This pair, along with Brenda Campbell, Bernard Condon and Seán Guerin, all came at it from different perspectives, but all emphasised that the jury should return a verdict of unlawful killing.

Condon referenced the *Titanic* and Roy Keane in his closing submission, quoting the latter by saying 'fail to prepare, prepare to fail' in relation to the lack of staff training or fire drills at the Stardust. On the issue of the wall coverings, he simply said in a derisive tone: 'Carpet tiles. On a wall. You don't really need to go much further. On a wall. On all the walls.'

Guerin, going last, was the most sombre. He said that the Stardust families have waited longer than Moses had wandered in the desert without justice.

He told the jury that they could offer these families a path out of the wilderness after all these years by returning a verdict of unlawful killing. 'There is no promised land for the families of these victims,' Guerin said. 'For as long as they live, they will live with their loss and their grief. But it may be, after all this time, and when they go to their rest, they can know why their children and their sisters and brothers never came home.

'Why did none of them come home? Why will they not grow old as their mothers and their families have grown old waiting to find out how they died? It has taken a very long time. Justice delayed may yet not be denied. Justice may yet be done.'

With these submissions to consider, as well as the plethora of evidence, the jury began deliberating on Wednesday, 3rd April 2024. The wait started off patiently.

Some questions would come in from the jury, and they would go off again to consider. This was the most important of deliberations in Ireland's longest-ever inquest. They had to take their time. The secrecy of the jury room is absolute. No one else can know what's going on in there. In the vacuum outside, journalists and legal teams began to fill it with their own predictions based on nothing. 'It'll be Thursday . . . Friday . . . next week.'

The jury entered its third week of deliberations on Monday, 15th April. Even with the dearth of information, the sense was building that it was close. The questions seemed to be geared around the tests for unlawful killing. One of the jury members had asked whether they should consider Caroline Carey's unborn child the 49th Stardust victim, with the coroner clarifying the inquests were about investigating the deaths of the 48. But slowly, an end was in sight.

* * *

The Pillar Room was packed for a day so very, very long in the making.

It was a day in the making, almost 24 hours on from the jury saying they had reached a majority verdict. It was 40 hours in the making, as that was how long the jury had spent deliberating on their verdicts. The patience displayed at the start – from the families and the legal teams – to give them the space to come to this momentous decision had begun to fray as the hours ticked on into days and weeks.

This was a year in the making. April 2023 marked the start of the inquests with the very first pen portraits. And here we still were, a year later. Gertrude Barrett had been in court every single day it sat across that year and she was there every day of the jury's deliberations. She was here again for the final day.

This day was five years in the making. Almost five years since the Attorney General had granted the fresh inquests in the first place, saying there'd been an 'insufficiency of inquiry' at the original inquests, and it was in the public interest to look at this again. As Seán Guerin had told the jury in his closing submission, there was no question of there being an insufficiency this time.

And, of course, this was 43 years in the making. It had been 43 years since that awful night that took away everything from them. As families travelled from far and wide to be in Dublin city on that cloudy and brisk April day, they did so with hope that the truth they'd sought for so long was finally within their grasp.

Families were invited to attend from 11am that morning, with the coroner's staff scrambling to accommodate everyone. Where she had predominantly posed the questions to witnesses throughout the inquests, Gemma McLoughlin-Burke was now mucking in with the other coronial staff, trying to sort out chairs for everyone who needed them. There was no question of the legal teams taking their usual seats; these were given up to help accommodate the hundreds of family members who had shown up on the day. The table that usually accommodated Brabazon Solicitors, representing the Kennedy family, was given to some of the parents of the deceased, poignant in that so very few of them would be able to be here on this day.

More and more people were logging in online for this moment, the number of attendees on the Zoom call ticking up and up. Suddenly, a message on screen: so many people had joined that it was now full.

So many faces in the courtroom were recognisable from their campaigning over the years or their appearances at the inquests. Antoinette Keegan and her family. Maurice and Phyllis McHugh. Bridget McDermott, in her late eighties but here all these years on with her children. Samantha Curran, who lost her mother Helena Mangan. Lisa Lawlor, who lost both her parents – Francis and Maureen – to the Stardust fire. Alison Croker, whose sister Jacqueline died. Pat Dunne, whose brother Brian died. Susan Behan, whose brother Johnny died. The Frazers. The Barretts. The Buckleys. All of them. All here for this most important of days. They embraced and talked. Nervous, anxious, apprehensive. Eyes constantly on their watches. The time ticked ever towards 2pm, when they'd find out at last.

Less than a handful of journalists had regularly attended the inquests throughout the year it had sat, but there was a veritable media scrum building from before 11am, with cameras and microphones galore. While they may not have paid the closest attention while it was ongoing, every news outlet in the country knew the significance of this day. The BBC and Sky News were among the foreign outlets in attendance. The regular media attendees were granted seats inside the packed courtroom, while others found space at the edges of the hall. Some people doubled up, sharing seats with each other. At the back of the room, people stood shoulder to shoulder, wedged in tight. Some ended up in the lobby, where the receptionist played an audio feed off her phone. One reporter opted to crouch outside in the cold with a laptop balanced on his knees,

THE LAST DISCO

peering in through a door opened to let air into the courtroom.

It had become something of a running joke among the reporters covering the inquests that the proceedings never started on time. That it was incapable of doing so, that if they had been told an 11am start the day before, it would be best to add on another 15 minutes or half an hour at least. This would not do today. This was already so long in the making. The families had waited long enough.

And so with the call of 'all rise', the coroner and the jury entered the courtroom just after 2pm. 'Good afternoon,' Dr Myra Cullinane began. Her first question to the foreman was to reiterate what we'd learned a day before, that the jury had reached majority verdicts in this case. The foreman said they had.

The next question sent a ripple through the crowd. So striking that after so long, such a simple question could mean so much.

'Have you reached the same verdict in relation to each of the deceased?' Dr Cullinane asked.

'We have,' the jury foreman said. As one, there was a collective intake of breath. The families and the lawyers knew what this meant. The same verdict for each person. No equivocation. No grey area. This was all or nothing.

Then it went through each person. Starting with Michael Barrett. Their cause of death. The date of their death. The location of their death. The date they were identified. In most cases, the Stardust victims had died as a result of rapid incapacitation due to fire, fumes and heat. One of the desperately sad facts of the Stardust played out when the date of identification was given as 2007 for five of

278

the deceased: Richard Bennett, Michael Ffrench, Murty Kavanagh, Eamon Loughman and Paul Wade, who were all buried together and not identified until years later. It brought back memories of the pen portrait for Murty, where his sister Terry Jones recalled how their father was a 'broken man' after the fire and would always say, 'I would love to know where my son is buried'.

After finishing with Paul Wade, the coroner then turned to the general questionnaire that the jury had been given and what their answers to that had been.

The answer to each would cause a sharp intake of breath. Again, after so very long, the impact of each of these answers for the families cannot be overstated.

'Are you able to establish where the fire started? The answer given by the jury is yes,' the coroner said. 'If so, where? The answer is the hot press in the dispense [main] bar.

'Are you able to establish the cause of the fire? You have answered the cause was an electrical fault in the hot press.'

The sense of relief was palpable. Arson, that horrible stain on the victims and their loved ones for so long, was gone. The jury had found that the Stardust fire had started as an electrical fault in the hot press of the main bar. That's what started all of this. There was also a sense of gratitude to the jury. 'We knew it wasn't arson,' one family member said. 'And they believed us.'

There was more to come. The jury was not able to establish the time at which the fire started. But they could say that it was first spotted outside the Stardust between 1.20 and 1.40am. They could also say that it was first spotted inside between 1.35am and 1.40am.

THE LAST DISCO

The jury said that the polyurethane foam in the seating and the height of the ceiling in the West Alcove contributed to the spread of the fire. They also said that those carpet tiles – those desperately dangerous carpet tiles that Eamon Butterly had said 'looked well' – contributed to the spread of the fire.

When asked about the factors that impeded the deceased in their ability to escape the building, they said the lack of visibility because of the black smoke, the toxicity of the smoke, the heat of the fire, the speed of its spread and the lack of staff preparedness all contributed to this.

The next one was a big one. At the time of the fire, were any of the exits to the Stardust locked, chained or otherwise obstructed? The answer to this was yes. Did the state of these exits impede the ability of the deceased to access emergency exits or to exit through them? Again, the answer was yes.

The families could see what way this was going. All the signs were pointing one way. As the last few questions addressing the actions of the emergency services were run through, the groundswell began to build. They held each other's hands. The moment was near. The anticipation almost unbearable. Forty-three years of hurt, of pain, of frustration and of grief brought to this point. To the five seconds it took for the coroner to invite the foreman to announce the verdict of the jury to its delivery.

Unlawful killing.

As one, they rose. They rose shouting. They rose crying. They rose holding on to one another. It seemed to last an eternity. The dam bursting. The pain of four decades released. Amidst the din, one voice shouted clearly, 'At last'. At last, they had the truth that had long been denied to them. At last, the justice they had sought for their loved ones. At last, the Irish State would acknowledge what they had always known. The 48 should have come home. This should never have happened. They were unlawfully killed.

No one who was in that room when those two words were said will ever forget it. It'll be a memory that stays with them for the rest of their lives. It wasn't just the families shedding tears. It was the legal teams, the media, the members of the jury, who had all been here for a part of this journey too. To see the long journey of so many vindicated at long last. The working-class people who were ignored and told to go away but would never go away. Could never. Their love for The 48 was so strong, their grief so raw. They couldn't bear the smears against them. They would fight and fight, and never give up. And, on 18th April 2024, they would do them proud.

Antoinette Keegan, who would give her life to fight for her two sisters and her parents, who never gave up, vindicated. Gerty Barrett, there every single day for her son Michael, vindicated. Bridget McDermott. Maurice Frazer. Maurice and Phyllis McHugh. Samantha Curran. Every single one of them, all vindicated. Their loved ones buried in the black smoke of the Stardust brought out into the light. They were unlawfully killed.

After a few seconds, Dr Cullinane asked for quiet inside the courtroom. A hush fell over the room again. She then read out the jury's recommendations, which said building regulations in Ireland should be frequently revised and that the target of inspections for places of public resort should be increased from 70% every two years to 100% annually to prevent something like this from ever happening again.

THE LAST DISCO

'These were the longest inquests in the history of this State,' Dr Cullinane said, paying tribute to the great act of public service the jury had undertaken. She said that the passing of the years hadn't diminished the horror of the evidence they'd heard; she praised them for listening intently throughout. This prompted the families as one to give a standing ovation to the jury.

She acknowledged that the Stardust fire was a source of ongoing grief and was the defining loss of their lives. She urged them to take solace from these fresh inquests.

'The fact they've been held is in no small part due to the persistence and commitment of families over the years,' she said. 'We remember the 48 people who lost their lives. It is their lives we've sought to vindicate by way of these inquests.'

When the coroner rose for the last time, the mood gave way to jubilation in the Pillar Room. People went to and fro to embrace each other. They'd been together on this journey; this was a true moment to savour and celebrate. Everyone wanted to hug Darragh Mackin. It was he who had set them on this path to inquests. They had been promised so much over the years and then delivered little. Mackin had been true to his word and had brought them along to reach this most important of days. Standing on a chair, he was applauded by the families as he addressed them on what would happen now.

Just a few minutes' walk from the gate of the Pillar Room on the eastern side of Parnell Street is the Garden of Remembrance. Opened for the semicentennial of the Easter Rising in 1966, it was dedicated to the memory of 'all those who gave their lives in the cause of Irish freedom'.

It felt like a fitting place for the Stardust families to march after they got justice, at last, for their loved ones. With a dozen or more photographers and camera crews outside, they marched up the road holding a banner bearing the portraits of The 48 with the words 'They Never Came Home'. A loudspeaker was quickly set up and played 'You'll Never Walk Alone' as they walked as one, singing, with those not holding the banner holding framed photographs of their loved ones. Given the similarities between the tragedy of the Stardust and Hillsborough, the song's significance was not lost on anyone.

With the cameras rolling and the media assembled, one by one, they took to a makeshift podium with the kind of 'unbending clarity' that Gertrude Barrett had shown on the very first day of the inquests a year before.

Maurice Frazer was among the first to call for a 'meaningful public apology' from the Irish State. 'For 43 long years, we've been relentless in a quest for justice for our dear sister Thelma, her boyfriend, Michael, and 46 others,' he said. 'We tirelessly battled against the barriers and the closed doors of Ireland's political and justice systems, clinging to hope, even when it seemed futile. Finally, those doors were broken open.

'Throughout this journey, families have endured the unbearable pain of losing parents, siblings and cherished friends, even decades later. For those decades, our hearts and minds have been shattered, and the mental toll has been overwhelming and exhausting, persisting day after weary day. In 2009, the finding of the Stardust Tribunal 1981 of probable arson was finally removed. That's 28 years later, 28 years of our loved ones' names smeared with a label of arson.

'This is why we, the families, need a meaningful public apology from the Irish State. Today marks a turning point, a step towards closure, healing, towards a future where justice prevails.'

Gerty Barrett said there are no boundaries 'when you're driven by desire'. 'This day belongs to my son Michael and the 47 others that perished with him,' she said. 'This is their day.' She also thanked the people who had stayed with them and never given up, 'because I know I never did'.

Pat Dunne said that her brother Brian Hobbs had been 'number 29' for years, but now he was Brian again. She said the jury had been fantastic because 'they were regular people on the street like all of us'.

Samantha Curran said she'd fought to find out the truth of what had happened to her mother Helena. 'It's just devastated me that much,' she said. 'But hopefully, now, we can move on. For me, it was to be a better parent to my kids. Now I've got justice, I can focus on my own family and make sure my kids have the parents I never had.'

Susan Behan said she wanted families to maybe find some peace from all of this now. 'They've done everything they possibly can,' she said. 'And justice has been served. [My parents] are here in spirit as is my brother and the 47. I know they'd be proud. And they'd be saying "well done".'

* * *

A week is a long time in politics. In March 2024, Simon Harris began the week after St Patrick's Day as the Minister for Higher Education and ended it as the Taoiseach-in-waiting following Leo Varadkar's shock departure.

The families of the 48 Stardust victims would scarcely have thought that within a week of the verdicts, they'd not only have long, detailed conversations with Harris in Government Buildings, but they'd also receive such a comprehensive apology in Dáil Éireann.

They barely had time to digest the verdicts delivered on Thursday, 18th April before their meetings with the Taoiseach the following Saturday. He said he was very keen to meet the families to assure them that he was listening as he knew they had felt they were unheard for decades. From that early stage, Harris was indicating that an apology could and would be forthcoming. After getting justice from the verdicts, this move was vital.

He stood up in the Dáil just a few days later to deliver it. Families had long been let down by taoisigh and politicians. Harris, not even born at the time of the Stardust fire, appeared to want a clean break from that, to try to right those wrongs. Families packed into the small public gallery to watch.

'Today, we say formally and without any equivocation, we are sorry,' he said. 'We failed you when you needed us the most. From the very beginning, we should have stood with you, but instead, we forced you to stand against us.'

Harris said he hoped the verdicts marked a turning point and a time when the State finally began to put things right. Well prepared to a fault, he then spoke a few words about each of the deceased, echoing what was said in the pen portraits. He acknowledged the injured and the mental scars so many bore from the Stardust.

'Being accused of telling lies, the smear of arson attached to their loved ones,' he said. This in itself was an extraordinary assertion – the Taoiseach of Ireland calling the finding of a government-established Tribunal of Inquiry a 'smear'. It felt significant.

He went on: 'Having their grief and sadness misconstrued as madness. A sense of threat and suppression when you simply started looking for answers. Stigma heaped upon sorrow bred shame and silence. The intergenerational and communal ripple effect of so much agony and the lack of closure.[. . .]

'For all of this, as Taoiseach, on behalf of the State, I apologise unreservedly to all the families of the Stardust victims and all the survivors for the hurt that was done to them and for the profoundly painful years of struggle for the truth. I apologise to the families that those present on the night of the fire were wrongly criminalised through the allegation of arson, which was an attack on their reputations. I say today clearly in Dáil Éireann, every person there was innocent. I say today, the truth is now known. I say today, not only were they innocent, they were unlawfully killed.'

Harris added that he had told his ministers to report back on the implementation of the jury's recommendations. Over four decades on from the Stardust, campaigners would welcome a long-overdue focus put on fire safety and prevention in Ireland to ensure no tragedy like this ever happened again. 'We need to make sure there's no delay,' Lynn Boylan said. She added that Dublin Fire Brigade remains 'completely under-resourced', and part-time retained firefighters in other parts of Ireland remain underpaid. 'Maybe that would be a fitting tribute for the government to actually fund the fire services that have been such great supporters of the families throughout the years.'

The Taoiseach also said he had asked his department to prepare proposals for how to 'appropriately commemorate the disaster'.

There would be many speeches in the Dáil that day. Seán Haughey, local TD and son of former taoiseach Charles, acknowledged that he had not done enough for the families over the years. 'I also admit that my relations with the committee were at times fraught,' he said. 'I do regret that. I admit too that when Pat McCartan issued his finding in 2017 to the effect that no new inquiry was warranted, I could not see how the case could be advanced further.' His words were, to put it kindly, not well received.

Sinn Féin leader Mary Lou McDonald – who had also met with the families after the verdicts – said that successive governments had hoped that the families would eventually stop, eventually shut up, eventually give up and eventually go away. 'Those governments forgot one very important thing,' she said. 'You do not mess with Dublin ma's; you do not mess with Dublin da's. You do not mess with Irish mammies, daddies and families, not when they are fighting for justice for their children, because you will lose and they will win, even if it takes them 43 long years. They will win.'

The speeches lasted hours. But it was only right, too. Too often, politicians had said there was nothing they could do for the Stardust families. The least they could do after all this time was say sorry.

* * *

'For our family, I know they couldn't be more proud of my mother. All of us. It's done. We can move forward.

Whatever happens now. We've got unlawful killing. We've gotten the [State] apology. I remember coming out of the Dáil and getting into the fresh air and just feeling "Oh my god, this is done".'

Selina McDermott felt like a weight had been lifted off her shoulders that week. It had been a whirlwind. Unlawful killing followed by a meeting with the Taoiseach in Government Buildings and then Simon Harris's Dáil apology. The verdict of unlawful killing was a release of decades of frustration and heartache.

'There's been happy times and sad times,' she said. 'There were many arguments between the families through those 43 years about the direction to go in getting the truth. I remember meetings in my ma's kitchen. In Gertrude Barrett's kitchen. I'd be making the tea and the sandwiches. I remember spilling the buckets from the collections we'd have at the supermarket and we'd count it to see how short we were of paying a solicitor.

'It's still so hard to believe it took this long. You pinch yourself to make sure that it's actually happened.'

In her chats with various politicians, Selina was told the 'way it was' on those days throughout the years when the Stardust families would march with their placards and their calls for new inquiries. Or simply their calls just to be listened to.

The conversations were 'Ah here, listen, don't touch them, just ignore them, what they want they're not going to get and they're very hard to deal with, what they want, we can't give them,' she said. 'That was the lingo in the Government Buildings behind the doors. "They'll go away in the end". By jaysus. But they were so determined, the mothers and fathers.'

Such treatment of a group of working-class people who have now been vindicated so many years later speaks for itself. It's to their eternal credit that they never gave up, despite all the promises and false dawns and roadblocks in their way.

It's a day Errol Buckley will never forget. 'Dynamite' is the word he uses to describe the unlawful killing verdict. 'The relief I got when I came out of that place,' he said. 'I hope we can all relax now. I was under pressure but I'm finished with it now. It's been lingering on and on and on. The light at the end of the tunnel is brilliant.'

In the aftermath, Errol in particular felt grateful to the witnesses who came forward to tell their story at the inquests. For some, it was the first time they had talked about it. 'I'd like to thank all of them,' he said. 'There were loads of different stories that went into them deciding it was unlawful killing. If this was all done right at the start, that would have happened.'

Linda Bishop now also reflects on this new process, with an inquest that was respectful and gave dignity to the families and the survivors. This was a dignity denied to them in the past.

'I was one that Mary Lou McDonald was talking about – the 18-year-old who felt bullied and intimidated,' she said. 'It felt then like the barristers had made their mind up. We were so scared. We were traumatised. No one asked if I was okay. This time, I was ready to come out swinging with both hands. But they were respectful. They listened to us. They believed what we were saying.'

The story of the Stardust fire now also has a vital element that was missing for so long: the cause of the fire. This hung over the story like few other elements did, casting a dark shadow every step of the way. This cloud is lifted, but absolute certainty is still out of reach. The jury decided that, on the balance of probabilities, an electrical fault in the hot press started the fire; 'balance of probabilities' is a less stringent measure than beyond reasonable doubt. However, the evidence of the fire experts was clear and gave credence to the roof space theories that the families put forward repeatedly in the 2000s and 2010s, theories that were so frequently dismissed. It can never be said with 100% certainty what caused the fire – but it is clear what the most likely cause was.

But there are so many other things about the Stardust fire that we will never know. The testimony on who locked, or unlocked, or didn't lock or didn't unlock, the emergency exit doors was given as honest, sworn evidence in court by a number of people, but it is still a difficult picture to piece together. There are elements, too, lost to the sands of time: the talk of a sprinkler system installed when the building was a factory being removed prior to its conversion into a nightclub, the motor pumps used turning up for sale years later. It wasn't a requirement, and the system was possibly unsuitable for the building, but it's just one small part of the story that has slipped through the cracks if ever it was the case. What has fallen into those cracks doesn't necessarily need to be recovered; truth is to be found in so many other areas now.

The legacy of the Stardust inquests could be far-ranging beyond just those involved in this terrible tragedy. A whole raft of new legislation was needed to ensure that the inquests could go ahead at all due to the issues around means tests for legal aid and for the jury to be chosen and compensated for their time. The inquests featured pen portraits, an unprecedented approach that put families at the centre of the process. And what the Stardust inquests showed more than anything else is that they are a means to get to the truth. To get justice.

'We've changed this once; it works. Let's change it again,' said Darragh Mackin a week on from the verdicts. 'We've made submissions to the coronial reform that's ongoing in the Department of Justice and we hope this will be listened to.'

Mackin doesn't think that inquests should replace larger-scale inquiries and says there's still a place for them. He said thinking that the Keane Tribunal was 'done wrong' isn't the way to look at it. For him, it was simply a case of 'Keane didn't work' and the correct question to ask was why these inquests worked.

Maurice Frazer agreed that the coronial system clearly needs updating on the back of the inquests. He said it was only down to the individual decision by Myra Cullinane that allowed pen portraits at the inquests but that it should be the norm to humanise the deceased at proceedings such as this.

Frazer also believes that the work done by the families can be a guide to others in Ireland who are fighting historical wrongs in this country, citing the Tuam babies – where hundreds of babies were buried in a disused septic tank at a mother and baby home – and the Whiddy Island disaster. 'It's opened up all those injustices that have been swept under the carpet,' he said, adding that Michael Kingston, the son of a Whiddy Island victim, stood with the families on the day of the unlawful killing verdict.

Frazer thinks that unlawful killing and the State apology are 'steps towards justice'. He said that it was a day that the doors were finally opened for all of the families. 'We are free now,' he said. 'God knows what'll happen down the line. That's another day's work.'

There are other potential legal avenues this story could take. When Eamon Butterly lost his bid to take a judicial review at the last gasp of the proceedings in March 2024, his barrister Paul O'Higgins SC pointedly requested the audio recording of the proceedings as they wrapped up. Whether any legal challenges will be taken against the verdicts in the inquests remains to be seen.

Both Frazer and Errol Buckley said they would like to see the matter looked at by the gardaí and Director of Public Prosecutions. It can't be left hanging, they said. Garda Commissioner Drew Harris said in the aftermath of the verdicts that gardaí are reviewing the files submitted to the DPP, both in the 1980s and in 2016. In both cases, the DPP recommended that no charges be brought. However, cold-case detectives were ordered to re-examine the potential for a criminal prosecution in the wake of the unlawful killing verdicts.

On the potential for criminal charges in the future, Mackin acknowledged that historical prosecutions in Ireland are usually very difficult to achieve. 'We have to be realistic in understanding the difficulties the DPP faces in prosecuting historically,' he said. 'But in many ways, whether or not a decision is taken to prosecute, it does not detract from the truth and does not detract from the truth of the verdict that was returned at the inquests of unlawful killing.'

That road will be followed, just like all the other roads through the years. But Mackin also acknowledged just what it's taken from people to get here. Redress from the government is the very least that should be forthcoming, he said, to ensure that families are compensated for the loss they have sustained over all these years.

'Some of these families have dedicated their entire lives,' he said. 'Their entire lives. They have given up everything to try and campaign for justice. We know now that should never have happened. Some of these families have given up decades of their lives to try to overturn that label of arson. We know now that's not true. The very least the government needs to do is put that right and ensure those who dedicated their time are adequately compensated.'

The government has already made clear that there will be a redress scheme, with the details still being worked out at the time of publication.

The Taoiseach's statement in the Dáil that he would now stand by the Stardust families was followed with action within a few days of his apology. Families received an email that same week giving details of the counselling that would be made available. It recalled the words of the late Eugene Kelly five years before, sitting in his Dublin home holding his brother Robert's jacket: 'First you need closure, and then you get counselling.'

As the dust settles, some might find that grief is still waiting in the wings to be felt, psychologist Niamh Fitzpatrick said. Grieving is a complicated and chaotic process, but this would have been heightened for the Stardust families by the many obstacles they faced in their quest for the truth, and compounded by the length of time it has taken to overcome them. 'Not having to chase the truth can clear a space for that grieving to continue as it needs to,' she said. It's a deeply personal experience; some may want to seek professional support. 'When you have traumatic loss, when you have circumstances like this, when you have investigations and

THE LAST DISCO

inquests which will plunge people back into that space, then it's entirely understandable.'

Selina said that many of the bereaved will take up the option. But it comes far too late for their mother Bridget. 'Our concern always was that my ma was okay,' she said, adding that doctors who see her didn't know until recently that she had lost three children. 'No matter where my mother went, she'd never mention the Stardust. My ma told us never to. She was always so dignified in that way.'

The McDermotts were invited into the Dáil along with all of the other families for the State apology. 'It was a victory, but I felt very sad as well,' Selina said. 'You're full of mixed emotions. I felt sad looking down. How different my life could've been. Everybody's lives. My family's. Everyone up in the gallery thinking the same. It was so sad to think it took this length of time and put us through all of that torment.'

As Seán Guerin said in his closing statement, there will be 'no promised land' for the bereaved families of the Stardust, even with an unlawful killing verdict. And Fitzpatrick agreed the truth may only go so far, with the residual feelings of grief and loss difficult to shake for some people.

Fitzpatrick added that it was important to say that while loss and grief can change us forever, it is possible to live, to enjoy life again after loss. 'There is hope,' she said. But it may take some time.

'It's going to take a while,' Linda Bishop agreed. 'It's bittersweet for everybody. I can imagine we'll all meet each other in the street years from now and say "did we go through all that? How did we go through all that?" Like it will have all been so surreal.'

It's still so hard for it all to sink in as, even at the end of this process and the long, long battle they should never have had to fight, families still wake up every day without their loved ones. At the end of this long road, their loved one is still gone. That can never change.

The truth can offer some comfort. They now know, and will always know, that they shouldn't have died. That they were unlawfully killed. They fought to the bitter end to vindicate their names and have done so.

The Stardust story, partially through the actions of the State, has become one of the most enduring tragedies in Irish history. As a nation, Ireland can never, and should never, forget it.

As when that smear of arson was finally struck from the record in 2009 and long-time Stardust campaigner Tommy Broughan TD stood up in the Dáil, he quoted the verse from a World War I poem on the memorial stone in tribute to the Stardust victims at Beaumont Hospital:

They shall not grow old, as we that are left grow old;
Age shall not weary them, nor the years condemn,
At the going down of the sun and in the morning.
We will remember them.
('The Fallen', Laurence Binyon, 1914)

* * *

The following are the names of all of those who died in the Stardust fire:

Michael Barrett
Richard Bennett

THE LAST DISCO

Carol Bissett
James Buckley
Paula Byrne
Caroline Carey
John Colgan
Jacqueline Croker
Liam Dunne
Michael Farrell
Michael Ffrench
David Flood
Thelma Frazer
Josephine Glen
Michael Griffiths
Robert Hillick
Brian Hobbs
Eugene Hogan
Murtagh Kavanagh
Martina Keegan
Mary Keegan
Robert Kelly
Mary Kennedy
Mary Kenny
Margaret Kiernan
Sandra Lawless
Francis Lawlor
Maureen Lawlor
Paula Lewis
Eamon Loughman
Donna Mahon
Helena Mangan
George McDermott
Marcella McDermott

William McDermott
Julie McDonnell
Teresa McDonnell
Gerard McGrath
Caroline McHugh
James Millar
Susan Morgan
David Morton
Kathleen Muldoon
George O'Connor
Brendan O'Meara
John Stout
Margaret Thornton
Paul Wade

All of them were unlawfully killed.

* * *

The inquests were the first time that an Irish coronial court had heard pen portraits of all the victims – something that will hopefully happen more in future proceedings. For practical reasons we could not include all of these in the book, but we would encourage readers to seek them out. They can be read on the Phoenix Law website or viewed on the RTÉ Player, where they are read out by the loved ones of the people who died.

Acknowledgements

The authors would like to thank the families and loved ones of The 48. In the name of truth and closure, you were willing to relive the most painful experience of your lives over and over to the public and to the media over four decades. This takes unfathomable courage, and to do so with such dignity throughout. The Irish public owe you a debt of gratitude. We want to thank and pay tribute to the survivors too, and acknowledge what you have been through over the decades. Journalists bear huge responsibility in the retelling of these stories to ensure that they are approached in a sensitive, careful and faithful way. It is something we have always kept at the front of our minds, and we hope we have achieved it in this book.

Thank you to everyone who spoke to us for this book. Your stories are so important, and we appreciate your trust in us.

We would like to thank Eriu for the opportunity to transform our work into this book and Deirdre Nolan in particular for making it happen. A massive thank you to everyone else involved in the publishing process, including Lisa Gilmour, Neil Burkey, and the Bonnier Books and Gill Hess teams.

An important thank you is owed to *The Journal* for giving us the time and space to record the Stardust documentary podcast in 2019 (including all the unsung voice actors we pulled from the newsroom to take part), and for supporting us in writing this book. Particular thanks to DCU's School of Communications, the Mary Raftery Prize, the Celtic Media Festival and the New York Radio Festivals for recognising the importance of the story and encouraging us.

We would like to thank the inquests team for being very accommodating throughout the process, particularly during our endless requests for more seating in the Pillar Room.

We'd also like to thank the incredible colleagues we've worked with over our years in journalism, particularly all at *The Journal*. In true newslist fashion, we'd like to thank AB, AC, AD, AR, BP, CDB, CF, CJB, CK, CMC, CR, CSF, CT, DB, DE, DMG, DP, ED, EMC, EML, GMN, GNA, GR, HH, HOC, IC, JHJ, JM, JMAT, JMC, JW, LAB, LB, LMS, MF, MH, MM, MOC, MSM, NB, NOC, OD, ÓR, PB, PH, QOR, RD, SCOX, SD, SMD, SOC, SR, TMN, VF, VL, MD and PD on NW (and NS and AC), all of the *Daily Edge* and *Fora*, AA, SC and KB, and everyone at *The 42* (special mention to NK, GC and ED).

Sean Murray I would like to thank my colleagues past and present at *The Journal* and the *Irish Examiner* for all of their support and guidance over the years. From the *Examiner* gang in Cork, I'd like to thank Tom Fitzpatrick, John O'Mahony, Ronan Bagnall, Stephen Rogers, Kevin O'Neill, Susan O'Shea, Paudie Hoare and Deirdre O'Shaughnessy for giving the time and space to write about Stardust in the paper over the last few years. A special thanks to Cianan and Kev for listening to me talk endlessly about the inquests while they were ongoing. Also thanks to Mick Clifford for having me on the podcast to talk about Stardust as things were developing. A thanks too to Kitty Holland and Conor Hunt for their company and support during those long days and weeks and months in the Pillar Room.

I'd also like to thank Christine, for being your usual listening, supportive self when I came to you with an idea for a podcast about the Stardust. And to Nicky for being an incredible partner to spend those long hours in the studio with. And to the both of them for helping bring this project to fruition.

To my family, I'd like to say 'you will always Whelans'. I also would like to thank Róisín, Joanne and my ma and da for putting up with me during the writing process, particularly in those last few weeks before its completion. And for their endless encouragement and love over the years.

Christine Bohan Thanks to Sean and Nicky, first and foremost, for your hard work, your diligence, your constant optimism, and your way with words. For the people who kept me going, even if they didn't realise it: The Cool Gang, Aoife, Maeve, Chiara, Rebecca, Sinéad O'C, Kate, Paul H, Cathy, Lisa, Hannah, Aoife B, Sinead C, the Wesley crew, the Labour Mas, the cousins, the book club gals, Lovely Ladies 2.0, Charleville Tennis Club, Hypno Girls, and everyone whose DMs I have repeatedly slid into over this past year. I owe you all a drink. Massive thank you to the early readers: Ann Marie, Sinéad, Órla and Andrew, you are probably the only people I would ever willingly let edit me and I deeply appreciate your skills. Thank you to Tony Canavan for solving a mystery for me. Thanks to my colleagues at *The Journal*, both past and current, the soundest, funniest, hardest-working and best people I have ever known.

To my family: Mam, Ann Marie, Rob, Breda, John, Marc, Mia, Michelle, Keith, Cara, Oliver, Ted, Katherine, Domhnall, Liam, Aileen, Edel, Billy, Mattie, Sam, Jack, Anthony, Maureen, Neil, Margaret, Ian, Rachel, Emily, Isla and Pab. You are the best bunch. I would have loved for Dad to be around to see this.

Massive thanks to the people who made it physically possible for me to do this while simultaneously working and navigating a baby: Links Childcare and Bruna for keeping the house in order, and Kelly from Sleepy Stars. And the people I owe so much to: the teachers at Dominican College Griffith Avenue, the CSC and Trinity News (and my lecturers, for those times when I actually attended class), everyone at DCU's School of Comms, and the editors and teams who took a chance on me at the *Sunday Tribune*, the *Irish Times*, *The Guardian* and *The Journal*.

And finally, for Andrew and Molly. I don't know how I got so lucky twice, but I am so grateful for you every single day of my life. I love you both more than anything.

Nicky Ryan I would like to thank Eimear, for not only putting up with my nonsense but also supporting me in more serious efforts too, and always with endless love and advice. I couldn't have done this without you. My parents Jan and Liam, for the lifetime of encouragement you have given me and the unwavering support that sustains me. I love you both so much. Aileen, Liam, Harvey and Stan

THE LAST DISCO

– Niall too, maybe – for giving me a place to lock myself away so I could get the final run on the book started (and for everything else over the past 13 years, of course). All the Ryans, all the Kavanaghs, all the McGarrys (especially Bernie) and Louis, Joanne, Alannah, Adalynn and Joseph. Ciara Doris and Stephen McDermott, for their careful attention to detail (please don't invoice me). Christine and Sean, never did I think that when we first stepped into that horrifically stuffy podcast studio in 2019 we would be here today with this book. A simple 'a' to Leah Kieran, Valerie Loftus and Derek O'Brien. A special mention to Kate Dillon, Hazel Mc Partlan, Shane Murphy, Gráinne Murphy, but also to everyone who keeps me sane and who understands the dangers of launching in a long list of names (everyone in Primadonnas, Midwheel, WNW, DT, Snack and beyond). Edward Denniston and Ciarán Kavanagh for the seeds of inspiration they sowed years ago. All lecturers in DCU and past colleagues at RTÉ for the invaluable skills they taught me. Everyone at *The Journal* (including the diaspora), it would be near impossible to find better colleagues.

And lastly, Nick Sheridan. The memory of your enthusiasm for this book drove me on. I wish you were still here so I could share it with you.

References

Prologue

Years after the Stardust disaster: Apps, P. (2022) *Show me the Bodies – How we let Grenfell happen* London: OneWorld

Chapter 1

1. **Dickie Rock at the Stardust:** RTÉ Archives (2020) *I've Got The Music In Me* https://www.rte.ie/archives/2020/0424/1134563-dickie-rock-in-concert/
2. **When the owners applied for the licence:** Butterly, P. (2000) *From Radishes to Riches* Self-published.
3. **Eurovision star Dana:** Irish Independent (30th April 2023). *Stardust fire families still seeking a semblance of peace*
4. **When boys and girls went to a disco:** Leahy, W. (2015) *From Dancehall Days to Boogie Nights: 50 Years of the Irish Disco.* [Podcast] Available at https://radiotoday.ie/2015/01/leahy-documentary-marks-five-decades-of-irish-disco/ (Accessed 19th May 2024).
5. **It still would have been considered a very new suburb:** Interview with Cormac Moore, 26th April 2024
6. **I've heard stories myself:** Dublin Inquirer (17th January 2018). *Suburban stories*
7. **The historian Erika Hanna:** The Irish Times (17th December 2017). *How Dublin became a city of sprawling suburbs*
8. **The emergence of showbands:** Paul Tarpey speaking on Leahy, W. (2015) *From Dancehall Days to Boogie Nights: 50 Years of the Irish Disco* [Podcast]

THE LAST DISCO

9. **As this migration to Dublin's suburbs:** Central Statistics Office (2000) *'That was then, this is now: Change in Ireland 1949–1999'.* Dublin: Stationery Office.

10. **At their peak:** Leahy, W. (2015) *From Dancehall Days to Boogie Nights: 50 Years of the Irish Disco.* [Podcast]

11. **U2 are listed:** U2 Gigs (no date) *The Stardust.* Available at https://www.u2gigs.com/The_Stardust-l590.html (Accessed 19th May 2024)

12. **The Specials played a gig:** The Irish Times (30th December 2022). *'No violence – we hate violence,' Terry Hall pleaded the night The Specials played Dublin*

13. **Far more people have gone to a disco:** Leahy, W (2015) *From Dancehall Days to Boogie Nights: 50 Years of the Irish Disco* [Podcast]

14. **One of the first discos in Ireland:** *ibid*

15. **The club called Sound City:** Brand New Retro (no date) *Map and timeline of the first Dublin discos (1965–1980)* https://brand-newretro.ie/2021/09/08/map-and-timeline-of-the-first-dublin-discos-1965-1980/ (Accessed 19th May 2024)

16. **Almost 1 in 8 young people:** Walsh, J. (1991) 'Changing Ireland – The Turn-around of the Turn-around in the Population of the Republic of Ireland' *Irish Geography*, 24(2), 117–125.

17. **It cost £3:** Central Statistics Office (2016) *Historical earnings 1938–2015 – The average industrial wage and the Irish economy.* Available at https://www.cso.ie/en/releasesandpublications/ep/p-hes/hes2015/aiw/ (Accessed 19th May 2024)

18. **Butterly was not of the entertainment world [and other auto-biographical notes about Patrick Butterly]:** Butterly, P. (2000) *From Radishes to Riches.* Self-published.

19. **He had some limited experience:** *Report of the Tribunal of Inquiry on the fire at the Stardust, Artane* (1982). Dublin: Stationery Office.

20. **Accounts for the Butterly Business Park:** Butterly Business Park Ltd: Abridged accounts for the year ended 3rd December 2010 (CRO (2024))

21. **Colm Keena noted:** The Irish Times (16th February 2006) *Former nightclub owners have assets of over €10.9m*

304

Chapter 2

22. **Taoiseach Charles Haughey had set a grime tone:** *RTÉ Archives (2015) A Ministerial Broadcast by An Taoiseach 9th January 1980* https://www.rte.ie/archives/2015/0109/671262-haughey-warns-we-are-living-beyond-our-means/ (Accessed 20th May 2024)

23. **Gene McKenna wrote:** Irish Press (13th February 1981). *RDS gets a facelift for Ardfheis*

24. **back to work after a five-week strike:** Irish Press (13th February 1981) *£2000 deal for strikers*

25. **some as young as 15:** Evidence heard at the Stardust Fire Inquests 16th October 2023

26. **Like "Alcatraz":** Evidence heard at the Stardust Fire Inquests 24th October 2023

27. **a venue had to serve a substantial meal:** Intoxicating Liquor Act 1962

28. **A schoolteacher named William Bassett:** Evidence heard at the Stardust Fire Inquests 5th October 2023

29. **massive steel plates were welded over the windows:** *Report of the Tribunal of Inquiry on the fire at the Stardust, Artane* (1982). Dublin: Stationery Office.

30. **Martin Donohoe wasn't too impressed:** *ibid*

31. **"The fact that there was no inspection:** *ibid*

32. **Eamon Butterly had considered his options and a decision was made between him and the senior staff:** *ibid*

33. **"total inadequacy of qualified fire prevention staff, to seek, find and remedy the fire safety inadequacies of all types of premises in this country":** Irish Independent (14th August 1980) *Inspection Staff Needed*

34. **using forged tickets to get in:** *Report of the Tribunal of Inquiry on the fire at the Stardust, Artane* (1982). Dublin: Stationery Office.

35. **The Beat lead singer Dave Wakeling told Ed Power in the Irish Times** Irish Times (30th December 2022) *'No violence – we hate violence,' Terry Hall pleaded the night The Specials played Dublin*

36. **"Outside, four lads were trying to sneak in":** *Report of the Tribunal of Inquiry on the fire at the Stardust, Artane* (1982). Dublin: Stationery Office.

THE LAST DISCO

Chapter 3: This chapter draws extensively on the authors' own interviews with survivors, evidence heard at the recent inquests, and the 1981 Keane Tribunal report.

37. **their prize, a voucher from K-Tel Records:** Dublin People (15th February 2014) *Memories of Stardust on 33rd anniversary*
38. **In Ireland, it spent a week:** The Irish Charts (irishcharts.ie)

Chapter 4: This chapter draws extensively on the authors' own interviews with survivors, evidence heard at the recent inquests, and the 1981 Keane Tribunal report.

Chapter 5

39. **The city latest edition of the Evening Herald:** Evening Herald. (14th February 1981). *Why? Oh Jesus why?*
40. **The Irish Press led with "Disco fire disaster":** Irish Press (14th February 1981). *Disco fire disaster*
41. **"The pontiff said".** Irish Press (17th February 1981). *Pope prays for the dead and injured.*
42. **Condolences also came from Britain's Queen Elizabeth IIL** New York Times (15th February 1981). *Toll rises to 49 dead, 129 injured in blaze at dance hall in Dublin.*
43. **"A list of the injured was compiled in each hospital:** The Stardust Disaster: The background and the physical consequences. Emer B Shelley, Medico-Social Research Board (1983)
44. **The Irish Press reported on the Tuesday:** Irish Press (17th February 1981). *Mournful task on a Sutton hillside.*
45. **The Irish Times reported on Monday 16th February:.** Irish Times (16th February 1981). *Inquiry will 'satisfy public concern'*
46. **Haughey said:** Dáil record (18th February 1981). *Artane (Dublin) Fire: Tribunal of Inquiry.*
47. **Minister for the Environment Ray Burke:** Murphy, G. (2021) *Haughey* Dublin: Gill Books
48. **Made against Dublin Corporation:** Irish Press (21st February 1981). *Claims for Stardust now over £4m*
49. **An editorial column:** Sunday Independent (22nd February 1981). *Stardust a lesson for the future*

306

Chapter 6

50. **When Taoiseach Charles Haughey:** The Irish Times (16 February 1981). *Inquiry will 'satisfy public concern'*

51. **The 18th-century building:** Law Society Gazette (Jan/Feb 2006) Vol 100 Issue 1

52. **The stained glass window:** The Irish Times (11th April 1981). *Young people uncowed by august surroundings*

53. **One newspaper described how:** *ibid*

54. **The 48-year-old:** The Irish Times (5 March 1981). *Judge decision queried*

55. **He was a star:** Mac Cormaic, R. (2016) *The Supreme Court* Dublin: Penguin Ireland

56. **In his 20s:** *ibid*

57. **Mr Justice Keane was seen:** *ibid*

58. **Mr John Lovatt Dolan:** The Evening Herald (6 April 1981). *How disco killer fire began*

59. **An editorial:** The Irish Independent (6 April 1981) *Editorial*

60. **Crucially, the Tribunal heard [and all other references to what the Tribunal heard and decided]:** *Report of the Tribunal of Inquiry on the fire at the Stardust, Artane* (1982). Dublin: Stationery Office.

61. **McKenna's comments:** Mullaney, J., Barry, S., and McGuinness, M. (1991) *Report on the psychiatric sequelae to the Stardust fire* https://www.lenus.ie/bitstream/handle/10147/572679/thestar-dustfire.pdf

62. **One newspaper praised:** The Irish Independent (3 July 1982)

63. **There were some positives:** Evidence of the Chief Fire Officer for Dublin Fire Brigade at the Stardust Fire Inquests, 7th February 2024

64. **This tell us what:** Irish Times (23 April 2024) *Prejudice at heart of Kerry Babies and Stardust cases*

Chapter 7

65. **It was a night like any other:** Irish Press (13th September 1982) *Locks Again On Stardust Doors*

66. **Butterly and barman John Dignam appeared:** The Evening Press (4th April 1984) *Silver Swan doors case opened*

THE LAST DISCO

67. **Both men were acquitted:** The Irish Times (6th April 1984) *Butterly found not guilty of having exit doors of bar locked*

68. **Taoiseach Charles Haughey phoned:** Irish Independent (17th February, 1981) *Disaster fund swelling*

69. **Frank McDonald's article on the press conference:** Irish Times (12th March, 1981) *Disaster families allege neglect*

70. **a statement issued by the Butterly family:** Irish Independent (5th June 1981) *Re-opening soon for Silver Swan*

71. **a disco would never be held at the site again:** Irish Press (25th November 1981) *Stardust owner is granted liquor licence*

72. **'Subterfuge':** Irish Press (30th September 1982) *Stardust buyer granted licence for one month*

73. **'not a bona fide sale':** Irish Independent (10th November 1982) *Swan licence transfer is refused*

74. **The Butterlys sought compensation:** Evening Herald (10th June 1983) *Stardust in claim for £3m*

75. **The judge, Sean O'Hanrahan:** Irish Press (14th June 1983) *Stardust: ratepayers face huge bill*

76. **These cases, potentially worth:** Irish Examiner (5th July 1982) *Arson likely—and owner also indicted*

77. **They were stalled for a range of reasons:** Irish Independent (14th February 1984) *Many Stardust victims may never get a penny*

78. **By September 1983, the decision:** Irish Press (21st September 1983) *Stardust fund is wound up*

79. **except for Danny Hughes, the DJ:** Anglo-Celt (23 November 1984) page six

80. **One publican, while making it clear:** Evening Press (3rd May 1985) *Fire regulations anger publicans*

81. **A slew of known fire traps:** Irish Independent (12th October 1984) *Stardust could happen again, says fire chief*

82. **His son Damien said:** Pen portrait heard at the Stardust Fire Inquests, 4th May 2023

83. **John appeared in court:** Evening Press (24th October 1983) *Accused of assault on Butterly*

84. **In June, the committee attended:** Dáil record (6 June 1985) *Estimates 1985, Vote 23*

308

85. **Although no punishment was imposed:** Irish Independent (10th August 1985) *Court bans song about Stardust disaster*
86. **A memo written by an official:** Irish Examiner (31st December 2015) *State archives: Taoiseach's office wanted to avoid Stardust compensation, records reveal*
87. **It followed a meeting with:** Irish Press (25th September 1985) *'Relatives 'will be happy'*
88. **The team received 953 applications** to **five were awarded between £100,000 and £200,000:** Report of the Stardust Victims' Compensation Tribunal (1991). Dublin: Stationery Office.
89. **This Tribunal's team were praised in the media:** The Irish Press (12th February 1987)
90. **Some 195 people made submissions:** Report of the Stardust Victims' Compensation Tribunal (1991). Dublin: Stationery Office.
91. **It was able to award a maximum of £7,500 under legislation from 1961 for 'mental distress':** *Ibid*
92. **The Tribunal found a solution:** *Ibid*
93. **This judgement was used as:** *Ibid*
94. **John took his anger to:** Sunday Press (20th April 1986) *Father wins Stardust appeal case*
95. **It rumbled on until the end of July:** Irish Press (1st August 1986) *Stardust father's case fails*
96. **They took the case to a higher court:** Irish Press (2nd August 1986) *Stardust case for Supreme Court*
97. **On 16th December 1986:** Keegan v Stardust Victims' Compensation Tribunal (1986 WJSC-SC 871)

Chapter 8

98. **was opened to the public:** Stardust Park, dublincity.ie
99. **Families were promised it in 1986:** Irish Press (8th April 1986) *Stardust memorial agreed*
100. **and Haughey turned the sod in 1991:** Irish Independent (31st May 1991) *Relatives welcome Stardust memorial blueprint*
101. **Threatening to picket the Dáil:** Sunday Press (10th February 1991) *Memorial committee to picket Taoiseach*
102. **'This is sacred ground to us,'** Irish Press (18th September 1993) *Stardust memories for those who remain behind*

THE LAST DISCO

103. **Articles around the 10th anniversary detail:** Irish Press (7th and 11th February 1991)

104. **'chaotic' control room at Tara Street:** Evening Herald (5th February 1991) *Flynn gets attacked on fire safety*

105. **By 1999, you still find similar articles:** Irish Examiner (6th May 1991) *18 years after Stardust another tragedy is just waiting to happen*

106. **Fitzsimons spoke to *Irish Times*:** Irish Times (10th February 2001) *1981 fire safety recommendations not yet implemented*

107. **silk floral tributes laid at the:** Irish Press (15th February 1994) *Thugs vandalise Stardust tributes*

108. **drug use plagued the park:** Irish Examiner (10th September 1997) *Stardust Park has become haven for drug dealers*

109. **a private developer dumped silt:** Sunday Independent (27th May 2001) *Stardust Memorial flooded with silt*

110. **the *Evening Herald* death notices:** Evening Herald (24th January 2000) page 88

111. **The intention was to highlight:** Evening Herald (2nd May 2002) *Living with Stardust pain*

112. **Critics questioned her lack of:** Report of the Assessment Into New and Updated Evidence Into The Cause Of The Fire At the Stardust, Artane (2007)

113. **The Dáil heard that she was:** Dáil debate (14th December 2017) *McCartan Report on the Stardust: Statements*

114. **Taoiseach Bertie Ahern made it clear:** Evening Herald (9th August 2003) *Way now open for new Stardust probe*

115. **The committee submitted a report:** Dáil debate, (3rd February 2009) *Stardust Fire Tragedy: Motion*

116. **They shared that they had:** Irish Independent (11th February 2006) *Taoiseach told to stay away from Stardust Mass by families*

117. **right down to the cast list:** Evening Herald (2nd January 2006) *Revealed: The secret cast list in Stardust blaze drama storm*

118. **Listeners flooded the Liveline switchboard:** Irish Independent (6th January 2006) *Stardust relatives anger at RTÉ*

119. **News and current affairs programme *Prime Time*:** *Prime Time* (14th February 2006) RTÉ

310

SEAN MURRAY, CHRISTINE BOHAN AND NICKY RYAN

120. **it was suddenly rebranded:** Irish Independent (11th February 2006) *Stardust site superpub fury*

121. **the opening night was to be:** Irish Independent (14th February 2006) *Anger over Butterlys' opening of bar on site*

122. **There were accusations that this:** Irish Independent (12th April 2006) *Protesters mount picket as Stardust pub opens again*

123. **protests were called off once:** Sunday Independent (20th August 2006) *Stardust protests to end after deal on memorial*

124. **he got one regardless:** Evening Herald (28th March 2006) *Taoiseach confronted in local pub*

125. **in the first meeting with Ahern:** Irish Times (19th September 2006) *Formal response to Stardust inquiry request in six weeks*

126. **'Nothing But The Truth' convinced them:** Irish Independent (21st February 2007) *Stardust families near probe*

127. **a 48-hour ultimatum to announce a name:** Irish Times (12th April 2007) *Taoiseach given 48-hour ultimatum over Stardust*

128. **barrister John Gallagher emerged to:** Irish Times (13th April 2007) *Expert in new Stardust inquiry named*

129. **Confidential meetings were held:** RTÉ News (22 January 2008) *Expert hears from Stardust relatives*

130. **The committee accused the government of:** Irish Independent (28th March 2008) *Stardust families call halt to probe*

131. **Work began on exhuming their remains on 30th January 2007:** Irish Examiner (30th January 2007) *Families of unidentified Stardust victims 'confident exhumations will succeed'*

132. **We could finally go to visit Michael:** Irish Independent (31st January 2007) *Gardai began exhumation of unnamed Stardust victims*

133. **The samples were sent to the:** Irish Times (27th April 2007) *DNA tests identify Stardust dead*

134. **one of Ahern's last acts as Taoiseach:** Irish Independent (23 June 2008) *Stardust probe to get new chairman*

135. **a Leinster House sit-in protest:** Irish Independent (11 July 2008) *Stardust fire probe gets new chairman*

THE LAST DISCO

136. **'It pointed to the fact that' to 'In so concluding and in':** Report of the Independent Examination of the Stardust Victims Committee's Case for a Reopened Inquiry into the Stardust Fire Disaster, 2009

137. **Photographer Julien Behal captured the emotional scenes:** Irish Independent (24th January 2009) *Stardust report is hailed as 'a victory for the dead'*

138. **'We were right,' McDermott told the *Irish Times*:** Irish Times (24th January 2009) *Families express relief at findings*

139. **Five parents who had lost children:** European Court of Human Rights (23213/09, 62652/09)

140. **Ultimately, the court decided in 2012:** Ibid.

141. **There was an investigation by gardaí:** Irish Times (18th January 2016) *DPP says no prosecution from 1981 Stardust inquiry*

142. **The financial crash wasn't kind:** Business Post (22 July 2012) *Receiver appointed to Stardust site*

143. **An earlier draft of the:** Irish Times (7th May 2013) *Stardust families demand new inquiry*

144. **Swans at the Stardust Memorial Park:** Irish Times (12th November 2013) *Swans 'badly contaminated' by pollution at Dublin park*

145. **The same year, a disciplinary board:** RTÉ News (30th September 2013) *Dublin solicitor guilty of professional misconduct*

146. **Another sit-in, this time:** The Journal (5th February 2014) *Stardust campaigners are refusing to leave Government Buildings*

147. **Minister for Justice Alan Shatter said:** The Journal (22nd January 2014) *No new inquiry into Stardust tragedy*

148. **His successor, Frances Fitzgerald, was:** 'A safe, fair and inclusive Ireland: Department of Justice and Equality strategy statement 2016–2019

149. **The persistent pressure eventually led:** RTÉ News (25th January 2017) *Evidence found by Stardust relatives to be assessed*

150. **Retired judge Pat McCartan was appointed:** Irish Independent (2nd July 2017) *Stardust tragedy judge in quit threat*

151. **'McCartan looked at the evidence' to 'McCartan also included a quote':** Report of the Assessment Into New and Updated Evidence Into The Cause Of The Fire At the Stardust, Artane (2007)

152. **Opposition politicians later defended Foy's work:** Dáil record (14th December 2017) *McCartan Report on the Stardust Fire: Statements*

153. **McCartan found nothing in it:** Ibid

Chapters 9, 10, 11, 12 and 13 draw extensively from the authors' own attendance, notes and reports on the inquests and related court hearings.

Chapter 9

154. **Including the Ballymurphy inquest and the Glennane Gang inquest:** Statement from Phoenix Law, 11th May 2021

155. **They were also involved in a court bid claiming:** The Guardian (6th January 2022) *'Gay cake' row: man loses seven-year battle against Belfast bakery*

156. **In his submission to the Attorney General:** The Journal (12th January 2020) *Attorney General: Decision to open fresh Stardust inquest drew on 'analogies' from Hillsborough disaster*

157. **Darragh Mackin didn't feel like mincing his words:** The Journal (14th October 2020) *There was 'State-sponsored effort to cover up' what happened at Stardust disaster, solicitor tells first inquest hearing*

158. **Darragh Mackin returns to court saying:** The Journal (24th March 2021) *'There's a further bump in the road. It's deeply regrettable': Stardust inquests hit with more delays*

159. **Compounded in 2022 with a High Court case:** Irish Examiner (25th February 2022) *Stardust owner launches judicial review ahead of inquest into 48 deaths*

160. **It wasn't until November that the High Court:** Irish Examiner (2nd November 2022) *Eamon Butterly's challenge to new Stardust inquest fails*

Chapter 13

161. **He stood up in the Dáil:** Dáil record (23rd April 2024) *Acknowledgement and Apology to the Families and to the Victims of the Stardust Tragedy*

162. **Garda Commissioner Drew Harris:** Irish Times (25th April 2024) *Stardust deaths: Cold-case gardaí ordered to examine possibility of criminal inquiry*